FRENCH CONNECTIONS IN THE ENGLISH RENAISSANCE

French Connections in the English Renaissance

Edited by

CATHERINE GIMELLI MARTIN
University of Memphis, USA

HASSAN MELEHY
University of North Carolina, Chapel Hill, USA

LONDON AND NEW YORK

First published 2013 by Ashgate Publishing

Published 2016 by Routledge
2 Park Square, Milton Park, Abingdon, Oxon OX14 4RN
711 Third Avenue, New York, NY 10017, USA

Routledge is an imprint of the Taylor & Francis Group, an informa business

Copyright © Catherine Gimelli Martin and Hassan Melehy and the contributors 2013

Catherine Gimelli Martin and Hassan Melehy have asserted their right under the Copyright, Designs and Patents Act, 1988, to be identified as the editors of this work.

All rights reserved. No part of this book may be reprinted or reproduced or utilised in any form or by any electronic, mechanical, or other means, now known or hereafter invented, including photocopying and recording, or in any information storage or retrieval system, without permission in writing from the publishers.

Notice:
Product or corporate names may be trademarks or registered trademarks, and are used only for identification and explanation without intent to infringe.

British Library Cataloguing in Publication Data
French connections in the English Renaissance.
    1. English literature – French influences. 2. English literature – Early modern, 1500–1700 – History and criticism.
    I. Martin, Catherine Gimelli. II. Melehy, Hassan, 1960–
    820.9'003–dc23

The Library of Congress has cataloged the printed edition as follows:
French connections in the English renaissance / edited by Catherine Gimelli Martin and Hassan Melehy.
    pages cm
  Includes bibliographical references and index.
  ISBN 978-1-4094-6625-3 (hardcover: alk. paper)
    1. English literature—French influences. 2. French literature—English influences. 3. English literature—Early modern, 1500–1700—History and criticism. 4. French literature—16th century—History and criticism. 5. French literature—17th century—History and criticism. 6. Influence (Literary, artistic, etc.) I. Martin, Catherine Gimelli, editor of compilation. II. Melehy, Hassan, 1960– editor of compilation.
  PR129.F8F737 2013
  820.9'358—dc23

2013007740

ISBN 9781409466253 (hbk)

Contents

List of Figures	*vii*
Notes on Contributors	*ix*
Permission Acknowledgmerts	*xi*

Introduction   1
Catherine Gimelli Martin and Hassan Melehy

Part 1   Translating and Transferring Gender

1   "La Femme Replique": English Paratexts, Genre Cues,
    and Versification in a Translated French Gender Debate   15
    A.E.B. Coldiron

2   Isabelle de France, Child Bride   27
    Deanne Williams

Part 2   Textualizations of Politics and Empire

3   Spenser's *Mutabilitie Cantos* and Du Bellay's
    Poetic Transformation   51
    Hassan Melehy

4   Utopia Versus State of Power, or Pretext of the Political
    Discourse of Modernity: Hobbes, Reader of La Boétie?   65
    Timothy J. Reiss, translated by Hassan Melehy

5   Milton and the Huguenot Revolution   95
    Catherine Gimelli Martin

Part 3   Translation and the Transnational Context

6   Cross-Cultural Adaptation and the Novella: Bandello's
    Albanian Knight in France, England, and Spain   119
    Dorothea Heitsch

7   Life, Death, and the Daughter of Time: Philip and Mary
    Sidney's Translations of Duplessis-Mornay   143
    Roger Kuin

vi *French Connections in the English Renaissance*

8   From "Amours" to *Amores*: Francis Thorius Makes Ronsard
       a Neolatin Lover   161
       Anne Lake Prescott, with Lydia Kirsopp Lake

Appendix: Ronsard in England, 1635–1699   *179*
       Anne Lake Prescott
Bibliography: Scholarship on the Anglo-French Renaissance   *193*
Index   *205*

List of Figures

1   Title page from *Interlocucyon, with an argument, betwyxt man and woman, & which of them could proue to be most excellẽt.* Anon. (London: de Worde, 1525). © British Library Board, Shelfmark W.P.9530. All rights reserved.   19

Notes on Contributors

A.E.B. Coldiron is Professor of English, Florida State University; author of *English Printing, Verse Translation, and the Battle of the Sexes, 1476–1557* (Ashgate, 2009) and *Canon, Period, and the Poetry of Charles of Orleans: Found in Translation* (Michigan, 2000); and editor of *Christine de Pizan in English Print, 1478–1549* (Modern Humanities Research Association, in progress).

Dorothea Heitsch is Senior Lecturer in French, University of North Carolina at Chapel Hill; author of *Practising Reform in Montaigne's* Essais (Brill, 2000); and co-editor, with Jean-François Vallée, of *Printed Voices: The Renaissance Culture of Dialogue* (Toronto, 2004).

Roger Kuin is Professor of English (Emeritus), University of York; author of *Chamber Music: Elizabethan Sonnet-Sequences and the Pleasure of Criticism* (Toronto, 1998); and editor of Robert Langham, *A Letter* (Brill, 1983) and *The Correspondence of Sir Philip Sidney* (Oxford, 2012).

Lydia Kirsopp Lake, formerly of the classics and philosophy faculty at Tufts University, is an independent scholar providing, directly or through her *Still Waters Arts and Services*, advice to Renaissance scholars on Greek and Latin languages and cultures. Her chief area of expertise is Greek Stoicism.

Catherine Gimelli Martin is Professor of English, University of Memphis; author of *Milton Among the Puritans* (Ashgate, 2010) and *The Ruins of Allegory: Paradise Lost and the Metamorphosis of Epic Convention* (Duke, 1998); editor of *Milton and Gender* (Cambridge, 2004); and co-editor, with Julie Robin Solomon, of *Francis Bacon and the Refiguring of Early Modern Thought: Essays to Commemorate "The Advancement of Learning" (1605–2005)* (Ashgate, 2005).

Hassan Melehy is Professor of French and Francophone Literature at the University of North Carolina at Chapel Hill and author of *The Poetics of Literary Transfer in Early Modern France and England* (Ashgate, 2010) and *Writing Cogito: Montaigne, Descartes, and the Institution of the Modern Subject* (SUNY, 1997).

Anne Lake Prescott is Professor of English (Emerita) and Senior Scholar of English, Barnard College; author of *Imagining Rabelais in Renaissance England* (Yale, 1998) and *French Poets and the English Renaissance: Studies in Fame and Transformation* (Yale, 1978); and co-editor, with James M. Dutcher, of *Renaissance Historicisms: Essays in Honor of Arthur F. Kinney* (Delaware, 2008).

Timothy J. Reiss is Professor of Comparative Literature (Emeritus), New York University; author of *Mirages of the Selfe: Patterns of Personhood in Ancient and Early Modern Europe* (Stanford, 2003), *Against Autonomy: Global Dialectics of Cultural Exchange* (Stanford, 2002), *Knowledge, Discovery, and Imagination in Early Modern Europe: The Rise of Aesthetic Rationalism* (Cambridge, 1997), *The Meaning of Literature* (Cornell, 1992), *The Uncertainty of Analysis: Problems in Truth, Meaning, and Culture* (Cornell, 1988), *The Discourse of Modernism* (Cornell, 1982, 1985), *Tragedy and Truth: Studies in the Development of a Renaissance and Neoclassical Discourse* (Yale, 1980), and *Toward Dramatic Illusion: Theatrical Technique and Meaning from Hardy to Horace* (Yale, 1971); editor of *Music, Writing and Cultural Unity in the Caribbean* (Africa World Press, 2005), *Sisyphus and Eldorado: Magic and Other Realisms in Caribbean Literature*, 2nd ed. (Africa World Press, 2002), and *For the Geography of a Soul: Emerging Perspectives on Kamau Brathwaite* (Africa World Press, 2001); and co-editor, with Patricia Penn Hilden and Shari N. Huhndorf, of *Topographies of Race and Gender: Mapping Cultural Representations*, 2 vols. (Annals of Scholarship, 2007).

Deanne Williams is Associate Professor of English, York University; author of *The French Fetish from Chaucer to Shakespeare* (Cambridge, 2004); co-editor, with Ananya Jahanara Kabir, of *Postcolonial Approaches to the European Middle Ages: Translating Cultures* (Cambridge, 2005); and co-editor, with Kaara Peterson, of *The Afterlife of Ophelia* (Palgrave, 2012).

Permission Acknowledgments

A.E.B. Coldiron, "'La Femme Replique': English Paratexts, Genre Cues, and Versification in a Translated French Gender Debate": excerpted by permission of the publishers from part of Chapter 3 (pp. 116–30) of *English Printing, Verse Translation, and the Battle of the Sexes 1476–1557* (Farnham, UK; Burlington, VT: Ashgate, 2009). Copyright © 2009.

Timothy J. Reiss, "Utopia versus State of Power, or Pretext of the Political Discourse of Modernity: Hobbes, Reader of La Boétie?": this chapter is a translation in abridged form of Timothy J. Reiss, "Utopie versus état de pouvoir, ou prétexte du discours politique de la modernité: Hobbes, lecteur de La Boétie?," *EMF 4: Utopia 1 (16th and 17th Centuries)* (1998): 31–83. © 1998 Rookwood Press. Published with the kind permission of Rookwood Press.

Introduction

Catherine Gimelli Martin and Hassan Melehy

French-English Connections

Anglo-French literary exchanges were a frequent occurrence in the Middle Ages, but toward the end of the sixteenth century they became a particularly vexed issue for many English authors. Mainly proceeding westward across the Channel in the early modern period, textual borrowings often functioned in the interest of establishing a literary canon in support of the emerging English nation-state; the problem lay in the awkward requirement of giving credit to a principal political and cultural rival for supplying key source material. French authors themselves had confronted similar problems only a few decades earlier as the literary movement centrally preoccupied with creating a new national literature, the Pléiade, found itself caught up in both international and local rivalries. While acknowledging the benefits of borrowing not only from the verse of Greece and Rome but also the thriving national and vernacular literatures of Spain and Italy, the Pléiade and its allies were chiefly concerned with promoting a distinctly French language and national culture.

The creation of the French Petrarchan sonnet exemplifies many of the problems involved in this effort. Although in many ways the "new" sonnet merely marks the completion of a cultural program begun by François Ier in the early sixteenth century, it is immersed in the complexities surrounding France's conquest of Italy. Even while affirming French political superiority, the king's Italianization of French royal court manners and fashions implicitly acknowledged Italian cultural ascendency. Thus when Clément Marot first translated Petrarch and introduced the sonnet into French in the 1520s and 1530s, he was indeed simply responding to François's Italianizing tastes, but at the same time he was paving the way for the sonnet to become the Pléiade's distinctly French poetic form of choice, especially through the very widely read sequences of Joachim Du Bellay and Pierre de Ronsard. Ironically, Du Bellay's defense of this and similar adaptations in what would become the Pléiade's manifesto, *La Deffence et Illustration de la Langue Françoyse* [*The Defense and Illustration of the French Language*] (1549), responds to this situation by explicitly rejecting the translation of Greek, Latin, and other foreign-language verse in favor of what he calls "imitation." Citing a stiffness of poetic language when verse is removed from its native context, Du Bellay nevertheless advocates, through prescriptive statement and a fortiori through the example of his own textual composition, the borrowing of at times wholly intact pieces of prior authors' works, thus showing that he understands imitation to involve some translation. Du Bellay justifies this perplexing compromise by insisting that imitation, or a reworking of foreign texts in the French language and with French themes, is only a provisional if necessary step in the case of both modern and ancient poetry. The ultimate goal is to allow the French literary canon to surpass all prior models, hence all rivals, eventually leaving them in the oblivion of history.

Like his contemporaries, Du Bellay understood this development as directly related to the consolidation of French imperial power, although the relationship of poetry to political domination in Pléiade poetry and poetic theory is often a more complicated one than it at first appears. At least one poet influenced by both the Pléiade and the Italian cultural revival in France, Louise Labé of Lyon, was more focused on reconfiguring and playfully attacking the widely used masculinist tropes of Petrarch's poetry than in supporting a new hegemony. Not so with Du Bellay, however, who in *La Deffence et Illustration de la Langue Françoyse* at once describes and prescribes the imperative of surpassing rival models in order to bolster the ascension of the imperial state; whatever role textual translation may play in this dynamic, the procedure involves a broader cultural translation whereby literary materials from one national context are transferred to and claimed by another. That goal also required elevating the national language to a higher international status, thereby effectively degrading the status of others.

Rivalries and Conflicts

Given the national and international rivalry inherent in this program, those who imported French literary material into England, if they didn't completely disavow their sources, tended to maintain an overt distance from them, usually playing down their importance. To different degrees and with somewhat varied rationales, some quiet admission of French sources characterizes the work of Philip Sidney, Edmund Spenser, William Shakespeare, Mary Wroth, and a number of others involved in creating an English national literature worthy of the burgeoning empire developed during the reigns of Elizabeth and James I. A similar approach characterized non-poetic borrowings even when they were actually used to contest state authority, whether that of France or its one-time island conquest. In political theory generally, failure to acknowledge vital French sources persisted even when it had achieved wide popular renown, as it had in the case of Etienne de La Boétie, well known both through the praise he received from his close friend Michel de Montaigne and the international dissemination of political tracts, among which La Boétie's *Discours de la servitude volontaire* [*Discourse of Voluntary Servitude*], appropriated in France by the Huguenot faction, figured prominently. Yet in England precisely as in France, what Richard Helgerson terms "discursive forms of nationhood" were "mutually self-constituting. Each made the other."[1]

---

[1] Richard Helgerson, *Forms of Nationhood: The Elizabethan Writing of England* (Chicago: Chicago University Press, 1992), 11.

France's intellectual and cultural lead was due to two well-documented factors: its much earlier and more successful attempts to establish its empire, and England's self-consciously belated participation in both the "new learning" of humanism and the new theology driving the Protestant Reformation. Despite the high profiles of Sir Thomas More and his close friend Erasmus, humanists strongly concerned with educational, moral, and especially in the case of Erasmus, religious reform, and despite the high hopes accompanying the sadly brief reign of Edward VI, the Tudor monarchs proved notoriously cautious, or in the case of Edward's father, Henry VIII, actually reluctant religious reformers. The latter circumstance frequently troubled the more progressive spirits of his age and beyond, when the specter of Spanish and French imperialism and the threat of religious re-conquest haunted first Elizabeth and then her heirs, the Stuarts. Both dynasties nevertheless presided over the rise of England's "golden age" literature, which continued to expand and thrive during the "silver age" of the seventeenth century.

Both at home and abroad, these English developments proved remarkable, even startling achievements, given the combination of political and religious insecurity that troubled this small and relatively unpromising European outpost. France nevertheless retained its hegemony by taking little note of English authors aside from the positive exception of Sidney, whose *Arcadia* was soon translated into French, and the negative exception of Milton, whose anti-monarchical tracts stirred such deep fears of rebellion that they immediately provoked a lengthy reply from the French Protestant Claude de Saumaise. Milton's relative success in this controversy—or Saumaise's failure—seems to have prepared the way for the extensive and almost immediate European translation of his belated epic, *Paradise Lost*, but even then, most of its cultural capital continued to remain at home. In politics as well, English advances proved precarious until the end of the century, and intellectual unrest was even more of a constant; both contributed more to enduring fears of national failure than to hopes for further progress. Throughout most of this period, the return of French cultural or actual "captivity" remained a national obsession, and even as it began to wane, Dutch naval power reinvigorated English insularity and xenophobia, as did Charles II's "Frenchified" court. Initially hailed as a return to stability, the Stuart Restoration soon proved equally precarious and, after James II's ascent to the throne, finally ended with the "Glorious Revolution," which in 1689 declared England's ultimate preference for the Dutch House of Orange. Yet even in the very midst of her rebellion against her great continental forebear, none of England's most respectable writers, neither John Dryden nor John Dennis, could ignore French literary theory and practice, which, in the form of a neoclassical revival, would dominate English literature throughout most of the following century.

Throughout the early modern period, then, France served as a prime model for English expansion, political reform, and literary progress, even when—as in the case of the carnage of the French religious wars—it mainly supplied unheeded warnings against taking the wrong direction. As such, France may be considered a primary locus or source of a general English "anxiety of influence." With the rise of nationalist sentiment on both sides, these closely related and competing nations simultaneously attempted to reclaim the preeminence both associated with Rome, whether imperial or republican. Options included imitating the great epic poets on either side of the Roman civil wars, chiefly, Virgil, Statius, and Lucan, or drawing on the works of a wide range of Roman moralists, lyricists, and satirists, Horace, Ovid, Catullus, Juvenal, to name only the most prominent. On the English side of the channel, this national competition seemed to end when both Milton's friend Marvell and his poetic rival Dryden differently but also similarly claimed that in *Paradise Lost* their bard had surpassed Homer and Virgil combined, as Dryden's famous encomium declared. Ironically, these claims responded to Milton's stated fear that his epic might never surpass its southern European or classical models owing to being born in "an age too late" or a climate too damp (*PL* 9.44–5). Much as one might expect, his French rivals seized on these fears as just intimations of its shortcomings; Voltaire cleverly reversed Dryden's estimation with a long diatribe against Milton's Italian models, his "barbaric" verse, and its fatal effects on the last English epic written in full-blown classical style.

As Helgerson has perceptively shown, in the earlier Renaissance nationalist competition was just as intense if not always so overt since England's literary and political architects ostensibly took Greece and Rome as the locus of their cultural anxieties. Just like France and Italy before her, England began its national self-articulation with "a sense of national barbarism, with a recognition of the self as a despised other, then moved to repair that damaged self-image with the aid of forms taken from a past that was understood as both different from the present and internally divided" by a kind of "semiotic necessity." Spenser typifies this in asking why, if the "Greeks had a kingdom of their own language" why can't England do the same? One way of accomplishing this goal was to imitate Greek poetic forms in English, another was to "go native," but both techniques required a considerable degree of selective memory about France's contribution to native forms. Although rhyme had been borrowed from the French "little more than two centuries earlier," its English defenders conveniently identified not just rhyme but the sonnet itself with "immemorial custom," thereby inventing a non-existent literary history in which "French and Italian poetic form came to stand for the customary and the unmade, for the purely English."[2]

Similar claims to ideological monopoly hiding simultaneously behind classical veils and a denial of closer rivals to authority underlie Michael Drayton's *Polyolbion*, much of Sir Walter Raleigh's poetry and his *History of the World*, Shakespeare's history plays, particularly *Henry V*, Spenser's *Faerie Queene*, and even Sidney's less obviously chauvinistic *Defence of Poesie*, which merely declares the privilege and duty of present and future English poets to serve as their nation's teachers and leaders, as the poets of France and Italy had long since done.[3] Yet even here, Sidney's

---

[2]   Helgerson, *Forms of Nationhood*, 2, 3, 39.

[3]   On *Polyolbion,* see Helgerson, *Forms of Nationhood*, 120; on Shakespeare's history plays, 195–245. Helgerson does not discuss other texts noted above in any detail but his

dependence on their example is largely a silent one since he mainly cites classical defenses of poetry, a strategy that paved the way for later English literary critics to follow. Like their poets, these critics would claim to return to the classical "font" for inspiration rather than to their nearest cousins, the French—and this despite some very obvious borrowings and a long and barely suppressed rivalry.

Transnational Considerations

The principal aim of this volume is to move beyond such fictions and begin reconstructing the national crossing of religious, literary, political, and other cultural influences traveling mainly from France to England in the early modern era. This task will include reexamining not just disguised borrowings but also more open if strangely overlooked uses of non-native sources. All the essays in this book must and therefore do address the differing functions of translation, including its broader role in literary and cultural transfer. Important to the volume's overall conception is the recognition that long-established and more recent critics alike, critics usually working in institutions that organize literary studies according to national boundaries, have often been even more guilty than their poets in over-emphasizing the unique "English-ness" of the texts they study. In fact, even French critics of British literature have been slow to overturn this long-standing critical tradition. Examples on both sides include ignoring Spenser's obvious debts to Du Bellay and the French Neoplatonists and instead stressing his emulation of Chaucer; seriously underestimating or not going further than a brief documentation of Shakespeare's extensive borrowings from Rabelais, Du Bellay, and Montaigne; and overlooking Milton's extensive Italian *and* French models by stressing his overwhelming debt to Spenser, his "great Original," as Dryden early named him. There are and of course always have been numerous exceptions to this tendency, exceptions amply represented by the scholars included in the present volume, a number of whom have already contributed major works to the field of Anglo-French Renaissance studies. But it remains generally true that even more than the Italian and especially Petrarchan sources of English poetry (always cited for England's two true "greats," Shakespeare and Milton), French connections have more often than not been deeply underestimated.

Reasons for these oversights vary widely, ranging from culture to politics to individual personality; the latter is in fact the sole reason that Milton's nephew and early biographer Edward Phillips gave for his uncle's scant attention to French travel, literature, or customs, all of which he claimed were uncongenial to his uncle's "natural" taste. Yet even the brief overview above should strongly suggest that more salient reasons include national insecurity as well as fierce competition

---

examples from choreography and legal, travel, and apocalyptic history (far too numerous to be included here) are equally instructive. On similar shifts in ideological attitudes toward the English language and its "polishing" through French borrowings, see Richard Foster Jones, *The Triumph of the English Language* (Stanford: Stanford University Press, 1953).

between these contiguous national stocks who share so much, perhaps too much, of the same linguistic and literary heritage. Ever since Chaucer chose to write in English rather than French, and typically to prefer Italian literary prototypes to previously dominant French imports, and ever since Thomas Malory aggressively "Englished" the Arthurian legends long circulating in France, English writers have tended to cite influences anywhere but there, at least until the nineteenth and twentieth centuries. Even then, Coleridge would turn to the German Romantic poets and theorists in preference to foundational French Romantic figures such as Rousseau, while Wordsworth would spend a great deal of his career repenting his early admiration of the French Revolution.

There is, nevertheless, no denying the fact that both nations drove real cultural wedges between themselves in the process of striving to claim the Roman and imperial mantle—that is, to succeed in becoming what Milton would call the "new Rome in the West." As this struggle developed throughout the Renaissance and Reformation, English intellectuals increasingly, and in some cases legitimately, viewed France as a negative example of its hopes and dreams of enlightenment: as a class-divided, priest-driven, authoritarian, and ultimately absolutist nation that had taken the wrong fork in the path toward individual freedom and true religion. The persistence of this outlook through the eighteenth century is most evident in such writers as the exiled Voltaire, who savaged many reactionary tendencies of the state and society of his home country through ironic comparisons to English progressivism in his *Lettres anglaises* or *Letters Concerning the English Nation*, published in 1734 in both English and French. Yet that hardly prevented him from belittling both the style and religious outlook of England's premier poet at the time, Milton, and giving mixed praise to Shakespeare. Similar biases on both sides were if anything more predominant in popular literature.

Channel Crossings

These biases should not, however, obscure many countervailing tendencies during the Anglo-French Renaissance. In the very act of seeking to solidify the authority of his own nation and queen, Spenser would significantly begin his very English poetic career by translating Du Bellay, and he would later reiterate phrasing and themes drawn from this poet in pivotal expositions of metaphysics, morals, and poetics in *The Faerie Queene*. Even more ironically, Milton would refute Saumaise and launch his European political reputation by translating the French monarchomachs and, with them, the Conciliarist tradition derived from Paris and its great university. These borrowings are clearly detailed in the chapters by the editors of this volume, who like its other contributors demonstrate the depth of these Anglo-French connections despite the propaganda wars that have separately defined each nation in its own unique terms. Of course, much of this propaganda accurately reflects the realities behind the conflicts, but only when its highly tendentious nature is taken into account. The secondary point of this volume will thus be to demonstrate how different such distinctions look when French and English traditions are examined together rather than apart. When placed in this perspective, even the ideological vantage point adopted in *King Henry V*, the Shakespearean touchstone of much propaganda to follow, loses much of its authority.

The plot outlines of *Henry V* are overwhelmingly familiar in both stage and cinematic incarnations: it features a far-sighted if also semi-Machiavellian, proto-"democratic" monarch who values his troops, commoners, and aristocrats alike, for what they individually dare to accomplish on the battlefield, while their French counterparts are fatuously preoccupied with titles, privileges, and customs that separate their ranks and doom them to defeat by Henry's rugged, highly principled English troops. When attacked by effeminate Frenchmen who take more pride in their fancy horses than in their actual military ethos, and who scurrilously slaughter innocent noncombatants (soldier boys outside the main lines of attack), the English both morally and militarily defeat the French even while outnumbered ten to one. Ironically, then, as English literati like to remember, only an inspired French *woman*, Jeanne d'Arc, could regain their lands, while the French clergy "thanked" her by burning her as a heretic. As Shakespeare's first tetrad of history plays further details, even Jeanne's initial victory was enabled more by internecine warfare on the part of English nobles than by French heroism alone, at least as he tells the story. Yet scholars who recall only these large outlines may well overlook the real military hero Sidney's spiritual debts to his French counterpart, the great Huguenot writer Phillippe Duplessis-Mornay, a visionary whom Milton himself politically followed in writing his antimonarchical tracts for a primarily Anglo-French but also pan-European audience.

Beyond Nation-Based Criticism

The contributors to this volume engage these and other literary connections in a variety of ways, in each case shedding light on the historical contexts in which they took place. As noted above, all the essays address the dynamics of translation, in its strict sense as well as in its broader meaning of literary or cultural transfer. Reflecting distinct aspects of this set of problems, the essays are presented in three topic divisions. Part 1 treats the sphere of social relations, examining how conceptions and evolutions of gender take shape in the movement of literary texts from one language and culture to another. Part 2 moves to the realm of politics and statehood, focusing on the conception and theorization of national culture and the state in both England and France, as these operations are inflected by the movement and rereading of texts. Extending into transnationalism, the third part explicitly addresses the operation of textual translation in literary transfer, demonstrating a paradoxically broad implication of more than two nations and languages as part of the process of contributing to a national literary canon. Within each part of the book the essays are arranged in the chronological order of the appearance of their English material.

Under the heading of "Translating and Transferring Gender," A.E.B. Coldiron examines how printers' decisions affected the large amount of French poetry that circulated in translation, often heavily rewritten, in England in the first half of the sixteenth century. She considers the implications of this phenomenon for the understanding of the formation of the English literary canon, especially in connection with early modern gender relations. She accomplishes this through an original reading of the French and English versions of the same poem, Guillaume Alexis's *Debat de l'homme et de la femme*, or *Interlocucyon, with an argument, betwyxt man and woman*. In a chapter that extends her previous groundbreaking work, Deanne Williams re-examines the critical problem of Shakespeare's Queen Isabel in *Richard II*, taking issue with accepted interpretations of the playwright's transformation of the historical Isabelle, a child bride of the French nobility, into an adult. Here Williams demonstrates not only that the understanding of the character of Isabel as a girl stems from culturally based notions of girlhood and womanhood, but also that these notions may be traced to an early modern English cultural break with France.

In the following part, "Textualizations of Politics and Empire," challenging dominant understandings of the *Cantos of Mutabilitie* with which Spenser concludes *The Faerie Queene*, Hassan Melehy considers textual affinities between them and the poet's translations of Du Bellay, the latter bearing the clear political purpose of bolstering the English state through both modeling and surpassing its French counterpart. Melehy shows that Spenser's preoccupation with the transformative power of time is bound up with notions of the transformation that poetry undergoes between one national context and another. In the following chapter, through a careful reading of a vast array of primary texts in early modern political thought, Timothy J. Reiss reconstructs the intellectual environment that Hobbes met when writing the work that virtually defined the authority of the modern state. Reiss shows that the problems to which the English philosopher responds may be traced to the formulations of La Boétie—that is, to a conceptual framework that emerged during the period of the consolidation of the French state against the backdrop of religious conflict. In the third essay in this part, Catherine Gimelli Martin clearly establishes Milton's dependence on French Huguenot political writers, further arguing that a reconsideration of this relationship goes a long way toward explaining many of Milton's own attitudes toward the English political situation.

The third part, "Translation and the Transnational Context," returns to the problem of textual translation with which the collection opens, dramatizing the extension of literary culture across multiple countries and languages as it travels from France to England. Dorothea Heitsch looks closely at the translation and dissemination in different national contexts of Matteo Bandello's *Novelle*—which were, among other things, an important source for several of Shakespeare's plays—from Italian, to French (as *Histoires tragiques*), and then to both English (as *Tragical Discourses*) and Spanish (as *Historias trágicas*). Heitsch takes the migration of Bandello's tale of the Albanian knight as a model of the development, in respective national literatures, of key generic and thematic concepts and

Introduction 9

conventions, and of the progression of a story from *fait divers* to moral exemplum. In the next essay, Roger Kuin examines the efficacy, exemplary nature, and reasons for the translations that Philip and Mary Sidney undertook of works by Duplessis-Mornay; given the missionary nature of these works in the spread of Protestantism throughout Europe, a European scope is inevitable, and the translation from French encounters the more widely circulating Latin version of Duplessis-Mornay's work. Finally, continuing the transnational challenge to dominant understandings of the composition of literary canons, Anne Lake Prescott (with Lydia Kirsopp Lake) counters the idea that Renaissance poetics promoted the notion that poetry was best and, ideally, longest-lasting in its original language through a study of Flemish poet Francis Thorius's translations of Ronsard into Latin, in which form they were appreciated by Sidney and his various circles. To round out the volume, and as a follow-up to her chapter, an appendix by Prescott is included on imitations of and allusions to Ronsard in England from 1635 to 1699; this catalogue offers a wealth of information on the continuing and vast role of the French Renaissance in English poetry.

The Scope of Literary Scholarship on French Connections in the English Renaissance

As a whole, these discussions teach us to beware critics of both English and French literature who fall into the older dichotomizing tradition, especially since this habit of mind remains so well entrenched even now that, in seeming to reflect the objective state of things, it continues to license glaring omissions in the guise of comprehensiveness.[4] In particular, the legacy of nineteenth-century nationalism has been so powerful that the conventions of treating the literatures of England and France as neatly divided by national borders remained almost unshakable for most of the twentieth century. It was only at the very end of the nineteenth century that small recognition was given to the French role in late sixteenth-century English letters: in *Shakespeare in France*, Jean Jules Jusserand devotes a few pages to the wide reception of French literature in London, the popularity of Marot, the Pléiade, and Rabelais, and some of the borrowings by Spenser and Shakespeare.[5]

---

[4]   Deanne Williams points out that a number of recent efforts to examine the multiple tributaries of early modern British identity have tended to focus on England, Ireland, Scotland, and Wales, omitting considerations of France altogether despite centuries of conquest going both ways and continuous cultural exchange; see *The French Fetish from Chaucer to Shakespeare* (Cambridge: Cambridge University Press, 2004), 237–8 n. 6. Williams gives two examples, David J. Baker, *Between Nations: Spenser, Marvell, and the Question of Britain* (Stanford: Stanford University Press, 1997), and David J. Baker and Willy Maley, eds., *British Identities and English Renaissance Literature* (Cambridge: Cambridge University Press, 2002).

[5]   Jean Jules Jusserand, *Shakespeare in France under the Ancien Régime* (London: T. Fisher Unwin, 1899), 18–24.

A few years later, in 1902, a more complete account of one important connection appeared in the *PMLA*, Elizabeth Robbins Hooker's "The Relation of Shakespeare to Montaigne." In this assessment the author provides newly gained, compelling evidence of the playwright's familiarity with John Florio's translation of the *Essais* in manuscript. Within the first decade of the twentieth century, the first full-length comparative study of French connections in the English Renaissance appeared, Alfred H. Upham's *The French Influence in English Literature*, which covers the major figures of the French Renaissance and their reading and textual incorporation by writers in England. Two years later, in what seems to be a competing volume, Sidney Lee offers a more broadly historical and comprehensive treatment of the topic in *The French Renaissance in England*.

Yet for many decades afterwards, in the atmosphere of resurging nationalism in Europe and North America accompanying the two World Wars, scholarship on French connections in the English Renaissance issued forth, at best, as an intermittent trickle. In 1933, Huntington Brown's *Rabelais in English Literature* treats the influence of the magisterial French Renaissance writer's work from its first appearance in England through Laurence Sterne, with special emphasis on Shakespeare. The following year saw Harold Stein's *Studies in Spenser's Complaints*, the first book on what were then called Spenser's "minor" poems, and one that addresses the importance of the poet's translations of Du Bellay to these lyrics. But it wasn't until 1960 that the next Anglo-French "Renaissance comparison" appeared, Alfred W. Satterthwaite's *Spenser, Ronsard, and Du Bellay*. What is notable about this book is not only the author's detailed treatment of Spenser's translations of Du Bellay and how they figure in both the *Complaints* and *The Faerie Queene*, but his similarly erudite examination of Du Bellay and Ronsard on their own terms, which places them on equal footing with their English counterpart.

The real turning point in Anglo-French Renaissance studies is nevertheless Anne Lake Prescott's 1978 *French Poets and the English Renaissance*. This remarkable book is foundational to current trends in the area: the author seriously engages translation as a key part of literary production and meaning, conducting detailed interpretations that are at once imaginative and rigorous, and making myriad interconnections between the two literary traditions. Her by no means dated book inaugurated a proliferation of studies. In 1983, Margaret W. Ferguson's *Trials of Desire* appeared, in which the author examines Renaissance defenses of poetry as foundational gestures. Her masterful theoretical perspective includes political, legal, aesthetic, and psychoanalytic ramifications, and in addition to Sidney and Spenser, she covers Torquato Tasso and the Italian tradition. Since then, there have been numerous books on the Anglo-French Renaissance, most of which will be familiar to readers of this volume, as well as a number of important European comparative studies that include French and English components. Although this is by no means an exhaustive list of even the best works in which the Anglo-French Renaissance figures, among outstanding titles are Thomas M. Greene's *The Light in Troy* (1982), Timothy Hampton's *Writing from History* (1990) and more recently

Fictions of Embassy (2009), William J. Kennedy's *Authorizing Petrarch* (1994) and *The Site of Petrarchism* (2003), William M. Hamlin's *The Image of America in Montaigne, Spenser, and Shakespeare* (1995), Prescott's *Imagining Rabelais in Renaissance England* (1998), Timothy J. Reiss's *Mirages of the Selfe* (2003), and David L. Sedley's *Sublimity and Skepticism in Montaigne and Milton* (2005). Most recently, the journal *Montaigne Studies* has devoted an issue to "Montaigne in England" (2012). (Readers will find a comprehensive bibliography of scholarship on French connections in the English Renaissance at the end of the volume.)

During the last decade, one of the most important books in the field is contributor Deanne Williams's prize-winning *The French Fetish from Chaucer to Shakespeare* (2004). Williams's work illustrates the revisionist turn toward transnational literature in which this volume participates. This turn marks the emergence of truly balanced portraits of English-French connections, in part, because when works such as Prescott's and Frances Yates's equally seminal *French Academies of the Sixteenth Century* first came out, they had to compete with the antithetical views of Robert Ellrodt, the distinguished French comparatist who denied that Shakespeare or Spenser, and especially the latter's *Faerie Queene*, were at all influenced by contemporary French or Italian Neoplatonism. Yates's work was especially hampered by the fact that, as she explains, she researched her study during the Second World War, when many primary sources were unavailable in England. Only recently have Jon Quitslund, Kenneth Borris, and Carol Kaske (among others) clearly demonstrated that Yates was correct and Ellrodt wrong: Spenser was "decisively influenced" (as Ellrodt himself contradictorily conceded in passing) by Louis Le Roy and the Pléiade as well as by Marsilio Ficino.[6] This late development again indicates the long persistence of old prejudices and dichotomizing tendencies that characteristically disavow French influence in an attempt to give a "backdated permanency"[7] to the English literary canon as we know it.

In keeping with recent contestations of these tendencies, this collection intervenes in a growing discourse on transnational and especially French-English connections. Much work has been done on parallel feminist or female interactions and developments in the Anglo-French tradition, such as (most notably) Margaret Ferguson's *Dido's Daughters: Literature, Gender, and Empire in Early Modern France and England* (2003). Carolyn Collette's *Performing Polity: Women and*

---

[6]   Jon A. Quitslund, *Spenser's Supreme Fiction: Platonic Natural Philosophy and "The Faerie Queene"* (Toronto: University of Toronto Press, 2001), 120–21, 240. Quitslund, Kenneth Borris, and Carol Kaske recently edited a special issue of *Spenser Studies* on Spenser and Neoplatonism (vol. 24, 2008), to which Martin (in this volume) also contributed. For the opposing position, see Robert Ellrodt, *Neoplatonism in the Poetry of Spenser*, 2nd ed. (Folcroft, PA: Folcroft Press, 1969).

[7]   This expression is from Paul Suttie, who uses it in connection with Spenser's mythologizing legitimation of Elizabeth's reign: *Self-Interpretation in* The Faerie Queene (Cambridge: D.S. Brewer, 2006), 209. The editors find the expression equally appropriate to retrospective nationalizations of literary traditions.

Agency in the Anglo-French Tradition, 1385–1620 (2006), and A.E.B. Coldiron's *English Printing, Verse Translation, and the Battle of the Sexes, 1476–1557* (2009) (in which the author's contribution to this volume, in somewhat different form, previously appeared), but few monographs or essay collections have approached the far broader scope of cultural interactions surveyed in the present anthology. Although the editors would not claim to offer an exhaustive overview of French-English Renaissance connections, they provide work from some of the most outstanding scholars in the field. Several contributors have published elsewhere on other connections that have not been included in this volume, such as Montaigne and Shakespeare (Melehy), Louise Labé and English poets (Prescott), and the reception of Marguerite de Navarre in England (Prescott); these and many other texts relevant to French-English Renaissance connections are listed in the bibliography. This volume nonetheless offers a wider range of topics than any other current anthology dealing with the subject; the few that have most recently appeared have focused more on particular (usually political) aspects of this cross-cultural phenomenon. The eight essays in this collection aptly reflect a wide variety of approaches to a field that so far continues to be slighted or sketchy, yet clearly deserves more cohesive and vibrant attention and will continue to do so in the foreseeable future.

PART 1
Translating and Transferring Gender

Chapter 1
"La Femme Replique":
English Paratexts, Genre Cues, and Versification in a Translated French Gender Debate

A.E.B. Coldiron

Some of the first and strongest connections between France and England in the early modern period are to be found in the many poems translated personally by, or under the general auspices of, the earliest printers in England. Before the mid-century organization of the Company of Stationers, many early printers in England were francophone appropriators of the materials, texts, and textual aesthetics of French print culture. William Caxton, Wynkyn de Worde, Richard Pynson, Robert Wyer, and others generated the first century of English printed poetry in significant measure from French raw materials and literary habits. Before 1557, many more English printed poems were translated from French than were translated from Italian—about six times more, according to William Ringler's count—and this fact has a number of far-reaching implications for the periodization and canons of English Renaissance poetry (and for the practice and theory of literary history more generally).[1] But this essay only looks across the English Channel at one especially curious instance of that wider appropriative process, an early gender-debate poem translated from French. Examined as a pair, the *Interlocucyon, with an argument, betwyxt man and woman* and the *Débat de l'homme et de la femme* exemplify the filtered, altered, individuated character of many of the early printer-translators' appropriations from France. Here I argue that the verbal and visual strategies of translation in the *Interlocucyon* reveal the early

---

[1] A version of this essay appears in Chapter 3 of my *English Printing, Verse Translation, and the Battle of the Sexes, 1476–1557* (Farnham, UK; Burlington, VT: Ashgate, 2009) on translations of poetry about gender in the early modern period. Excerpted by permission of the Publishers; © 2009, Ashgate Press. For fuller discussion see my "Translation's Challenge to Critical Categories," *Yale Journal of Criticism* 16.2 (October 2003): 315–44. For examination of early francophone printers in terms of the work of Habermas and Pratt, see my "Public Sphere/Contact Zone," *Criticism* 46.2 (2004): 207–22. All translations here are mine except as otherwise noted. Thanks to seminar participants at the Attending to Early Modern Women Conference (2006) at the University of Maryland for discussion of these poems. For William Ringler, see *Bibliography and Index of English Printed Verse 1476–558* (Mansell), p. 6.

16   *French Connections in the English Renaissance / Coldiron*

English printers' varied, experimental appropriations of certain elements of French gender discourses and their refusal of others. The French and English versions participate in their respective literary cultures, but these elements position each differently within its own culture. In other words, the same content comes to mean something rather different because the apparently slight interventions of the printer and translator have much larger stylistic and literary-aesthetic consequences.

One of Wynkyn de Worde's many imprints about women and gender relations, the *Interlocucyon betwyxt man and woman* ... is a translation of *Le Débat de l'homme et de la femme* written by Guillaume Alexis in about 1460 and printed at least seven different times before 1530.[2] Unlike most of Wynkyn's other output, however, this little book is notable for giving the woman the last, longest word. Well before Gosynhill's *Schole House for Women* and *Mulierum Paean* break out the traditional arguments into separate he-said-she-said treatises, this work voices a male and female speaker in direct debate, flinging stanzas at each other inside one poetic work. The work's early appropriation of French gender discourses, and particularly its amplified female interlocutor, anticipates the better-known English debates of the mid and late sixteenth century.[3]

---

[2]   Alexis, *Le debat de lome et de la fe[m]me* (Lyon: Pierre Mareschal s.d. [v.1490]); *Le debat de lhomme et de la femme* (Paris: Trepperel 1493); *Sensuyt le debat de lomme et de la femme* (Paris: Jehan Trepperel, s.d. but probably c.1500); *Le debat* ... (Paris: Guillaume Nyverd, s.d. [v. 1520]); *Le debat* ... (Paris: s.n., s.d. but c.1520); another, (Paris: s.n. s.d., c.1525); fuller bibliographical details, pp. 127–31 in *Oeuvres Poétiques de Guillaume Alexis, Prieur de Bucy*, eds. Arthur Piaget and Émile Picot (Paris: Firmin Didot, 1896–1908; rpt SATF 1968), I. 121–44. The full title of the English translation is *Here begynneth an interlocucyon, with an argument, betwyxt man and woman* ... (London: Wynkyn de Worde, 1525), facs. rpt., ed. Diane Bornstein, *The Feminist Controversy of the Renaissance: Guillaume Alexis, An Argument Betwyxt Man and Woman (1525); Sir Thomas Elyot, The Defence of Good Women (1545); Henricius Cornelius Agrippa, Female Pre-Eminence (1670)* (Delmar, NY: Scholars' Facsimiles and Reprints, 1980); Piaget and Picot also reprint the English poem, pp. 145–55. Priscilla Bawcutt explores a Scots translation written in the Aberdeen Sasine Register II. 480–81 (1502–1507) and explains that "the two works [in English and Scots] were translated independently" from the French (40), offers information about dating and authorship, and clarifies several readings. She finds that this abbreviated, reordered version "appears more misogynistic than the French work. It not only displaces the woman's climactic speech from its final position, but ends with the man's denunciation of female trickery" (39); "An Early Scottish Debate Poem on Women," *Scottish Literary Journal* 23.2 (Nov. 1996): 35–42.

[3]   Diane Bornstein, ed., pp. v–vii and xi, places the work in the venerable line of "woman question" publications, between classical or medieval tracts and the Renaissance prose treatises—between, on the one hand, Jerome, Theophrastus, Mathéolus, Deschamps, Boccaccio, Christine de Pizan, and Map, and on the other, Gosynhill's pamphlets, Elyot's *Defence of Good Women*, the *Prayse of All Women*, the *Treatise of Nobilitie and Excellencie of Woman Kynde,* and several others. See also Blamires; Wright; Utley, especially pp. 339–41; Gay; Linda Woodbridge, *Women and the English Renaissance: Literature and the Nature of Womankind, 1540–1620* (Urbana and Chicago: University of Illinois Press,

"La Femme Replique" 17

Michel-André Bossy and Diane Bornstein have provided excellent, foundational readings of this work, well worth brief review here. Bornstein summarizes the positions of the two speakers:

> In the debate both the man and the woman base their arguments mainly on scriptural authority. The man begins with Eve to demonstrate the evil of women. In turn the woman counters with the Virgin Mary, an example she uses several times.... The man uses all the traditional anti-feminist jibes: women paint their faces and waste money on clothes; they deceive men, flatter, and lie; they speak too much, scold, gossip, contradict men, and reveal their secrets; they are avaricious ... The woman ... [enumerates] the virtues of women: they are chaste, religious, and merciful; they are good nurses and mothers; and they are generous patrons when they own property. (viii)

Bornstein points out that "for most of the debate the woman is on the defensive" until the long final section in which "she cites a series of negative male examples ... men are aggressive, violent, deceitful, and ungrateful; they often act as murderers, tyrants, criminals, and war mongers; instead of slandering women, who are their mothers and nurses, they should be grateful to them" (ix). Bossy, writing about the French version, explains that while Alexis's oeuvre is generally anti-feminist, this work defends women even though it appears to debate the question.[4] The long final section's unanswered condemnations of men and the French version's verbally adept female speaker create this unusual result.

In their content, the French and English versions differ very little. But the English translation, even while preserving content, makes meaningful changes to the French text. Paratextual changes, for instance, may not alter a work's content, but they matter a great deal in how French gender debates are conveyed to English readers. In the case of the *Interlocucyon*, the printer and translator create a complex and specifically literary set of frames for the English version of the debate. First, the translation passes itself off as an English work: in the framing paratexts, at least, there is no mention of a source or of the French version. (In Lawrence Venuti's terms, it is an "invisible" translation, pretending to be a native; this debate is to be claimed as English.) While most extant French imprints include in the title or colophon Guillaume Alexis's name and status as a monk (the "Prieur de Bucy"), Wynkyn's edition bears no author's name. Many of Wynkyn's other translated works are invisible in the same way, so this suppression of Frenchness

---

1984); Pamela Joseph Benson, *The Invention of the Renaissance Woman* (University Park: Pennsylvania State University Press, 1992); Katherine Henderson and Barbara McManus, *Half Humankind: Contexts and Texts of the Controversy about Women in England, 1540–1640* (Urbana and Chicago: University of Illinois Press, 1984); Lloyd Davis, ed., *Sexuality and Gender in the English Renaissance: An Annotated Edition of Contemporary Documents* (New York: Garland, 1998).

[4]   Michel-André Bossy, "Woman's Plain Talk in *Le Débat de l'omme et de la femme* by Guillaume Alexis," *Fifteenth Century Studies* 16 (1990): 23–41; see pp. 23–5.

and of authorship are not unusual in Wynkyn's output.[5] Wynkyn's habit, like that of many early English printer-translators, was to adopt not only texts but layouts, page design, woodcuts, book design, typefaces, and so on; this imprint is no exception. The English *Interlocucyon* does include two woodcuts, and Wynkyn may have taken the design concept of this work from one of the many extant French imprints.[6] The title cut Wynkyn uses (Figure 1) resembles a stock woodcut found in French marriage complaint poems, and its male figure also appears in the title cut of another early translated French debate poem (*The Seyenges of Salomon and Marcolphus*, 1529). Bornstein thinks that the title cut to the *Interlocucyon* signals the printer's understanding of the work as anti-feminist (vii). I think it also indicates his understanding that both imprints are part of a general area of interest for his readers—"woman questions"—a topic that can be usefully advertised to customers with such commonly reused woodcuts, part of a strand or sub-genre of discourse that will be identifiable and marketable. The title woodcut depicts the poem exactly: a debate between a man and a woman; but it may do more than that, whether as part of a plan or because of a technological problem in the woodcut.

Several colleagues have suggested to me that the blank speech banner above the woman's head is a sign that she is silenced, but I would argue the contrary: blank banderoles were common above early interchangeable cuts. Furthermore, the woman has both a speech banner and a speaking hand gesture, while the man, who does have a speaking hand gesture, has clearly had his speech banner obliterated by two pieces of border design that are asymmetrical, obvious additions. Other uses of this same factotum man, such as the *Salomon and Marcolphus* title cut, do allow him his speech banner. (Perhaps it was thought easier to debate a king than a woman; or perhaps the speaking figures supplicate, while the silent figures are the more powerful.) Was it really a selling point for Wynkyn's book that the woman silences the man on the title page? Was it even deliberate on Wynkyn's part—or might the inserted, asymmetrical border design have merely been used to try to cover a problem with the woodblock or in the printing process? (The male figure's

---

[5]   I think that Martha Driver's point about printer Robert Wyer, regarding the tendency of early printers to suppress source authorship, extends to Wynkyn as well. See "Christine de Pisan and Robert Wyer: *The .C. Hystoryes of Troye, or L'Epistre d'Othea* Englished." *Gutenberg Jahrbuch*, 1997: 125–39.

[6]   It may not be possible to determine with certainty which one. The title cut to the edition of c.1490 (Lyon) shows a courtly interior scene between an aristocratic man and woman. The title cut to the first Paris edition by J. Trepperel, c.1493, offers a typical border design with large-lettered inscription moving clockwise from bottom left. The second Trepperel edition, Paris c.1500, seems to me the best candidate to have been the version imitated by the English printers: the title cut features two stock figures separated by a tree. An undated Trepperel and a Paris edition by Nyverd (c.1520) are missing their title pages. A Paris edition of 1530 has the famous clerk-at-desk woodcut as its title, like the one Wynkyn uses as a title-verso cut, and two other cuts within showing a man with a sword speaking to a woman. See the notes to Piaget and Picot's edition, and Tchemerzine I.74–8. Not every banderole is a speech banner (some bear names), but in a debate poem, the speech function seems more appropriate.

"La Femme Replique" 19

Fig. 1   Title page from *Interlocucyon, with an argument, betwyxt man and woman, & which of them could proue to be most excellẽt.* Anon. (London: de Worde, 1525). © British Library Board, Shelfmark W.P.9530. All rights reserved.

reappearance in 1529 appears to be a re-cut, but I have not examined the original to be certain.) What is certain is that the title cut to the *Interlocucyon* is not only a more direct representation of text than Wynkyn usually gives, but also a more specific one, since regardless of the printer's motives, the image illustrates, with the obliterated speech banner above the male factotum figure, that the woman will be the dominant speaker in this debate (which she in fact turns out to be, in her long last-word finale section). That important final element of the French debate poem, the woman's long unanswered catalogue of bad men, is not only translated verbally but is represented visually in the title image.

The next woodcut in the work, on the title verso, is a famous, oft-used cut of the cleric-at-desk. However odd it seems to modern readers at first glance, this cut may be a visual gesture to the authorship, genre, and literary history of the French source. The French versions generally mention Guillaume Alexis as author in colophons or titles, if not by name, then as the Prieur de Bucy. While there is no mention in the English version of Alexis or of any French author, this verso image at least puts a monk-figure at the threshold, thus placing the work in a clerical or scholarly tradition of "woman question" treatises, perhaps in the line of Mathéolus or Jerome. This dual-woodcut presentation makes a certain kind of sense, signaling readers first that the work is a gender debate in which the woman dominates strongly, and next that the work may have clerical origins and may be expected to trot out the standard misogynist topoi for popular consumption.

However, while the poem itself fulfills entirely the promise of the debate-scene title cut that the woman's part will overpower the man's, and while the male speaker's part of the poem fulfills the verso cut's promise of clerical misogyny, the poem's verbal frame—a frame added by the English translator—adds a third, rather more complex implication. The new English framing speaker overhears the man and woman debating as if in a *chanson d'aventure* or (day)dream-vision poem. The new verbal frame thus positions the work differently still: this will indeed be a debate, with male misogyny silenced by female speech, but it will also locate itself against courtly as well as scholarly traditions. The English-added frame begins

> When Pheb[us] reluysa[n]t / most arde[n]t was a shene
> In the hote sommer season / for my solace
> Under the umbre of a tre / bothe fayre [&] grene
>   I lay downe to rest me / where in this case.
>
> As after ye shall here / a stryfe there began
> Whiche longe sys endure / with great argument
> Bytwyxte the woman / and also the man
> Whiche of them coulde proue / to be moost excellent.
>
>   The man.
> The fyrst whiche I herde: was the ma[n] that sayde
> ...

At this point the actual debate begins. After 49 quatrains (the last 11 of which are spoken by the woman), the translator adds the following framing lines to end the poem:

> The auctor.
> Of this argument / the hole entent
> I marked it / effectually
> And after I had herde / them at this discent
> I presed towardes them / incontynently
> But when they sawe me / aproche them to
> Lest I wolde repreue / theyr argument
> Full fast they fledde / then bothe me fro
> That I ne wyst / whyther they went
> Wherfore now to iudge / whiche is moost excellent
> I admyt it / unto this reders prudence
> Whyther to man or woman / is more conuenyent
> The laude to be gyuen / and wordly [sic] magnyfycence.

The *chanson d'aventure* frame is also, of course, French-born. Related to the medieval dream vision (even though this speaker never actually admits to falling asleep), this frame places explicit responsibility on the readers to draw their own conclusions ("I admyt it unto this reders prudence"). Both dream-vision and *chanson d'aventure* frames allow the narrating or authorial speaker a safe distance from the topic and an appearance of neutrality. So the translator frames Alexis's bare debate with a revised authorial persona—not the author named in the source or even the Prieur de Bucy implied in the inner woodcut, but a quasi-courtly "Auctor" persona. This "Auctor" strongly re-frames the debate of the title cut's bourgeois factotum figures as if they were courtly speakers in a romance, romantic, or even sexual encounter. The mixed signals of these paratexts—the gender-debate woodcut, the clerical-line woodcut, the courtly-literary framing device, the forensic format and versification—open the work quite curiously in English. Except that they each represent the work as in some way "literary," the paratexts don't really reflect a coherent presentational strategy for this work. Like other early printer-translators, Wynkyn, an active intervener in and re-packager of French gender discourses, may have been experimenting with representational strategies for the material. Printers and readers in 1525 were still setting out the horizons of expectation for the new English poetry, and poems on gender, as this one suggests, proved to be an important line of experimentation.

In addition to these visual and verbal translations, the translator (who may also have been Wynkyn de Worde) intervenes with a new set of versification strategies for the *Interlocucyon*. As with so many English translations from French, the short French lines of the source—*octosyllabes* in this case—are rendered in longer English lines. However, this translator doesn't show much metrical skill. The lines turn out as approximate, irregular pentameters, despite the labored and clumsy visual marking of caesuras in nearly every line. Several stanzas in the final section are closer to tetrameter, and as in the above passage, some lines are short and some (the poem's final line, for instance) are hendecasyllabic or longer. This change is typical in early verse translations from French to English: instead of allusive, abstract, compressed, epigrammatic French lines, we find specific, verbally textured English lines, often with doubling or amplification. The body of the *Interlocucyon* is made up of quatrains in crossed rhyme (*abab*), not *rimes plates* (*aabb*) as in Alexis's poem. This results in a slower pace and a woven rather than a stacked or epigrammatic effect.

Alexis's stanzas are really remarkable—the repeated "ia" rhyme in the third line of each quatrain is very difficult to sustain. The English translator wisely chooses instead to vary his rhymes throughout the work, giving himself much more flexibility. However, this means that the snappy phonetics and the spirited dueling refrains of the French debate are missing from the start, losing most of the French version's rhetorical play and point. This loss is considerable, and when read in its full contexts, this aesthetic difference changes the balance and meaning of the gender debate. The opening lines, as edited by Picot and Piaget, will illustrate:

> LOmme commence.
> Adam jadis, le premier pere,
> Par femme encourut mort amere
> Qui tresmal le consilia :
> Bien eureux est qui rien n'y a.
> La femme respond.
> Jhesus de femme vierge et mere
> Fut fait homme, c'est chose clere ;
> Aussi nous reconsilia :
> Malheureux est qui rien n'y a[7]

In English, the corresponding stanzas are:

> The Man.
> The fyrst whiche I herde was the Man that sayde:
> Adam our forfather by Woman's shrewde councell
> To ete of an apple was pyteously betrayde.
> Well happy is he that with you dothe not mell.
> The Woman.
> Jhesu of a mayden and vyrgyn his mother
> Was incarnated to redeme that man had loste
> Set thou this one now agayne the other
> And Woman is more excellent in every coste

---

[7] "The man begins. Long ago, Adam, the first father, incurred bitter death because of a woman who advised him very badly; happy is he who has no part in it [i.e., relations with women]. The woman answers. Jesus was made man through a woman virgin and mother, that's clear; so it reconciles us: unhappy is he who has no part in it." Translations are mine unless otherwise noted; many thanks to Nancy Vine Durling for helpful corrections and suggestions on the translations.

Specificity (the apple), adverbial additions ("pyteously"), and doubling ("mayden and vyrgyn") are entirely typical changes in translating from the shorter French to the longer English line. The English version, especially with 10- and 12-syllable lines like these, loses the punchy rhythms of the *octosyllabe* couplets. Moreover, the English version drops the complex cross-stanza wordplay in which the woman repeats but revises the man's words in exactly the same verbal pattern, effectively flinging them back at him in a nearly stichomythic style. In French, the third line verbs ("consilia/reconsilia," and in other stanza pairs, for instance, "adulteria/ maria," "ydolitria/humilia," "on n'y a/supplia," "spolia/employa") tighten the verbal connection between stanza pairs, sharpening the tension between assertion and contradiction. The woman picks up the man's rhyme schemes, as well, using whatever rhyme he selects for the *aa* couplet in her own *aa*. The refrains powerfully reinforce this effect: "Bien heureux qui rien n'y a / Malheureux qui rien n'y a," sustained throughout the poem, form an important structural counterpoint lost entirely to the English. The rhyme scheme is in fact not just *aabb*, it is *aabb aabb ccbb ccbb ddbb ddbb* and so on, a showy, heightened performance indeed.

Also lost with these parallel refrains is a piece of fifteenth-century intertextuality: the French lines imitate almost exactly a double-ballade refrain set in Villon's *Le Grant Testament*.[8] English readers may not have had the same full, immediate mental access to those lines as French readers likely had; I suspect that a translator who added *chanson d'aventure* framing stanzas would have known them and could have decided to use them. Yet if the translator were aware of this echo, either he did not think his English readers would be aware of it, or he did not think it was worth the effort to convey—that, or such specifically allusive intertextuality is not something that is finally possible to convey in another literary tradition.[9] Sometimes translators bring French refrains straight into English verse without translating them at all, as in the *Beaute of Women* (1525, 1540), but Alexis's flashy, allusive refrains did not come across intact. In any case, along with the sound-play of the dueling refrains, the poem's gesture to (and joining of) the community of French readers and poets is gone. The poem can no longer signal itself as part of the Villon family nor engage with the sub-culture of late-medieval readers for whom debating was a staple poetic art.

Furthermore, the removal of the dueling refrains and answering rhymes from the English also removes rhetorical power from the woman speaker, who in the French version is the one we end up wanting to listen to, waiting to see how she will cap him *this* time. The verbal suspense and interest of the poem, in other words, rest with the energy of this remarkable female speaker, and the English

---

[8]   Piaget and Picot, eds, identify the allusion, pp. 121–2. Bossy, pp. 23–4, reminds us that it could have been Villon who borrowed it from Alexis. It seems likely that this was a commonplace, nearly proverbial refrain line.

[9]   One loss of deep context may in part explain some of the verbal differences: could English readers have brought the long echoing traditions of the Occitan and Provençal *tenzone* to their reading of gender debates in the same way French readers might have done?

woman, while offering almost exactly the same rebuttals as far as the content goes, doesn't come across as a particularly adroit or exciting interlocutor.

However, Michel-André Bossy points out that compared to its own literary milieu, the French poem actually features a relatively plain-speaking female persona.[10] Here is a case where a comparative historicist method can clarify distinctions that are otherwise lost. In Bossy's view, the French female speaker's plainness relative to the flashy French rhetoric of Alexis's literary world works out as an implied advantage for the woman. Too much verbal cleverness could substantiate charges of being "cauteleuse" or sneaky, flattering, lying, and verbally manipulative. If she is a plain-speaker, she exonerates herself of those charges with each unornamented stanza. She is very much plainer in English, but the advantage of plain-spokenness is lost when it is placed in a relatively flattened English context: *rhétoriqueurs* were not wildly popular in England (as they were in France), so instead of looking honorably plain-by-contrast, she risks seeming just commonly dull. And the English poem is much less verbally entertaining overall, which by the end renders its proto-feminist content less persuasive. In translation, then, the female speaker has lost both the advantage of relative plainness and any advantage a verbal dexterity could have given her in English.

However, in the remarkable final section of the French poem, the woman speaks 52 lines of nonstop couplets defending women and (mostly) attacking men. Titled "La femme replique" in both French and English versions, this final section lets the translator's cloak of invisibility slip, revealing the poem's French origins. It is notable that the visibly French origin pops out just at the moment the woman's speech dominates. This final section gives the woman the last word—many last words in fact. In French scholarship on the poem there has been some question about whether or not this final section might simply be another poem grafted on here; its ranting couplets in French make a real break with the flashy stanzaic dueling of the rest of the poem.[11] The content is very close between versions, but at this key point in the poem, the translation of rhyme matters: the English translator turns this final section's French couplets into eleven more *abab* quatrains. The new English rhyme-scheme thus makes for a more coherent result, unifying the woman speaker's long final section with the rest of the poem. In other words, what had seemed a postscript in French seems in English like the woman speaker's complete takeover of the form and content of the poem. Here we see another frequent habit of the early translator-printers: striving for a formal consistency in the English literary product, they often select one English verse form and stick with it, regardless of variations in the French source. In some cases this ruins certain effects of the French, but here it changes the woman's final speech from an afterthought to a more seamless part of the whole—from tacked-on coda to triumphant finale.

---

[10]   *Passim*, but some convenient examples are on p. 31.

[11]   Piaget and Picot, eds., pp. 122–3.

In its French milieu, the *Débat* does not stand out so much in terms of its rhetorical performance (such was the French emphasis on verbal effects in Alexis's day and for decades after), yet it is still much more rhetorically flashy than the English translation. In French the poem is one among many such *débat* exercises.[12] In the context of Alexis's oeuvre it is more exercise than sincere expression. Alexis cannot be thought of as having a feminist or even proto-feminist sensibility, but he did create an effective, rhetorically interesting female speaker. However, in the English context of Wynkyn's printed output (since we do not know the translator's identity), the poem looks decidedly literary and proto-feminist. It displays negative male exempla and men's culpable behaviors and gives the woman a much more real, effective, and integrated voice than she finds in other contemporary imprints debating gender issues.[13] In English the poem may lose rhetorical sparks, but its content is in some sense a special link, as Bornstein shows, between medieval and Renaissance treatises on women.

Despite the strong presence of Christine de Pizan in early English print,[14] the woman's side of the *querelie* is voiced relatively little in early English poetry (compared, that is, with French poetry). But in the *Interlocucyon*, at least, the verbal and visual interventions of the printer and translator do import from France the effective speaking woman and her long last word. But even though the English printer features her final tirade on the title cut, she is double-framed with competing genres and hobbled with clunky cross-rhymed pentameters. Indeed, she would seem to have lost her stylish wit in the crossing. While the content of the poem itself may successfully span some cultural distance between early modern France and England. the aesthetic and poetic distances are too great. As is so often the case in translations, the paratexts signal a bridging effort and are thus the mark of larger differences operating, at a particular moment, between the two literary systems.

---

[12] See Paul Meyer's list in "Mélanges de poésie française: Plaidoyer en faveur des femmes," *Romania* 6 (1877): 499–503. See also Utley, p. 54.

[13] Compare, for instance, Wynkyn's imprint from Lydgate, *The payne and sorowe of euyll maryage*, c.1530 (STC 19119). Outside the scope of this essay is an oblique complication to the matter of speaking women: the English suppression of two French stanzas about women and the priesthood.

[14] Christine's actual *querelle* documents do not appear in early English print, and her presence is less as a gender debater than as a powerful advisory authority on matters ranging from military strategy to political governance to the education of princes and the historiography and mythography of Troy. See my "Taking Advice from a Frenchwoman: Caxton, Pynson, and Christine de Pizan" in *Caxton's Trace: Studies in the History of English Printing*, ed. William Kuskin (University of Notre Dame Press, 2005), 127–66.

Chapter 2
Isabelle de France, Child Bride[1]

Deanne Williams

"J'étais une pucelle."
— Jacqueline Kennedy to André Malraux, about life before her
marriage to John F. Kennedy

For most readers, the queen in *Richard II* is an adult. As Jean Howard and Phyllis Rackin put it, Shakespeare "transforms the child [of historical record] into a mature woman," in a manner that is, like so much of Shakespearean history, "unhistorical."[2] In his Cambridge edition of the play, Andew Gurr states that Shakespeare's queen is actually a conflation of the historical Isabelle de France and her predecessor, Richard's first wife, Anne of Bohemia, a tradition that appears to stem from Horace Walpole.[3] Theatrical productions of the play thus tend to cast the queen as a grown woman: Kathryn Pogson, Anna Carteret, and Michael Brown, in an all-male production of the play, played the role in their thirties, and Sian Thomas and Ellen Tree (Mrs. Charles Kean) played it in their forties.[4]

---

[1] The author thanks the Social Sciences and Humanities Research Council of Canada, the Huntington Library, the Centre for Reformation and Renaissance Studies at the University of Toronto, Terry Goldie, David Goldstein, Hassan Melehy, and Stephen Orgel.

[2] Jean E. Howard and Phyllis Rackin, *Gendering a Nation. A Feminist Account of Shakespeare's English Histories* (London: Routledge, 1997), 157. Peter Ure refers to the "the unhistorical conception of Isabel as a mature woman" in his Arden edition of *King Richard II* (London: Methuen, 1956), xliii. Charles Kean writes, "Shakespeare has deviated from historical truth in the introduction of Richard's queen as a woman in the present piece." *Shakespeare's Play of Richard II Arranged for Representation at the Princess's Theatre With Historical and Explanatory Notes by Charles Kean* (London: John K. Chapman, 1857), 43.

[3] *King Richard II*, ed. Andrew Gurr. The New Cambridge Shakespeare (Cambridge, Cambridge University Press, 1984 updated 2003), 65. Edmund Malone credits Horace Walpole's suggestion in his 1821 edition of Shakespeare's *Plays and Poems*: *The Plays and Poems of William Shakespeare* vol. XVI (London, 1821), 53.

[4] The youngest queen I can find is Janet Maw, who was 24 when she appeared in Ian McKellen's 1978 TV production. Lily Brayton (b. 1876) also played the part in her twenties, from 1900–1909. In the 2007 RSC production of Shakespeare's histories, the youth of Hannah Barrie's twenty-something queen was highlighted by the much-older Jonathan Slinger. Interestingly, it was Fiona Shaw's performance of King Richard in Deborah Warner's 1995 production that was described as "girlish." Carol Chillington Rutter, "Fiona Shaw's Richard II: The Girl as Player-King as Comic" *Shakespeare Quarterly* 48 (1997): 314–24. On his 1988 National Theatre production, starring Derek Jacobi, Clifford

28 *French Connections in the English Renaissance / Williams*

The theatrical tradition of the adult Isabelle is illustrated by G.H. Broughton's painting, *Queen Isabella and Her Ladies*.[5]

The historical Isabelle de France, however, was famous for being a child bride. Isabelle de France (1389–1409) married Richard II (1367–1400) in 1396, when she was just 7 and Richard was 29. Isabelle was the daughter of the French King Charles VI, a member of the house of Valois, and his wife, Isabeau de Bavière. Devastated by the death of his first wife, Anne of Bohemia, in 1394, Richard II rapidly entered into marriage negotiations.[6] Charles VI had initially offered his daughter to Richard II when she was just five, in an effort to prevent the English king from marrying Yolande, the daughter of the King of Aragon.[7] Cheered by the prospect of marrying Isabelle, for whom he received a very large dowry, and eager to bring the long war with France to a conclusion, Richard dismissed all other prospects of a more suitable age. Agnes Strickland, who devotes a lengthy chapter to the girl queen in her *Lives of the Queens of England* (1851), conjectures that Richard expected his grief to have diminished by the time Isabelle was old enough to consummate their marriage (2).[8]

As Helen Ostovich observes, "historically, Queen Isabel's claim to fame was her age."[9] Jean Froissart's *Chroniques*, one of Shakespeare's major sources for the play, reveals a fascination with Isabelle's age that borders on obsession.[10]

Williams writes: "Clearly, it would be disastrous to invite a child of ten to play queen Isabel. The content of the poetic form of her speeches precludes such a notion." <http://www. sparrowsp.addr.com/theatre%20pages/richard_ii_1.htm>.

[5]   <http://www.english.emory.edu/classes/Shakespeare_Illustrated/Broughton. Isabella.html>. See, for comparison's sake, the contemporary image by Jean Fouquet: <http://commons.wikimedia.org/wiki/File:Isabelle_de_France.jpg>.

[6]   J.J.N. Palmer, *England, France, and Christendom* 1377–1399 (London: Routledge and Kegan Paul, 1972), 169–79 and his "The Background to Richard II's Marriage to Isabel of France (1396)" *Bulletin of the Institute of Historical Research* XLIV no. 109 (May 1971): 1–17.

[7]   Yolande, who had been engaged to the Duke of Anjou, was championed by the English. But the French were threatened by an English alliance with Aragon, and demanded that Yolande honor this previous engagement.

[8]   Agnes Strickland, *Lives of the Queens of England, from the Norman Conquest* vol. 2 (London: Henry Colburn, 1851), 2.

[9]   Helen Ostovich, "'Here in this Garden': The Iconography of the Virgin Queen in *Richard II*," *Marian Moments in British Drama*, ed. Regina Buccola and Lisa Hopkins (London: Ashgate, 2007), 21–34 at 21. Ostovich's argument, one of very few serious treatments of this character, links Shakespeare's treatment of the queen to medieval iconography of the Virgin Mary.

[10]   My edition is the Lord Berners translation, which was most likely Shakespeare's source: *Here beginneth the third and fourthe boke of Syr John Froissart of the cronycles of Englande, France, Spaygne, Portyngale, Scotland, Bretayne, Flaunders, and other places adioynyng, translated out of french into englishe by Johan Bourchier knight lorde Berners ...* (London, 1525). The most relevant chapters are CXCIX, CC, CCIII, CCX, CCXIII. On the subject of Froissart, Charles Forker writes, "It is therefore hard to disagree with Tillyard, who thought it 'scarcely conceivable that Shakespeare should not have read so famous a

Consistently referring to her youth, Froissart offers a series of anecdotes that reveal the little girl to be charmingly self-possessed and quite precocious. Strickland imagines it as quite the *cause célèbre*: "They [the people of England] saw with astonishment an infant, not nine summers old, sharing the throne as the chosen queen-consort of a monarch who had reached his thirtieth year" (1). Shakespeare had just created the imaginative, insightful, and intrepid Juliet, who was "not yet fourteen," and it is possible to imagine him turning, then, to a historical figure with intelligence and *sang froid* who just happened to be ten.

What happens to the queen in *Richard II* when we imagine her, not as a composite, but instead as a dramatic representation of her historical counterpart, Isabelle de France? Turning to Shakespeare's French sources, especially Froissart's *Chroniques*, which places heavy emphasis upon Isabelle's status as a child bride, this chapter recovers the historical and biographical information that shaped Shakespeare's conception of Richard's queen. It seeks to detach this character from the notion that she could only be an "unhistorical" adult, which appears to have its roots in Enlightenment and Victorian notions of childhood and girlhood as a distinct and protected space, and to return her to a medieval and early modern historical context in which it is possible—albeit highly unusual—for a little girl to be both a wife and a queen.[11] I am not, in the spirit of Philippe Ariès, seeking to deny Isabelle's childhood as an anachronism.[12] Rather, I am seeking to recover the girlhood of a historical figure and a dramatic character that has been lost as a result of theatrical tradition and habits of reading Shakespearean history that focus upon English nationhood.

---

book' (253), or with Bullough, 'It would be strange if Shakespeare did not look into' a work that conveys a 'sense ... of being in the situations described' (3.3.67)." *King Richard II*, ed. Charles R. Forker. *The Arden Shakespeare Third Series* (London: Thomson Learning, 2002), 153.

[11] In this way my chapter participates in recent attempts to recover early modern conceptualizations of girlhood. Sara Mendelson and Patricia Crawford, *Women in Early Modern England* 1550–1720 (Oxford: Oxford University Press, 1998). Discussions of girlhood in later periods include: Carolyn Steedman, *Strange Dislocations: Childhood and the Idea of Interiority* (Cambridge: Harvard University Press, 1995); Catherine Robson, *Men in Wonderland: The Lost Girlhood of the Victorian Gentleman* (Princeton: Princeton University Press, 2003); and *Secret Gardens, Satanic Mills: Placing Girls in European History, 1750–1960*, ed. Mary Jo Maynes, Birgitte Søland, and Christina Benninghaus (Bloomington: Indiana University Press, 2005). See also the chapter on "Theatres of Girlhood" in Seth Lerer, *Children's Literature: A Reader's History from Aesop to Harry Potter* (Chicago: University of Chicago Press, 2008), 228–51.

[12] Philippe Ariès, *Centuries of Childhood. A Social History of Family Life*, trans. Robert Baldrick (New York: Vintage, 1960). More recent studies of medieval and early modern English childhood, such as Linda A. Pollock, *Forgotten Children: Parent Child Relations from 1500–1900* (Cambridge: Cambridge University Press, 1983) and Barbara Hanawalt, *Growing Up in Medieval London: the Experience of Childhood in History* (Oxford: Oxford University Press, 1995) contest Ariès, claiming that childhood was conceptualized, and that children even enjoyed a special status.

To read Shakespeare's queen through the child bride of historical record is, therefore, to return attention to *Richard II*'s investment in French sources and representation of England's longstanding history with France and the French.[13] Following his deposition, Richard tells his queen, "Hie thee to France, / And cloister thee in some religious house (5.1.22–3).[14] Richard's almost obsessively repeated references to France ("Prepare thee hence for France" 37; "you must away to France" 54; "Weep thou for me in France" 87) reinforce Isabel's French origins and Richard's French affiliations, as well as England's pre-Reformation Catholic religion. France here serves not only as a refuge, but also as a site of nostalgia for both royal pomp, "… from whence, set forth in pomp, / She came adorned hither like sweet May" (78–9), and religious practice. The play's final reference to its dead king is Exton's: "Herein all breathless lies / The mightiest of thy greatest enemies, / Richard of Bourdeaux" (5.6.31–3). Returning him to his French birthplace, these lines also recast the play's depiction of civil strife in terms of England's ongoing military and territorial rivalry with the French.[15]

Elizabeth I famously quipped, "I am Richard II, know ye not that?" but the Virgin Queen in *Richard II*, whose very name, Isabel, is a French version of "Elizabeth," offers other opportunities for political allegory.[16] As confirmation, perhaps, of Elizabeth's wisdom in avoiding a French match, and as a figure identified with Catholicism as opposed to Elizabeth's Protestant faith, the queen functions as a symbol of England's open, fluid, and constant relations with France that Shakespeare's history plays seek, at least on the surface, to overcome.[17] She symbolizes, in particular, the hotly contested Anglo-French peace treaty, which ended one phrase of the Hundred Years War, and which Richard's critics felt illustrated the king's susceptibility to French influence. Given the play's careful emphasis upon the historical details that underpin the queen's French identity, it seems perverse to deny her the most salient aspect of her historicity, namely her girlhood. To imagine Richard's queen, neither as a redoubtable Victorian matron, nor as an anachronistic Bohemian hybrid, but as a little girl, as a pawn

---

[13] I discuss *Richard II* as part of the history plays' ongoing engagement with France in chapter 5 of my *The French Fetish from Chaucer to Shakespeare* (Cambridge: Cambridge University Press, 2004), 181–226.

[14] Here Shakespeare anticipates the cloistered Isabella in *Measure for Measure*: a character who, like Isabelle of France, was good at rejecting the offers of her admirers. My edition is *King Richard II, The Arden Shakespeare*.

[15] This detail is also mentioned in Froissart (fol. CC. xlvii r). Exton's words here also invoke, ironically, the hero of a famous French romance, *Huon of Burdeaux*, who manages to elude death by performing a series of Herculean tasks.

[16] Stephen Orgel, "I am Richard II," *Spectacular Performances* (Manchester: Manchester University Press,): 7–35 offers a full discussion of this event, the details of which can also be found in the Arden Two edition of *Richard II*, ed. Peter Ure (London: Methuen, 1956 rpt 1964), lvii–lix.

[17] For a discussion of Marlowe's *Dido, Queen of Carthage* in a similar context see my "Dido Queen of England" *ELH* 71 (Spring, 2006): 31–59.

Isabelle de France, Child Bride

in international politics, and as the undeserving victim of the play's political machinations, is to intensify our sympathy for her plight at a dramatic level, and, at an interpretive level, to recognize her status as a compelling French counterpoint to the play's overarching English nationalist teleology.

A French Princess

Nigel Saul writes:

> the predominance in the English royal line of French wives was a natural reflection of the longstanding Angevin or Plantagenet interests in France. For over two centuries ... it was through marital alliances between the English and French lines that differences between the two competing dynasties were accommodated.[18]

A list of French queens of England would include Eleanor d'Aquitaine (1122–1204), Eleanor de Provence (1223–1291), and another Isabelle de France (1292–1358), the wife of Edward II, who had been promised to Edward while still an infant. Shakespeare's history plays represent some of these French queens: there is Isabelle de France's little sister, Catherine de Valois (1401–1437), who married Henry V, and Margaret d'Anjou (1430–1482), the wife of Henry VI. Isabelle d'Angoulême (1188–1246), who, at 12, married King John, is strangely absent from Shakespeare's *King John* (although her mother-in-law, Eleanor d'Aquitaine, plays a prominent role).

According to Froissart's *Chroniques*, Isabelle's age was a major issue in the marriage negotiations with Richard II. There were even jokes made about it at the wedding.[19] Canon law allowed a girl lawfully to consent at seven, but marriages typically took place no earlier than the age of 12 (14 for boys).[20] Of course, medieval and early modern aristocratic and royal babes were often involved in marriage negotiations, virtually from birth: The young Elizabeth I of England, for example, had been offered to the French Dauphin when she was little more than an infant. Seven was, nevertheless, an unusually young age to become a wife. Froissart describes how Isabelle's mother Isabeau demurred, expressing her discomfort with the idea in the oblique terms of courtly politesse: "it was shewed them that they must be content how so euer they found her for they sayd she was but a yonge chylde of eyght yere of age wherfore they sayd there coulde not be in her no grete wysdome nor prudence how be it" (fol. CC lix.r).[21] Froissart also

---

[18] *The Three Richards: Richard I, Richard II, and Richard III* (London and Hambledon: Continuum, 2005), 136.

[19] Her young age is compared favorably to that of the cousin of St. Paul (Froissart, fol. CC lxxvi.v).

[20] Barbara J. Harris, *English Aristocratic Women, 1450–1550. Marriage and Family, Property and Careers* (New York: Oxford University Press, 2002), 43–61.

[21] Note the difference in contemporary and medieval calculations of age: when Isabelle was, for us, almost seven, her mother considered her to be in her eighth year.

relates Richard's rebuttal: "she shal yet growe ryght wel in age, and though he fast a season he shal take it wel in worth, and shal ordre her in the meane season at hys pleasur and after the maner of Englande, saying also howe he is yet yonge ynough to abyd tyll the lady be of age" (fol. CC liii.r). It was much more typical for a girl to marry as a teenager, as Anne of Bohemia did when she married the teenaged Richard II, at the age of 16 and 15, respectively. However, the older Richard imagined an alternative paradigm with Isabelle: a little girl that he could raise in his own image.

Certain practices protected children, especially girls, from being bound unwillingly to an early match, as well as from the premature loss of sexual innocence. Early marriages were not consummated at the time that they were solemnized: although Isabelle was married at seven, it would have been expected that she remain a virgin until 16, and records of her subsequent marriage negotiations to Charles d'Orléans express little concern for the state of her virginity.[22] It was also possible for girls who had been married before the age of 12, and boys before 14, to renounce their marriages. And there were provisions for the return of the dowry if either the bride or the groom died before the age of 16: provisions that the English sought to overlook in Isabelle's case. Of course, according to the historical record, Isabelle was most enthusiastic about her marriage to King Richard.[23] At 12, she could have refused her marriage, although she would have had to forfeit her dowry.[24] But she lost Richard before she could renounce him, even if she had wanted to.

By all accounts, the relationship between Richard and Isabelle was deeply affectionate: Anne of Bohemia had died childless, and the young Isabelle, paradoxically, fulfilled Richard's desire to have a child. For her part, Isabelle, whom Richard treated kindly, remained fiercely loyal to her husband throughout his troubles. When Richard left for Ireland, never to see his young queen again, their parting at Windsor was tearful. Isabelle was just ten. The historical record does not, given its obvious bias, mention whatever aspects of coercion were involved, but Froissart reinforces the idea that Isabelle was an entirely willing participant from the beginning. When asked her opinion about marrying Richard, Isabelle—in what is probably the most famous statement by her—was enthusiastic about what it meant for her: "than answered the yong lady well aduysedly without counsayle of

---

[22]   This practice lies behind the controversy concerning the consummation of Catherine of Aragon's first marriage, to Prince Arthur. Married by proxy at the ages of three and two, and then again at the ages of 16 and 15, they may or may not have consummated their marriage before Arthur died, five months later, of the sweating sickness.

[23]   Léon Mirot, "Isabelle de France reine d'Angleterre, comtesse d'Angoulême, duchesse d'Orléans (1389–1409). Épisode des relations entre la France et l'Angleterre pendant la guerre de cent ans," *Revue d'histoire diplomatique* 18 (1904): 546–73 and 19 (1905): 60–95, 161–91, and 481–522. For historical references to Isabelle's life see *Chronicles of the Revolution, 1397–1400: The Reign of Richard II*, ed. Chris Given-Wilson (Manchester: Manchester University Press, 1993).

[24]   Palmer, *England France and Christendom*, 174.

any other person. Syr quod she and it please god and my lord my father that I shalbe quene of England I shall be glad therof for it is shewed me that I shal be than a great lady" (fol. CC lix. r.).[25] Taking pains to advertise Isabelle's appeal to older people, Froissart sounds like a parent relating a well-rehearsed anecdote about his or her precocious child, and recalls, as well, depictions of the Presentation of the Virgin Mary, at the age of three, to the elders of the Temple: "The maner countenaunce and behavoure of this yonge lady plesed greatly the ambassadors and they sayd amonge them that she was lyke to be a lady of hyghe honoure and great goodnesse" (fol. CC lix. r). Strickland's account of the story imagines the young princess rehearsing her future position like an actress, complete with rapt audience: "She was, from that time, styled the queen of England. And I was at the time told it was pretty to see her, young as she was, practicing how to act the queen" (5).

At a very young age, Isabelle de France was both queen and child, carrying the symbolic weight of the rapprochement between France and England at the end of this particular phase of the Hundred Years War: a peace that was hotly contested in England. Isabelle not only symbolized a new peace treaty, but also England's longstanding relationship with France that was the legacy of the Norman Conquest.[26] Richard himself had spent his childhood in Aquitaine, a duchy that had been in English hands for centuries before it was returned to France at the end of the Hundred Years War. He read, fluently, from a book of French poems Froissart presented to him upon his engagement to Isabelle.[27] He maintained his childhood ties to France and preserved his status as a francophile by taking many cultural cues from France, embracing French language, French fashions, and French artistic and musical tastes in a manner that, as Nigel Saul puts it, "turned first into emulation and then into competition" (353). Indeed, the courtly excesses for which Richard received such sharp criticism constituted the king's attempt to impress his French in-laws in the feudal and aristocratic economies of gift exchange and magnificent hosting, as well as in the obsession with *bella figura*. The famous Smithfield tournament, held to celebrate the arrival of Queen Isabelle, sought to replicate the girl's spectacular entry, or "joyeuse entrée," into Paris, some months before.[28]

Richard's marriage to Isabelle also took place at a time when it was necessary to reassert his authority as king. There had been other destabilizing events, such as the Rising of 1381 and the Merciless Parliament, but the most important in this context was the perceived capitulation to France that ended this phase of the Hundred Years War. The symbolic value of France as a girl child—John Stow called her "the little queen"—reinforced both Richard's patriarchal authority,

---

[25]   We may compare the medieval campaign to present Isabelle as a precocious child with the public investment in Princess Diana's innocence, expressed by her legendary response to Prince Charles's proposal of marriage: "yes please!"

[26]   Williams, *The French Fetish from Chaucer to Shakespeare*.

[27]   Strickland, *Lives of the Queens of England*, 5.

[28]   Richard Saul, *Richard II* (New Haven: Yale University Press, 1997), 531.

and, following decades of punishing warfare, the supremacy of England.[29] In this context, France is diminished by its symbolic status as a girl child. The grandeur and sumptuousness of the English wedding celebrations, from Isabelle's entry into London, to the tournament at Smithfield held in her honor, to her coronation, would have underscored the diminutive size and great youth of the French guest of honor. However, as Stephen Orgel reminds us, early modern symbolism is characterized by its "notorious profligacy."[30] On the one hand, as a French girl queen, Isabelle flatters English notions of power. On the other, the idea of a ten-year-old girl styling herself the queen of England would have gratified the French by turning England and the English crown into child's play.

Isabelle symbolizes the culture of childhood that defined the Ricardian court.[31] Richard himself had become king at the age of ten: yet another reason why Richard did not consider Isabelle's age to be an impediment to becoming queen. When Richard's father, Edward the Black Prince, died in 1377, his mother, Joan, the Fair Maid of Kent, hurried to invest her son with Edward's titles, including Prince of Wales, so that he could be crowned king after the death of his grandfather, Edward III, which occurred later the same year. The Ricardian court embraced and celebrated its sovereign's youth as a strategy for justifying and valorizing the symbolic weakness and vulnerability of the boy king. Froissart capitalizes on this aspect of royal iconography when he reminds Richard II that that they first met when the king was a child: "in his youthe he hadde sene me, in the courte of the noble king Edwarde his father and with the quene his mother" (fol. CC xlxii.r). The Wilton Diptych, completed while King Richard was in his late twenties or possibly even 30, depicts King Richard as a beardless youth, paying homage to the Virgin and Child.[32] The 11 girlish angels it depicts, which are believed to represent the 11 years he had lived before he was crowned, also highlight the idea of the king as a child. The painting was produced in the context of Richard's marriage negotiations with Isabelle—the negotiations during which Richard asserted that he was "yonge enough to abyde"—and in this sense we may see it as an idealized, celestial image of the courtship, the court, and the eventual heir Richard envisioned for himself

---

[29] John Stow, *A Survey of London*, ed. William J. Thoms, Esq. (London: Whittaker and Co., 1842), 10.

[30] Stephen Orgel "Gendering the Crown" in *The Authentic Shakepeare and Other Problems of the Early Modern Stage* (New York: Routledge, 2002), 107–28 at 115. In "I am Richard II" 2011), Orgel writes: "But of course one can't control the implications of imagery, or close it off to interpretation" (19).

[31] James Simpson, "Contemporary English Writers," in *A Companion to Chaucer*, ed. Peter Brown (London: Blackwell, 2002), 114–33. Simpson writes, "the very means at its disposal to assert the king's power also expose his vulnerability" (115).

[32] Ostovich, "Here in this Garden," 21; Dillian Gordon, *The Wilton Diptych* (London, 1993), and "The Wilton Diptych: an Introduction" in *The Regal Image of Richard II and the Wilton Diptych*, eds Dillian Gordon, Lisa Monnas, and Caroline Elam (London: Harvey Miller, 1997), 19–26. <http://www.nationalgallery.org.uk/paintings/english-or-french-the-wilton-diptych.

and his bride.[33] Another portrait of Richard II, now in Westminster Abbey, and the earliest known portrait of an English monarch, depicts the king without a beard. Orgel writes, "[T]he image is so stylized that, though he is clearly in coronation robes, it could represent him at any point in his twenty-year reign." He also makes the point that "[a]ll the other representations of the king done during his lifetime, such as that in the Wilton Diptych, are similarly beardless."[34]

Some scholars have seen the representation of the Arthurian court as "berdles childer" (280) in *Sir Gawain and the Green Knight* as a reference to the Ricardian cult of childhood, while others have found Gower's *Confessio Amantis* and Geoffrey Chaucer's *Legend of Good Women* (among other works) to offer implicit criticisms of the limitations and even danger posed by a young king.[35] "Woe to thee, O land, when the King is a child," laments Ecclesiastes 10.16: a text quoted frequently by Richard's detractors. It appears in the Prologue of Langland's *Piers Plowman* (195a) and in the related text, *Richard the Redeless*: "Ye come to youre kyngdom er ye youreself knewe" (I. 32).[36] Gower's *Vox Clamantis*, an account of the Rising of 1381, calls Richard an "undisciplined boy." Adam of Usk's chronicle explains, "Many great things were hoped for in the time of this Richard's reign; but, because he was tender of age, other persons who had charge of him and of the kingdom did not cease to inflict wanton evils, extortions, and other intolerable injustices upon the realm."[37] Although Christopher Fletcher has recently made a detailed argument in support of Richard II's manliness, the fall of Richard and rise of Bolingbroke was imagined as a grown man taking over from a mere youth, even though Richard II and Henry IV were only eight months apart in age, and ages 32–33 in 1399: "wherefore then a boy rules, will alone rules, and reason is in exile."[38] Archbishop Arundel's sermon on the deposition refers to Richard as "puer" and to Henry of Lancaster as "vir." The accession of Henry IV thus constituted a wholesale rejection of the Ricardian culture of youth: after 1400, Ricardian magnificence and theatricality appeared as a childish game of dress-up. Most importantly for our purposes, however, the Ricardian culture of youth was

---

[33] The 11 angels may also represent the 11,000 Virgins in the story of the virgin martyr, St. Ursula, a story that concerns the story of a virgin, like Isabelle, crossing the sea to join her future husband.

[34] Orgel, "I Am Richard II." 1–2.

[35] Simpson, "Contemporary English Writers," and R. Voaden, "Out of the Mouths of Babes: Authority in *Pearl* and in Narratives of the Child King Richard," in *Youth in the Middle Ages*, eds P.J.P. Goldberg and Felicity Riddy (York: AMS, 2004), 61–72.

[36] William Langland, *The Vision of Piers Plowman*, The B-Text ed. A.V.C. Schmidt (London: Everyman, 1987) and *Richard the Redeless*, ed. James M. Dean (Kalamazoo, MI: Medieval Institute Publications, 2000).

[37] Simpson, "Contemporary English Writers" and *The Chronicle of Adam Usk*, ed. and trans. C. Given-Wilson (Oxford: Oxford University Press, 1997), 3.

[38] Christopher Fletcher, *Manhood, Youth and Politics 1377–1399* (Oxford: Oxford University Press, 2008). *Record and Process* in *Chronicles of the Revolution, 1397–1400*, ed. Chris Given-Wilson, 168–9 and Simpson, 116–17.

not *sui generis*, but a copy of the "milieu jeune" of the French court, of which Isabelle's father, the young Charles VI, was the centre.[39] As a girl queen, therefore, Isabelle reflected back upon her husband the French-inflected *mythos* of Richard II as boy king, *enfant terrible*.

Suiting Her Passions to Her Years

Agnes Strickland found Isabelle's history exciting enough to narrate in her *Lives of the Queens of England*, and she clearly found her story enchanting. While Strickland's admiration of the historical Isabelle can easily be explained by the Victorian cult of girlhood, other Victorian responses to Shakespeare's Queen are quite dismissive, regarding her as a pale contrast to the expressions of womanly power in more celebrated Shakespearean heroines.[40] Mary Cowden Clarke, for example, does not find her important enough to fictionalize in *The Girlhood of Shakespeare's Heroines* (1850), although she may have been confused by the fact that, in this case, the heroine was a girl. Anna Jameson's *Characteristics of Shakespeare's Women* (1832) asserts, "there is no female character of any interest" in *Richard II*, and claims that Isabel takes "the same passive part in the drama that she does in history."[41] Augustine Skottowe finds the whole part "feebly written," and John A. Heraud observes, "I do not perceive that he [Shakespeare] felt sufficient interest in the character to bestow any of his own touches upon it."[42] Beverley E. Warner importantly explains the perceived weaknesses of the character: "the scenes in which Isabel appears are the weakest in the tragedy" as a result of Shakespeare's transformation of Isabelle into an adult, an act which she calls "the gravest anachronism."[43]

The negative appraisal of the queen in these Victorian discussions of *Richard II* reinforces the idea that something is lost in the character when we

---

[39] Mirot writes: "Dans ce milieu jeune, où les soverains étaient quasiment des enfants, ce n'etaient que fêtes et plaisirs, que n'interrompaient pas de graves preoccupations politiques." I. 547.

[40] This Victorian image of Isabelle and Richard II illustrates a short story by Cecilia Cleveland called "A Child Queen," in the *St. Nicholas Magazine for Boys and Girls* (5, Nov 1877–Nov 1878): 1–3. <http://www.gutenberg.org/files/17513/17513-h/images/0136-1.jpg>.

[41] See Jameson, *Characteristics of Women, Moral, Poetical, and Historical* vol. II (London: Saunders and Otely, 1832), 238.

[42] Augustine Skottowe, *Richard II and the Truth of History*, vol. I. (London, 1824), 141, and John A. Heraud, *Shakespeare: His Inner Life as Intimated in his Works* (London: John Maxwell, 1865), 118–26. See *Richard II. Shakespeare: The Critical Tradition*, ed. Charles Forker (London: The Athlone Press, 1998).

[43] She goes on, "That knowledge and appreciation of womanhood which is one of the noblest components of his later works, is lamentably deficient here." *English History in Shakespeare's Plays* (New York: Longman's 1894), 60–61, 79–88.

Isabelle de France, Child Bride

read her as an adult.[44] The longstanding theatrical tradition of what Howard and Rackin call "the mature queen" may be traced to Nahum Tate's 1681 adaptation of *Richard II*, which offers an older reading of the character. Reflecting, perhaps, the recent appearance of professional actresses on the English stage, Tate's queen makes references to the king as her "lover" (33) and compares herself, as a traditional, faithful wife, to "Calpurnia" (37).[45] However, Samuel Daniel's *Civil War*, an important Shakespearean source, is usually cited as Shakespeare's source for the adult queen. Here is Daniel's account of Isabelle's story:[46]

> Now Isabell, the young afflicted Queene,
> Whose yeares had neuer shew'd her but delights,
> Nor lovely eies before had euer seen
> Other then smiling ioies and ioyfull sights:
> Borne great, matched great, liu'd great and euer beene
> Partaker of the worlds best benefits. (71)

Juxtaposing the delights of her youth and the depth of her sorrows, Daniel set off Isabelle's great status against her high tragedy.[47] By highlighting Isabelle's chronological age, and then contrasting it to the very adult situation in which she finds herself, Daniel was following his source, Froissart: "for all that she was but yonge, right plesauntly she bare the porte of a quene" (fol. CC lxvi.v). Curiously, however, Daniel's lines have been interpreted by scholars who read Shakespeare's queen as a mature woman, and who find in them evidence that Daniel raised her age.[48]

Yet Daniel makes it clear that he was seeking to express both Isabelle's young age and the complexity of her predicament, a challenge that he did not feel he met. In the "Epistle Dedicatorie" to the 1609 edition of the *Civil Wars*, addressed to Mary Herbert Sidney, "The Right Noble Lady, the Lady Marie,

---

[44]   The Victorians pay more attention to the queen than current scholars, for whom the queen is simply "marginalized." Jeremy Lopez, *The Shakespeare Handbooks: Richard II* (New York: Palgrave, 2009), 29. Lopez makes the interesting suggestion that Shakespeare downplays the relationship between the queen and Richard in order to avoid tainting it with Richard's performative inauthenticity.

[45]   *The History of King Richard the Second Acted at the Theatre Royal under the Name of the Sicilian Usurper* (London: Richard Tonson, 1681).

[46]   Samuel Daniel, *The First Four Books of the Civil Wars Between the Two Houses of Lancaster and York* (London, 1595), book II, stanzas 66–98.

[47]   Daniel is also very clear about the distinction between the public role and the private self. Isabel tells Richard: "I love thee for thy selfe not for thy state" (stanza 90).

[48]   George M. Logan, "Lucan – Daniel – Shakespeare: New Light on the Relations Between *The Civil Wars* and *Richard II*," *Shakespeare Studies* 9 (1976): 121–40. See also Gurr: "Daniel gave a precedent for Shakespeare's queen" (65) and "Like Daniel, Shakespeare unhistorically makes Isabel a grown woman" (2.2.0n). Forker concurs, "By making the Queen an adult (as did Daniel), Shakespeare can use her to draw sympathy to the King as well as to sound an effective voice of tragic foreboding." *King Richard II*, 274.

Countesse Dowager of Pembroke," Daniel makes the following apology: "if I have erred somewhat in the draught of the young Q. Isabel (wife to Ric. 2) in not suting her passions to her yeares: I must ... hope the young Ladies of England (who will think themselves sufficient, at 14 years, to have a feeling of their own estates) will excuse me in that point."[49] Here Daniel expresses the difficulty he found, as a poet, matching the complexity of her predicament as a queen to her very young age. Nodding to his readers, the "young Ladies of England" whom he imagines taking a particular interest in the story of this young queen, Daniel may be thinking in particular of Lady Anne Clifford: he was her tutor when he wrote *The Civil Wars*, and in 1599, when it was first published, she was only nine.

Daniel's depiction of Isabelle's final encounter with Richard, an unhistorical event that Shakespeare uses in *Richard II*, confirm his conceptualization of the character as a youth:

> But he whom longer time had learn'd the art,
> T'indure affliction as a usuall touch:
> Straines forth his words, and throws dismay apart,
> To raise up her, whose passions now were such,
> As quite opprest her ouerchardged hart,
> *Too small a vessel to containe so much*
> And cheeres and mones, and fained hopes doth frame,
> As if himselfe belieu'd, or hop'd the same. (98)

Daniel here highlights the difference in age between Richard and Isabelle, and describes the queen's young heart overwhelmed by adult tragedy. It is not, therefore, the idea of an adult queen that Shakespeare gets from Daniel, who presents her unwaveringly as a girl (albeit a girl with grown-up problems). Instead, what Shakespeare takes from Daniel is a challenge: to create a character that is both a young girl and a tragic queen. This is precisely the problem Daniel expresses in his preface, in which he also imagines his girl readers' willingness, however premature, to meet adult challenges: "who will think themselves sufficient, at 14 years, to have a feeling of their own estates." Daniel's words here, along with his representation of Isabelle in the *Civil Wars*, allow us to think about girlhood, not as a distinct and protected space, incommensurate with marriage or other forms of adult responsibility, but instead as occupying a more fluid position on a temporal continuum between infancy and adulthood, in which little girls imaginatively project themselves, like Froissart's little princess, into adult positions of power and prominence. The idea that young girls may have a "feeling of their own estates" before they reach adulthood allows us to consider medieval and early modern child marriage less as a coercive institution and more

---

[49]   *The First Four Books of the Civil Wars Between the Two Houses of Lancaster and York* (London, 1609), A3.

as a form of sanctioned projection into a future condition.[50] This may also allow us, moreover, to stop conceptualizing girlhood and womanhood as separate and distinct conditions, alienated from each other.

Taking up Daniel's challenge, Shakespeare endows his queen with lines that convey her experience and sophistication. Inspired both by Daniel's fascination with Isabelle's tragic pathos, and by Froissart's tales of the precocious princess, Shakespeare's queen speaks lines of such maturity that they, paradoxically, enable later readers to cast her as an adult. But her lines possess greater meaning, irony, and pathos when we imagine them delivered by a child actor. She thus dramatizes an ongoing and self-conscious tension, even dialectic, between her status as a girl and her status as a queen. For example, Bushy's description of the queen at Windsor Castle as "sad" (2.2.1) is the first adjective that describes her in the play. The *Promptorium Parvulorum* gives "sad" as the Latin equivalent of "maturus," and *A Short Dictionary for Beginners* by John Withals defines it "as he that is of gravitie," using another Latin root, *gravitas*, for seriousness, duty, dignity.[51] The implications of Bushy's adjective are developed in the queen's own description of herself as "heavy sad" (31).[52] Here, like Froissart and Daniel, Shakespeare highlights the contrast between Isabelle's chronological age and the maturity demanded by her status as queen.

In her line, "so sweet a guest / As my sweet Richard" (2.2.8–9), the queen attaches to her much-older husband the diminutive term, *sweet*, that conveys daintiness and delicacy, as well as a certain effeminacy, and recalls Richard's reputation as a boy king. Casting Richard as the child bride, and Isabel as host to her husband's guest, even though she is, of course, a guest in his country, her words undermine the categories of youth and age, bride and groom, calling into question binary between England and France that controls the play's dramatization of English nationhood. Shakespeare goes on to dramatize her plight by upsetting, reversing, and rewriting a series of categories, images, and narratives concerning maternity and motherhood, which highlight the extent to which her fate denies her her much-anticipated future as a wife and mother. Depriving this precocious princess, praised for acting like a little grown-up, of the very adult future that was promised her as a little child bride already wise beyond her years, Shakespeare also presents an alternate history of Anglo-French relations that will be denied by the fall of Richard.

---

[50] We may also use the idea of a temporal continuum to allow adult women access to the girlhood they may feel is lost to various forms of adult responsibility.

[51] Gaulfridus Anglicus, *Promptorium Parvulorum* (London: Wynkyn de Worde, 1516), I. ii. verso, and John Withals, *A Shorte Dictionary for Young Beginners* (London: Iohn Kingstvn, 1556), Z. i. verso.

[52] And in her later, feisty, "What, was I born to this, that my sad look / Should grace the triumph of great Bolingbroke?" (3.4.98–9). "Gravitas" is a Latin term, as well, for pregnancy, which fits this later scene's repeated references to pregnancy and childbirth.

Isabel's exchange with Bushy concerning the expected departure of Richard for Ireland develops the idea of her maternity:

Yet again, methinks,
Some unborn sorrow, ripe in Fortune's womb
Is coming towards me, and my inward soul
With nothing trembles. At something it grieves,
More than with parting from my lord the King. (2.2.9–13)

Those who would read Isabel as an adult point to these lines, which refer to the womb, as well as to the scene's attachment to the language of pregnancy and childbirth. Of course, at ten, Isabel could be expected to know about wombs, but in this case she is referring not to her own womb but to that of Fortune, popularly personified as the goddess Fortuna. These lines imply a fascinating kind of conception accomplished between women, as the Goddess Fortuna appears like the Archangel in the biblical story of the Annunciation, making the queen's inward soul tremble. Here, her lines make use of the traditional language and iconography of the Annunciation, which highlights the Virgin Mary's youth: prayers to the Virgin recalling the Archangel's address, "Ave Virgo," also praise her as "puella" [girl] and "ancilla dei" [handmaiden of God].[53] In the case of Isabel, however, the conception moves from Fortune's womb to the queen's soul, and thus from the physical to the spiritual, rather than from the spiritual realm to the physical womb of the Virgin. The Marian image of Isabel's "inward soul" trembling, which recalls the Magnificat ("my soul magnifieth the Lord"), transforms a biblical moment of joy and revelation into one of fear and trembling; her physical response is to sad tidings instead of glad. Most importantly, Isabel acknowledges that this "unborn sorrow" is also "nothing." The interplay here, between what is anticipated and what does not yet exist, refers to the bad news of Richard's departure for Ireland, which she expects but that is not confirmed until later in the scene. It also refers, by means of these references to the Annunciation, to the gulf that exists between the queen's status as Richard's wife, with all of the anticipated pleasures of marriage and family, and what she now knows is never to be. For Shakespeare, the particular sadness of the queen concerns, to quote from Wallace Stevens's "The Snowman," "the nothing that is not there and the nothing that is." Emphasizing the nothing that has taken place that makes her still a virgin, and the nothing that is the child that she will never bear, Shakespeare's conceptualization of this character's tragedy thus hinges upon her status as a girl.

Bushy's response to Isabel introduces the conceit of the perspective:[54]

---

[53] Ostovich reads the imagery of this passage in terms of the iconography of the *Mater Dolorosa* ("why I should welcome such a guest as Grief" [2.2.7]).

[54] From the Latin *perspicere*: to see through, look closely into, discern, perceive.

> For Sorrow's eyes, glazed with blinding tears,
> Divides one thing entire to many objects,
> Like perspectives, which, rightly gazed upon
> Show nothing but confusion; eyed awry,
> Distinguish form. (16–20)

Bushy compares Isabel's eyes to glass perspectives, which multiply an image, and also to perspective paintings such as Holbein's *The Ambassadors*, which offer an anamorphic image that confuses the observer if looked at head on, and are viewed correctly only at an angle or with a transforming device such as a mirror.[55] Bushy's argument is that human technologies, products of our seething and sorrowful brains, are deceptive, multiplying griefs, or creating confusion, "shadows / Of what it is not" (23–4). Thus, he advocates sticking to the facts: "More than your lord's departure weep not" (25). For Isabel, however, viewing askance prepares her for the truth: "But what it is, that is not yet known what, / I cannot name. 'Tis nameless woe, I wot" (39–40). Whereas the "form" that is distinguished through the perspective is, for Bushy, misleading, for Isabel it is the truth, although it is at the moment only a "nameless woe." Isabel is as prepared for the birth of her sorrow as the Virgin is prepared for the birth of Jesus, although it comes from Fortune, not from the heavenly Father, and heralds an ending, not a beginning.

Like an anamorphic painting, Shakespeare is drawing upon Marian imagery yet presenting it askance, transforming it from joy to sorrow, turning it from divine comedy to human tragedy. The language and iconography of the Annunciation and the Nativity, rendered askance, thus ask the audience to consider viewing the play's English history askance, and to find in the play a sympathetic acknowledgement of Ricardian court culture. Contrary to the investments of the Tudor line in the story of Henry IV's succession, Isabel's words evoke, even as they anamorphically transform, the cult of the Virgin that was violently suppressed during the Reformation. Recalling a religious figure and devotional practice that had been cut off, and that are now seen from a different perspective by a sixteenth-century audience, the anamorphic transformations of Marian imagery in this scene convey how the future of Isabel is, itself, cut off. She will never resemble the Madonna with child envisioned by the Wilton Diptych; she will become pregnant, instead, with grief: "for nothing hath begot my something grief."

Isabel gives birth to her "nameless woe" and "unborn sorrow" when she learns that Bolingbroke has "safe arrived / At Ravenspurgh," (2.2.50–51), where his many supporters have flocked. She calls Greene, the messenger, "midwife to my woe" (62) and refers to herself as "I, a gasping new-delivered mother, / Have woe to woe, sorrow to sorrow joined" (65–6). Along with the messenger as her midwife, and, elsewhere in the scene, Bolingbroke as her "sorrow's dismal heir" (63),

---

[55] For a detailed discussion of this passage from a different perspective see Scott McMillin, "Shakespeare's *Richard II*: Eyes of Sorrow, Eyes of Desire" *Shakespeare Quarterly* 35.1 (1984): 40–52.

the scene's metaphorics of conception and childbirth are detached from the realities of age as well as gender. Using maternity as a conceit for her tragedy, Isabel expresses her distance from, as well as her deprivation of, a maternal future.

Rather than reinforcing a reading of her character as older (or connecting her to Anne of Bohemia, who had no children), this scene reveals how Richard's fall has deprived Isabel of the future she expected, as her present tragedy serves as a substitute for her future heir.[56] When the queen next appears, in the Duke of York's garden, she distinguishes herself not from a maternal future, but from a girlish present. The garden setting, with its associations with love, youth, and pleasure, represents a world that Isabel is, paradoxically, both not old enough to enjoy and beyond enjoying. Highlighting the tension between her age and her status, the scene hinges upon Isabel repeatedly addressing her lady-in-waiting as a "girl," drawing upon the associations of the term "girl" with female domestic work as well as with female childhood. Here, "girl" is used, somewhat brutally, to emphasize the Lady's status as the queen's servant, but it also reinforces the girlish nature of the diversions that she offers to Isabel, which, as a whole, construct an image of carefree childhood: "Madam, we'll play at bowls" (3.4.3), "dance" (6), "tell tales" (10), and "sing" (18). By detaching herself from the term "girl," Isabel rejects her lady's suggestions as well as her chronological girlhood: "Therefore, no dancing, girl" (9). The images of happy girlhood and youth established by the Lady's proposals highlight the tension between what, as a girl, the queen should be doing at age ten, and the grief and sorrow that take their place. Emphasizing Isabel's distance from these pleasures, the word "girl" here highlights the extent to which she will never enjoy them: after all, the word "girl" would never be used to address a queen.[57]

Isabel's cantankerous responses to her lady explode into rage when she overhears the gardener talk of deposition. News of Richard's captivity provokes her resolution, "to meet at London London's king in woe" (97), and the gardener returns to his work, commenting on the queen:

> Here did she fall a tear. Here in this place
> I'll set a bank of rue, sour herb of grace.
> Rue, e'en for ruth here shortly shall be seen,
> In the remembrance of a weeping queen. (104–7)

---

[56] Some would read this passage as suggestion that the sexual relationship between the king and queen has been compromised by minions: "You have in manner, with your sinful hours / Made a divorce betwixt his queen and him / Broke the possession of a royal bed / And stained the beauty of a fair queen's cheeks / With tears" (3.1.11–15). However, Peter Ure points out that breaking the possession of a royal bed draws upon legal metaphors that refer to a "covenant"—the issue, then, is not about adultery but about a more legally inflected notion of a promise of something that will take place in the future (91–2).

[57] It is interesting that the play never refers to the Queen as Isabel. Perhaps this seeks to affirm the permanence of her royal status in a play in which kingship is fluid, in which the King is, by the end of the play, designated as Richard.

These lines, which develop the play's well-known imagery of England as a garden, also allude to Isabel's historical plight as a child bride. Recapitulating the Marian imagery of pregnancy and birth that defined Isabel's previous scene, the gardener plans to plant rue, a well-known abortifacient mentioned in Ophelia's mad scene ("there's rue for you; and here's some for me"), which is often paired with thyme, which symbolizes virginity. As a verb, however, "rue" means repentance or regret: the ancient ballad refrain, "Rue the Day," expresses regret for an untrustworthy man who has married another. The gardener is planting "rue even for ruth": *ruth* has an archaic meaning that links it to pity, care, and sorrow, remorse, grief, and lamentation.[58]

The gardener's "ruth" here recalls the biblical Book of Ruth, which concerns the death of a husband, who leaves behind a foreign wife. The Book of Ruth was more prominent in medieval France than England, making a regular appearance in religious art and biblical commentaries.[59] Like Isabel, Ruth engages in a cross-cultural marriage. A Moabite who marries the Israelite Mahlon, Ruth lives with Mahlon's family. When Mahlon and his brother Chilion die, their mother Naomi decides to return to her own hometown of Bethlehem. Orpah, the wife of Chilion, returns to her family, but Ruth says:

> Entreat me not to leave you, or to turn back from following you; For wherever you go, I will go; And wherever you lodge, I will lodge; Your people shall be my people, and your God, my God. Where you die, I will die, and there will I be buried. The Lord do so to me, and more also, if anything but death parts you and me. (Ruth 1:16–17, The King James Bible).

The gardener's reference to Ruth here alludes to Isabel's immediate plan to follow her husband to London, as well as, more generally, to her famous loyalty to her husband. Isabel quotes Ruth directly in her final scene of the play, "Then wither he goes, thither let me go" (5.1.85).[60]

The gardener's allusion to the book of Ruth also raises the question that dogged the new king Henry IV: who is going to marry Isabel? When Ruth and Naomi return to Bethlehem, they work in a field that belongs to Naomi's relative Boaz, who is obliged to marry Ruth in order to preserve his family line. Naomi sends Ruth to the threshing floor to uncover the feet of the sleeping Boaz. When Boaz awakens, Ruth reminds him that he has the "right to redeem." Boaz must first clear this, however, with another male relative who has the first right of refusal— with his blessing, and that of the elders, they marry. It is possible here to see parallels with Henry IV's plan to marry Isabel to his own son, the future Henry V, who was her cousin by marriage. Henry IV also considered marrying her himself.

---

[58]   J.A. Simpson and S.C. Weiner, eds *The Oxford English Dictionary* (2nd ed.) (Oxford: Oxford University Press, 1989), s.v. "ruth."

[59]   Anne Rudloff Stanton, *The Queen Mary Psalter: a study of affect and audience* (Philadelphia: Transactions of the American Philosophical Society, 2001), 114–16.

[60]   Ostovich also discusses Ruth in connection to the queen (30).

Here, the gardener's words reinforce the idea that Isabel and Richard are from different tribes, as different as the Moabites and Israelites, and gesture towards an alternative history in which Isabel remains under English control. On the one hand, the book of Ruth offers a paradigm for Isabel's devotion to Richard; on the other it proposes an image of Isabel as English chattel that she passionately resisted.

Rejecting the attentions of both Henry IV and Prince Henry, Isabel sought to return to France. Her return was delayed by a dowry dispute between France and England that hinged upon the ownership of the jewels and other treasures that had accompanied her from France. Eventually, Isabel was allowed to return to France without her jewels, where she married her cousin, the nine-year-old boy who would become the French poet Charles d'Orléans, and died in childbirth at the tragically young age of 19. Ultimately, the story of Ruth applies better to Isabel's little sister, Catherine, who married Henry V, and, after his death, remained in England to marry Owen Tudor, and found what would eventually become the royal Tudor line.

Isabel's final scene in the play is a fabrication. Historically, the two parted when Richard went off to Ireland. But Shakespeare follows Daniel in making the queen and Richard meet following his fall.[61] This scene contains references both to the Virgin Mary and to medieval poetry, firmly grounding Richard's deposition as a break with France as well as with Catholicism. When Isabel begs her ladies, "But soft, but see, or rather do not see / My fair rose wither" (5.1.6–7), her construction of Richard as the beloved, the rose, recalls her previous reference to "my sweet Richard." At the same time, the popular association of the rose with the Virgin Mary extends the play's pattern of defining Isabel against the Virgin, while also identifying Richard with the medieval tradition of courtly love poetry enshrined by the Old French *Roman de la rose*. Isabel's words here evoke not only Richard's reputation for youth and effeminacy, but also their association, as a couple, with a medieval history of Anglo-French literary and cultural connections. Continuing the scene's saturation with both personal and cultural nostalgia, Richard recalls Isabel's initial arrival in England, "My wife to France, from whence, set forth in pomp, / She came adorned hither like sweet May, / Sent back like Hallowmas of short'st of day" (78–80). Comparing Isabel to May reinforces Shakespeare's conception of the character as a young girl, while also recalling Chaucer's young female character, May, who marries the *senex amans*, January, in *The Merchant's Tale*. Recalling Isabel's arrival in England at the same time that he is telling her to return to France, "Hie thee to France, / And cloister thee in some religious house" (22–3),

---

[61]   Charles Knight observes that it allows for a sense of growth in the character: whereas Knight sees "scarcely more elevation of character than might belong to a precocious girl" in the garden scene, this scene allows the "majesty of the high-minded woman" to shine. *The Pictorial Edition of the Works of William Shakespeare*, ed. Charles Knight, Histories, vol. 1. (London: Charles Knight and Co., 1847), 147. Although he is among the very few to read her—to a certain extent—as a girl, Knight pictures her only once, a tiny figure in a group scene illustrating 5.1. The image appears on p. 137.

Shakespeare is highlighting the play's overarching fidelity to its historical sources, recalling the celebrated marriage of Isabel and Richard, while, at the same time, reminding the audience that Isabel's future will be not as Richard imagines. Presenting France as a refuge to which Isabelle can flee, Richard's words not only recall medieval and Catholic religious practices, but also nod to the contemporary status of France, in the late sixteenth century, as a refuge for English Catholic recusants.

According to a French source, *La Chronicque de la traïson et mort de Richart Deux roy Dengleterre*, Isabelle was a puddle of tears when Richard left her:[62]

> ... he [Richard] then took the Queen in his arms, and kissed her more than forty times, saying sorrowfully, 'Adieu, Madame, until we meet again: I commend me to you.' Thus spoke the King to the Queen in the presence of all the people; and the Queen began to weep, saying to the King, 'Alas! My lord, will you leave me here?' Upon which the King's eyes filled with tears on the point of weeping, and he said, 'By no means, Madame; but I will go first, and you, Madame, shall come there afterwards.' Then the King and Queen partook of wine and comfits together at the deanery, and all who chose did the same. Afterwards the King stooped, and took and lifted the Queen from the ground, and held her a long while in his arms, and kissed her at least ten times, saying ever, 'Adieu, Madame, until we meet again,' and then placed her on the ground, and kissed her at least thrice more; and, by our Lady! I never saw so great a lord make so much of, nor show such affection to, a lady, as did King Richard and his Queen. Great pity it was that they separated, for never saw they each other any more. Afterwards the King embraced all the ladies, and then mounted on his horse.

This passage, drawn from an eyewitness account, highlights the emotional and physical closeness between the king and queen and raises questions about sexuality within child marriage. The many, many sad kisses could be those exchanged by

---

[62] *The Chronicle of the Betrayal and Death of Richard King of England* [*Chronique de la traïson et mort de Richart Deux roy Dengleterre*], ed. Benjamin Williams (London: Historical Text Society, 1846), 167.

> il ... print la Royne entre ses bras tres gracieusement et la baisa plus de xl foiz en disant piteusement Adieu Madame jusques au reueoir Je me recommande a vous [27] ce dist le Roy a la Royne en la presence de toutes les gens et la Royne commenca adonc aplourer disant au Roy, helas monsieur me laissiez vous icy. Adonc le Roy ot les yeulx plains de larmes sur le point de plourer et dist nennil Madame maiz Je iray devant vous Madame y vendrez apres Adonc le Roy et la Royne prindrent vin et espices ensemble droit a luis de leglise et chacun qui en voulloit prendre. Et apres le Roy se baissa et print et leua de entre la Royne et la tint bien longuement entre ses bras et la baisa bien x foiz disant tousdiz Adieu Madame jusques au reveoir. Et puis la mist a entre et la baisa encores iii foiz. Et par notre Dame Je ne vy oncques si grant seigneur faire si grant feste ne monstier si grant amour a ne dame comme fist le Roy Richart a la Royne Cestoit grant pitie de leur departie car oncques puis ne virent l'un lautre Apres le Roy baisa toutes les dames et puis monta a cheual. (27)

lovers, by married people, or a parent and child, shedding light on the complexity of child marriage in the Middle Ages, as well as on the reasons why audiences have worked hard to imagine and to cast Shakespeare's Isabel as an adult. These lines dramatize a true and affectionate love that does not fit easily within the contemporary categories or tastes. Shocking as it is to contemporary sensibilities, the historical Isabel's affection for her husband truly may have been as genuine as it appears in this portrait, and in every other historical reference to their relationship: she may have loved her husband as well as any ten-year-old wife.

If the warm kisses exchanged by Richard and Isabel in their final scene in *Richard II* are faithfully historical, "We make woe wanton with this fond delay," murmurs Richard, "Once, more, adieu. The rest let Sorrow say" (101–2), so is their French valediction, "adieu." But Shakespeare makes a few important changes. Where the chronicle gives the young queen very little to say, apart from a little protest, and presents her mainly as the recipient of kisses, Shakespeare inserts the strong character revealed by the historical record: not only did Isabel refuse to acknowledge Henry as Richard's successor, and reject his plans for her future, but she also wrangled with him over the return of her dowry and trousseau.[63] Far from providing evidence of Shakespeare's creative license, Queen Isabel's fiery rhetoric in this scene is consistent with the personality of the historical Isabel: "What, is my Richard both in shape and mind / Transformed and weakened? Hath Bolingbroke / Deposed thine intellect? Hath he been in thy heart?" (5.1.26–8). Richard, who knows his wife's character, requests her to be his Horatio-like spokesperson, narrating, and thus preserving for posterity, "the lamentable tale of me" (44).

Their parting exchange is rendered as a series of rhyming couplets, in which the king matches the queen's rhyme:

> QUEEN: And must we be divided? Must we part?
> RICHARD: Ay, hand from hand, my love, and heart from heart.
> ... QUEEN: Then wither he goes, thither let me go
> RICHARD: So two together, weeping, make one woe. (81–6)

Recalling the famous rhymed exchange of the lovers Romeo and Juliet ("palm to palm is holy palmers' kiss," 1.4.213), in this exchange Richard, like Romeo, completes Isabel's rhymes.[64] In *Romeo and Juliet*, Juliet usually corrects or qualifies

---

[63]   We may compare her, in this respect, to Catherine of Aragon, a queen famous for her resolve, who accepted Henry VII's plans to marry her to Prince Henry after the death of Prince Arthur.

[64]   JULIET: Ay, pilgrim, lips that they must use in prayer.
   ROMEO: O, then, dear saint, let lips do what hands do;
      They pray, grant thou, lest faith turn to despair.
   JULIET: Saints do not move, though grant for prayers' sake.
   ROMEO: Then move not, while my prayer's effect I take.
      Thus from my lips, by yours, my sin is purged.

Romeo's words. Similarly, in this exchange, which also reflects a marriage of true minds, Isabel speaks for herself. And although she is clearly brokenhearted, Isabel once again bucks convention by not insisting that their kiss produce the proverbial exchange of hearts, but, instead, by insisting that Richard return her heart to her: "Give me mine own again; 'twere no good part / To take on me to keep and kill thy heart" (97–8). Once again defining his queen against traditional images and paradigms, Shakespeare reminds his audience of Isabel's treasures that Henry IV churlishly retained in England and divided up among his children: give me mine own again.[65]

What does it mean, finally, to give Isabel her own? This chapter has sought to give both the historical Isabelle de France and Shakespeare's queen their own, by recovering the historical details of a redoubtable child bride in order to enrich our understanding of a Shakespearean character. Recovering the historical Isabelle is also, therefore, to recover a series of French connections that Shakespeare dramatizes, and to which he alludes, throughout *Richard II*, thus shedding light not only on the character of the queen but also upon the play as a whole. To put it another way, while it is easy to see why readers and audiences may have embraced the unhistorical yet more palatable notion of an adult queen, to continue in this tradition is to deny both the historical Isabelle her due, and Shakespeare's play itself. By reading Shakespeare's queen as a girl, and by charting the complexity of his representations of her against, and in resistance to, a series of paradigms from Ruth to the Virgin to Shakespeare's own Juliet, we acknowledge not only the historicity and contingency of our own notions of marriage and childhood, but also the powerful break with a longstanding English history with France that Richard II's deposition signified within the terms of Shakespearean history. Concluding a long history of countless, inextricable, English connections with France, Shakespeare's queen reveals the old paradigms no longer working, the old hopes and expectations forever refused, and the individual promise of a child forever thwarted. While it may very well be time to see this character played by a child actor, it is certainly time to read and imagine her as a girl.

JULIET: Then have my lips the sin that they have took.
ROMEO: Sin from thy lips? O trespass sweetly urged!
   Give me my sin again.
JULIET: You kiss by the book. (215–23).
Romeo and Juliet, ed. Jill Levenson (Oxford: Oxford University Press, 2000).

[65]   She divided her remaining jewelry among the Englishwomen who accompanied her back to France. The astonishing volume of this dowry treasure that accompanied her to France is detailed in Mirot, "Isabelle de France reine d'Angleterre."

PART 2
Textualizations of Politics and Empire

Chapter 3
Spenser's *Mutabilitie Cantos* and Du Bellay's Poetic Transformation

Hassan Melehy

The interpretive challenge that Spenser's *Mutabilitie Cantos* have long posed to criticism points to the principal paradox that they raise. This paradox is most evident in the fact that the ostensible finality of the quelling of change, the overt purpose of the *Cantos*, is achieved in an "unperfite" or unfinished canto. The relatively small number of studies of the *Mutabilitie Cantos* often acknowledge both their elusiveness in connection with this "unperfite" state and the uncertainty of the reasons for their inclusion in the 1609 posthumous edition of *The Faerie Queene*.[1] One critic has pointed out how odd it is that Mutabilitie's final submission takes place so quickly after an elaborate exposition and demonstration of the vitality that she offers.[2] In stanza 58 of Canto 7, in issuing her final judgment, Nature describes the role of change in the order of the universe: when things undergo change, rather than departing from "their first estate," they "Doe work their owne perfection so by fate."[3] That is, their only transformation is into the finality of their first form,

---

[1] Angus Fletcher remarks, "Considered simply in formal terms, the *Mutablitie Cantos* are quite unlike any other part of the epic to which they were thought by the 1609 publisher to have made a 'parcell.'" "Complexity and the Spenserian Myth of Mutability," *Literary Imagination: The Review of the Association of Literary Scholars and Critics* 6.1 (2004): 3. According to Paul Suttie, "In one sense what the poem's closing stanzas express is an intense yearning to break free from mythical explanations, in favour of a genuinely authoritative vision, however deferred. But at the same time they demonstrate how even that yearning articulates itself as yet one more imaginative positing of a just and 'stedfast' basis of interpretation, securely prior to all that is 'fading' and 'fickle' (VII.viii.1–2)." *Self-Interpretation in* The Faerie Queene (Cambridge: D.S. Brewer, 2006), 3. See also Marion Campbell, "Spenser's *Mutabilitie Cantos* and the End of *The Faerie Queene*," *Southern Review* 15.1 (1982): 46–59.

[2] According to Kenneth Gross, "[I]t is somewhat surprising that critics find it so splendid a triumph. For we may justifiably feel that Nature's clever argument that Change cannot rule without destroying her part in that order which legitimates rule is just a little too pat. The fact that Nature herself disappears so hastily after her utterance … may be more than anything else a way of keeping us and everyone else at the trial from lingering over the real inadequacy of her words." *Spenserian Poetics: Idolatry, Iconoclasm, and Magic* (Ithaca: Cornell University Press, 1985), 251.

[3] Edmund Spenser, *The Faerie Queene*, ed. Thomas P. Roche, Jr., and C. Patrick O'Donnell, Jr. (London: Penguin, 1978), 7.7.58. Henceforth cited in the body of the text.

which according to Nature they always were in. The paradox, then, occurs when the final statement of this finality or perfection is itself "unperfite" or unfinished.[4]

If, as Harry Berger states, "Spenser presents the latest form of experience both *in* his work and *as* his work,"[5] then the form of the work is closely connected to the experience it describes, that of the relationship between stasis and change. (As the 1609 publisher indicates, the *Mutabilitie Cantos* "both for forme and matter" appear to belong to *The Faerie Queene*.)[6] If the final canto is "unperfite," and the judgment subjugating change to the ends of stasis hence unfinished, *The Faerie Queene* presents itself as open-ended and subject to change on the subject of change. The ambiguities that many critics cite throughout the epic and culminating in the *Mutabilitie Cantos* are thereby left in a state of affirmative irresolution—so Change seems to enjoy a certain victory after all, even if Nature forcefully insists on stasis.

How, then, do this condition and this determination affect the ostensible purposes of *The Faerie Queene*? This question is especially important in connection with the canonical status of the epic, which it holds in its reception as one of the most indelible books in the English curriculum, as well as in its production as national-cultural legitimation. Indeed, it is all the more canonical in that it constitutes an effort to found a new canon of English literature by incorporating the old and elevating it into a position of providing the service of glorification to the state; this is a canon in the etymological sense of a rule or measure by which all subsequent literature will be judged and through which social and cultural norms are propagated. As such, *The Faerie Queene* presents itself as a model, very much according to the proposals for models that Joachim Du Bellay made in the *Deffence et Illustration de la Langue Françoyse*,[7] which Spenser likely read at the Merchant

---

[4] Louise Gilbert Freeman provides an excellent discussion of the relationship between the "perfection" that Spenser identifies in 7.7.58 and the "unperfite" state of Canto 8: "Vision, Metamorphosis, and the Poetics of Allegory in the *Mutabilitie Cantos*," *SEL* 45.1 (Winter 2005): 66–7.

[5] Harry Berger Jr., *Revisionary Play: Studies in the Spenserian Dynamics* (Berkeley: University of California Press, 1988), 245.

[6] Spenser, 1025.

[7] Du Bellay writes, "Immitant les meilleurs Aucteurs Grecz, se transformant en eux, les devorant, et apres les avoir bien digerez, les convertissant en sang, et nouriture, se proposant chacun selon son Naturel, et l'Argument qu'il vouloit elire, le meilleur Aucteur, dont ilz observoint diligemment toutes les plus rares, et exquises vertuz …" *La Deffence et Illustration de la Langue Françoyse*, ed. Jean-Charles Monferran (Geneva: Droz, 2001), 91. Richard Helgerson's translation is as follows: "By imitating the best Greek authors, transforming themselves into them, devouring them, and, after having thoroughly digested them, converting them into blood and nourishment, selecting, each according to his own nature and the topic he wished to choose, the best author, all of whose rarest and most exquisite strengths they diligently observed …." *The Regrets; with, The Antiquities of Rome, Three Latin Elegies, and The Defense and Enrichment of the French Language*, trans. Richard Helgerson (Philadelphia: University of Pennsylvania Press, 2006), 336. Once the French language has been enriched by imitations of ancient models, it can in turn offer models to modern poets.

Taylors School and which contributed to shaping his poetic project from very early on. The purpose of such a literature in its functioning as a canon involves the cultivation of the subject of the state. As Spenser puts it, the goal of his epic is "to fashion a gentleman or noble person in vertuous and gentle discipline."[8] The glorification of the state here takes the form of the praise of Elizabeth or Gloriana, "the most excellent and glorious person of our souveraine the Queene, and her kingdome in Faery land" (16). It is certainly not an accident that in presenting the role of hazard and change in politics, culture, and poetry, Spenser presents the drama of the *Mutabilitie Cantos* as that of a trial, the goal of which is to pronounce judgment. The modern epic poem is the canon or measure by which aesthetic judgments, with their political ramifications, will be made.

By considering these well-known aspects of *The Faerie Queene*, I wish to explore the question of the canonical status of the poem, with the aim of making broader and more general observations on the function of a canonical poem. Although very few works that declare themselves great actually succeed at subsequently being regarded as such, it is quite interesting to examine a work that does succeed, since its strategies of self-promotion can indicate a lot about the operations and functions of canonical literature. *The Faerie Queene* is probably the best example in English of such success. It would be easy, as some have done, to see Spenser as nothing but a legitimator of the state and an apologist for royal power,[9] but I will insist here on examining the complexities and contradictions evident in the *Mutabilitie Cantos* as plainly revealing, in the fashion of all superb poetry, the functions of the interactions between politics and literature.[10]

As a model, *The Faerie Queene* necessarily functions paradoxically. It builds on the prior models of epic poetry that Spenser names in the "Letter of the Authors" (15), after the fashion that Du Bellay describes in the *Deffence* (see note 7). And much like the new poetry that Du Bellay projects, it will become a model for future poetry; as such, it will then surpass and reduce the importance of prior models if not lead to their oblivion. It will do all this in the service of glorifying and promoting the state. But at the same time, in instituting itself as a supreme model that nonetheless must take its place in a series of models, it also places itself in the position of being surpassed and hence risks contributing to

---

[8]   Edmund Spenser, "A Letter of the Authors," in *The Faerie Queene*, 15. Henceforth cited in the body of the text.

[9]   Karl Marx's judgment on Spenser furnishes a classic example. In notes on Henry Sumner Maine's *Lectures on the Early History of Institutions*, Marx refers to Spenser as "der Elizabeth's Arschkissende Poet (Elizabeth's ass-kissing poet)," using a curious anglicism (*kissende* for the correctly German *küssende*) that plays on Spenser's epithet, England's "Arch Poet." Editors and Anthony W. Riley, "Marx and Spenser," in *The Spenser Encyclopedia*, ed. A.C. Hamilton et al. (Toronto: University of Toronto Press, 1990), 457–8.

[10]   Cf. Fletcher: "Some will say that Spenser is too fully committed to an unchanging establishment. I think, however, that like all the more serious and powerful poets, he tries to give space to the pressures forced by contingent events upon any ideal of unshakeable stability" (5).

its own oblivion. This is the logic of poetic imitation that Du Bellay outlines in the *Deffence*, in which he briefly but unmistakably acknowledges the possibility of such oblivion.[11] However, Spenser doesn't make such an acknowledgement; furthermore, in making his own more overt and more aggressive gestures of legitimation, he cannot do so. Absolute state sovereignty necessitates the appeal to a higher, more permanent authority so as to forestall all questioning of current governing institutions. This authority of course culminates during the Christian era in assertions of the monotheistic divine right of monarchs that legitimate the durability of burgeoning global empires.

In Western Europe during the early modern era, an important purpose of poetry is to provide the mythological background on which such a legitimation may take place. However, in Spenser's case, we see a breach in the finality of the legitimation insofar as the final judgment is unfinished or "unperfite." *The Faerie Queene* remains unfinished, the cantos that finish it are unfinished, and the judgment that these cantos examine is incomplete. Whether material circumstances kept Spenser from finishing his epic or not, the nature of the judgment on the role and experience of Mutabilitie with respect to permanency is of necessity unfinished. The poem that would bring permanency to the state it supports, and to the poetry that is this state's cultivation and culture, must acknowledge the necessity of poetic change to its own existence. This poem hence also recognizes such change as the precondition of all future poetry, as the sine qua non of poetry with respect to the vagaries of language.

Spenser and Du Bellay

Most commentaries on the *Mutabilitie Cantos* treat them as a statement on metaphysics and/or morality, both of which are of course essential to the legitimating function that *The Faerie Queene* both engages in and interrogates. If it is addressed at all, their status as poetics isn't usually made central.[12] In the

---

[11] Du Bellay writes: "Le tens viendra (peut estre) et je l'epere moyennant la bonne destinée Françoyse, que ce noble, et puyssant Royaume obtiendra à son tour les resnes de la monarchie, et que nostre Langue (*si avecques Françoys n'est du tout ensevelie la Langue Françoyse*) ..." (*Deffence*, 82—my emphasis). The translation is as follows: "The time will come—and with the help of the good fortune of France, I have high hopes for it—when this noble and powerful kingdom will in turn seize the reins of universal domination and when our language (*if with François* [or the French—Du Bellay plays on the double entendre] *the French language has not been wholly buried*)" (*The Regrets*, 328—my emphasis). In this passage, he raises a slight doubt as to the survival of French. See Hassan Melehy, "Du Bellay and the Space of Early Modern Culture," *Neophilologus* 84.4 (October 2000): 508–10; also Hassan Melehy, *The Poetics of Literary Transfer in Early Modern France and England* (Farnham, UK: Ashgate, 2010), 17–29.

[12] In her superb article on the *Mutabilitie Cantos*, Freeman treats them as a reflection on the process of allegory: "I will argue, in fact, that the *Mutabilitie Cantos* is the work in Spenser's oeuvre in which his own anxieties about the accessibility of the divine (or even

following pages I would like to highlight this function of the *Cantos*, especially in relation to their legitimating force and canonical status. In so doing, I will consider the paradox of a poem whose ostensible purpose requires finality and permanency and that nonetheless remains open-ended.[13] I will also examine the related paradox of *The Faerie Queene*'s authorization of its own canonical status on the basis of the prior poetry of another nation, namely the work of Du Bellay. In its presentation of a mythological, allegorical version of England that provides a "backdated permanency"[14] to English sovereignty, *The Faerie Queene* borrows from Du Bellay. It does so by way of the translations and imitations that Spenser did of his predecessor's work. Spenser published these translations in his own 1590 *Complaints* and earlier in Jan van der Noot's 1569 *Theatre for Worldlings*. *Complaints* also showcases a number of poems that are clearly imitations of Du Bellay, in which Spenser develops the notion of imitation and its role in national poetry; he thereby anticipates the *Mutabilitie Cantos*, particularly their focus on poetics and transformation. Considered in connection with his work on Du Bellay, the *Cantos* offer an acknowledgement that the poetic production of the moral and political model of English culture builds on the strategy that Du Bellay proposed for French poetry. But just as Du Bellay made transformation a part of his own poetry, so his work is transformed in its migration to Spenser's; as such, this prior poetry offers to Spenser the very process of poetic transformation that he discovers to be necessary to his project of writing. The trial of Mutabilitie, in ways not suggested by most of its interpretations, thus provides a commentary on Spenser's project of *the* canonical English poem, as well as on the very notion of a literary canon in English.

The context of the *Cantos* suggests that the reason why Mutabilitie can't enjoy a formal triumph in the challenge she mounts to Jove is simple: her challenge claims a legitimacy based on a more permanent version of the very ground of his legitimacy, permanency itself. If she were successful in establishing her own permanency, the result would be the abolition of her continued operations of change.[15] Mutabilitie is not simply a rule of change within a fixed order, but rather a harsh threat of disruption to all rule and order. First appealing to chaos theory and then looking to its successor, complexity theory, Angus Fletcher sees her as integral to a "complex adaptive system," an ordering that is continually open to limited chaotic transformation.[16] Mutabilitie mounts her challenge not simply

---

the ideal) through the instrument of poetic allegory come closest to the surface. Here the poet reflects, self-critically, on his own program of allegory in a more explicit way than he has elsewhere in *The Faerie Queene*" (66). My approach shares a lot with Freeman's, although my interest is principally Spenser's transforming relationship with Du Bellay rather than that with Ovid.

[13]   On the conflict in *The Faerie Queene* between completion and fragmentation, see Campbell.

[14]   This is Suttie's splendid expression (209).

[15]   Ibid., 209.

[16]   Fletcher, 11–22.

to obtain recognition for the value of change but also "to gain status for what amounts to a new idea of change itself. If once change never changed anything, now it changes everything."[17]

Change and Permanency

Mutabilitie's appearance at the end of *The Faerie Queene* seems to function as a demonstration that, paradoxically, she has no place in it. If she is successful in her appeal, she makes herself permanent and is as such no longer Mutabilitie—that is, she destroys herself. If she fails in her appeal, the question remains as to what her role was in the first place, and the value of her prior contributions is nullified. Furthermore, given *The Faerie Queene*'s dependence on poetic transformation as I have outlined it, Mutabilitie's full defeat would render Spenser's epic impossible. However, in keeping with the legitimating function of the epic, Spenser accentuates the failure of Mutabilitie's effort to combat Dame Nature's arguments. Most critics have interpreted this failure as a real one, but a few see it otherwise.[18] A source of the minority opinion is the final judgment of Canto 8, in which the narrator presents his own wish for absolute permanency in eternal and eternally static life:

> When I bethinke me on that speech whyleare,
>   Of *Mutability*, and well it way:
>   Me seemes, that though she all vnworthy were
>   Of the Heav'ns Rule; yet very sooth to say,
>   In all things else she beares the greatest sway.
>   Which makes me loath this state of life so tickle,
>   And loue of things so vaine to cast away;
>   Whose flowring pride, so fading and so fickle,
> Short *Time* shall soon cut down with his consuming sickle.

Oddly enough, this apparent preface to the statement of Mutabilitie's final submission amounts to an observation of just the opposite idea, that despite all attempts to contain and subdue her she continues to exercise quite a bit of power: "In all things else she beares the greatest sway." The suggestion is that, although Mutabilitie can't touch Heaven's rule, it is ineffective in subduing her. Although the next stanza is apparently a prediction, it would sooner seem to be a wish, not necessarily on its way to fulfillment, and revelatory of its own contradictory nature:

---

[17]   Ibid., 7.

[18]   Arnold E. Davidson does an excellent and very succinct job of sorting out the logic of Dame Nature's argumentation, demonstrating its untenability: "Dame Nature's Shifting Logic in Spenser's *Cantos of Mutabilitie*," *Neuphilologische Mitteilungen* 83.4 (1982): 451–6.

Then gin I thinke on that which Nature sayd,
  Of that same time when no more *Change* shall be,
  But stedfast rest of all things firmely stayd
  Upon the pillours of Eternity.
  That is contrayr to *Mutabilitie*:
  For, all that moueth, doth in *Change* delight:
  But thence-forth all shall rest eternally
  With Him that is the God of Sabbaoth hight:
O that great Sabbaoth God, graunt me that Sabaoths sight.

The chief ambiguity here is in Spenser's spelling of *Sabbaoth*, which yields the dual meaning of "rest" and "hosts or armies." These two senses point to two different ways of arriving at final stillness: one of them involves a simple cessation of motion, and the other a violent imposition of immobility through divine triumph. Although the result is the same, the ambiguity suggests indecision between motion and rest; the finality of the words is hard to contest, except by their placement in an "unperfite" canto, which leaves all the room for a reply to this indecisive finality.[19] In other words, the formal lack of finality is a necessary disruption to rhetorical finality: the former results from the continued action of Mutabilitie, who promotes change by disallowing finality.

Nevertheless, Spenser cannot integrate an explicit affirmation of Mutabilitie's continuing operations, for to do so would amount to a statement of the failure of *The Faerie Queene* as a functioning canonical epic. In light of the Bellayan concerns on which Spenser partly authorizes his poetic project, the prospect of this failure looms, but Spenser's legitimating efforts must allow his epic to appear to be canonically permanent. The *Mutabilitie Cantos*, then, reflect and embody the struggle between permanency and change that both enables national epic and renders it unsustainable. Mutabilitie, effectively having *no place* in the poem, persists in a space beyond it, in a projected future utopia (or "no-place") of continued poetic transformation. Such creativity is a necessary outcome of the establishment of a poetry in English; but it also threatens this establishment, since part of its operation is to transform and unseat previous canonical models. In situating Mutabilitie as it does, *The Faerie Queene* suggests that, in the procedure of imitation integral to the development of English poetry, it will one day be left behind, no longer functioning as new poetry or model. With regard to procedures of state legitimation, *The Faerie Queene* offers illustrations of their operation, as well as, ultimately, a demonstration of their untenability.

---

[19] Raphael Lyne details many of the important critical positions on this ending: *Ovid's Changing Worlds: English Metamorphoses, 1567–1632* (Oxford: Oxford University Press, 2001), 102–3. Cf. also Harry Berger Jr., *Revisionary Play*, 269–70.

Rome and Mutabilitie

Du Bellay's mark is patent throughout the *Mutabilitie Cantos*, though with a few exceptions unmentioned in scholarship. Indeed, detailed appreciations of the relationship between Du Bellay and Spenser's imitative work in *Complaints* have been infrequent, although in recent years interest in them has grown. In general critics tend to treat Spenser's "shorter" (a term now used more often than "minor") poems apart from *The Faerie Queene*. This is unfortunate not so much because it entails a loss for source criticism (which has only limited interpretive value) as because it poses shortcomings to understanding the very process of poetic transformation that Spenser describes as he engages in it. This transformation is important to an adequate account of the emergence of modern Western poetry, as it is precisely what authorizes the creation of canonical works in states and empires that are still in chaotic flux. By considering the transformation of Du Bellay— both Du Bellay's development of transformation as an aesthetic principle and the transformation of his work in Spenser's appropriations—one can bring to light this essential aspect of Spenserian poetics, without which the implications of what he attempts to do for the institution of the literary canon cannot be fully understood.

In not examining the relationship between Du Bellay and Spenser as manifested in the *Mutabilitie Cantos*, even the most hermeneutically suspicious critic may to a degree be fooled by Spenser's canonical ambitions, willing to examine Spenser's conceptions of transformation but not the ways that these are bound up with the genealogy of his work. Part of this critical shortcoming has to do with the strong emphasis on national literatures in the institutionalized study of the very polyglot, transterritorial Renaissance. As part of its own function as national legitimation, present-day criticism often ends up taking the foundational gestures of modern canonical literatures at their word: it almost always presents the national literatures as already in full existence, when in fact their statements to this effect are a sign of struggle. Much has been said about Spenser's reworking of Ovid in *The Faerie Queene*, but there is very little on Du Bellay in the same context.[20] Instead of seeing Spenser's canonical products as in formation, critics attribute a permanency to them. This permanency is, of course, an important aspect of Spenser's work; but as I will show, another aspect of this work—its involvement with continual transformation—is just as essential. My main interest in what follows, then, is

---

[20] This is unfortunate, given that a key Ovidian notion of transformation appears in sonnet 3 of the *Antiquitez de Rome* and *Ruines of Rome*, which names time as the continual flow of transformation and ruin. The figure of the river in this sonnet is directly traceable to Du Bellay's translation of Ovid. Lyne is one of the few scholars to accord serious attention to Ovidian motifs in Du Bellay, which Spenser subsequently takes up (89–93). See Hassan Melehy, "Du Bellay's Time in Rome: The *Antiquitez*," *French Forum* 26.2 (Spring 2001): 10–11, and Melehy, *The Poetics of Literary Transfer*, 31–50. Reading Spenser as engaging with a nearly contemporary and canonically unstable Du Bellay, rather than as referring only to the more established works of antiquity, reveals some very dynamic aspects of his work.

in the parts of the *Mutabilitie Cantos* that engage and rework Du Bellay and transform his notions of transformation.

The complexity of Mutabilitie becomes evident when Spenser, through allusion, effects a certain identification between her and Rome as Du Bellay renders it. This rendition is of vast importance to Spenser, beginning with his earliest published work, the translations he did in 1569 for van der Noot of Petrarch's Canzone 323 (or rather of Clément Marot's translation of it), the principal intertext of Du Bellay's *Songe* (1558—also incorporated through Marot's version), along with 11 of the 15 sonnets from the *Songe*. Spenser acknowledges his debt to Du Bellay in *Complaints* by including a revised and much-improved text of his translation of the *Songe* under the title *Visions of Bellay*, as well as a translation of Du Bellay's *Antiquitez de Rome* (1558) titled *Ruines of Rome*. From these works Spenser derives a few key thematic words, namely *vision* and *vanity*. He is also evidently fascinated by the role that Du Bellay assigns to Rome. Du Bellay holds Rome to be the modern poet's dream of permanency, the source of political and poetic grandeur.[21]

But on closer examination, the poet and French diplomat who makes a pilgrimage to Rome realizes that the city he has idolized has become a complete ruin. If the supposedly eternal city can fall into ruin, then the poet infers that nothing on earth can have any kind of permanency. For Christians, the only certainty is in divinity, but even that is available only by way of fleeting signs and in the violence of a cataclysmic judgment that, in bringing everything to finality, effects the greatest disruption of earthly stability and threatens to continue to do so in cyclical fashion. Rome then becomes the emblem of earthly transformation, the greatest indicator that change is inevitable in the world. But at the same time, it is through this very transformation that the fluidity of language necessary to the construction of poetry becomes possible. For Du Bellay, the placement of words in a poetic text requires the malleability of signifier, signified, and their interrelationship. This placement also requires that the status of the poetic text be fleeting such that new poetry can continually be written in a rewriting of the old. From one point of view, poetry is a lamentation of its own continual decay and the decay of the world that it engages; from another it is the celebration of this decay as a creative transformation of poetry into exactly what is continually new. Rome, then, becomes the site of Du Bellay's meditations on poetic transformation, and its ruins become the embodiment of this transformation. Du Bellay's treatments of Rome and all that it entails turn up not only throughout Spenser's *Complaints*, but also in different places in *The Fairie Queene* and especially the *Mutabilitie Cantos*, Spenser's own contemplation of poetic transformation.

---

[21]   In my examination of Spenser and Du Bellay, I am extending ideas that I developed elsewhere: Hassan Melehy, "Spenser and Du Bellay: Translation, Imitation, Ruin," *Comparative Literature Studies* 40.4 (2003): 415–38; *The Poetics of Literary Transfer*, 75–117.

60   *French Connections in the English Renaissance / Melehy*

Early in Canto 6, Mutabilitie takes on some of the defining characteristics of Du Bellay's Rome. In stanza 7, Mutabilitie is very close to becoming the new name for old Rome and functioning as the latter's replacement:

> And now, when all the earth she thus had brought
>   To her behest, and thralled to her might,
>   She gan to cast in her ambitious thought,
>   T'attempt th'empire of the heauens hight,
>   And *Ioue* himselfe to shoulder from his right.
>   And first, she past the region of the ayre,
>   And of the fire, whose substance thin and slight,
>   Made no resistance, ne could her contraire,
> But ready passage to her pleasure did prepaire.

The use of the word *empire*, in allusion to the growing power of earthly kingdoms, evokes the model that continually recurs in early modern Europe, Rome. Du Bellay uses this word and related ideas throughout the *Antiquitez*, and it is very important for his depiction of ruin that Rome once dominated the whole world and then threatened the heavens. I quote first from sonnet 8 of the *Antiquitez* and then from Spenser's translation of it in *Ruines of Rome*:

> Par armes & vaisseaux Rome donta le monde,
> Et pouvoit on juger qu'une seule cité
> Avoit de sa grandeur le terme limité
> Par la mesme rondeur de la terre & de l'onde ...[22]

> Through armes and vassals *Rome* the world subdu'd,
> That one would weene, that one sole Cities strength
> Both land and sea in roundnes had survew'd,
> To be the measure of her breadth and length ...[23]

Both Du Bellay and Spenser use the word *empire* in line 10 of the sonnet (line 108 of *Ruines of Rome*). In these lines, which Spenser initially read and translated well before composing *The Faerie Queene*, there is an earlier version of the empire that has subjugated the entire world through force. Although Spenser's "vassals" for "vaisseaux" could be a misreading of the French, a misspelling in English, or an alternate spelling of *vessels*, it is nonetheless noteworthy that Spenser is extending the idea of feudal submission that Du Bellay develops. This extension through translation continues in the creation of Mutabilitie, who is able to conquer the earth through the seductive power of what is fleeting and vain. Just as the glory

---

[22] Joachim Du Bellay, *Les Antiquitez de Rome*, in *Les Regrets et Autres Oeuvres Poëtiques*, ed. J. Joliffe and M.A. Screech (Geneva: Droz, 1974), 281, ll. 1–4. Henceforth cited in the body of the text by sonnet number.

[23] Edmund Spenser, *Ruines of Rome: By Bellay*, in *The Yale Edition of the Shorter Poems of Edmund Spenser*, ed. William A. Oram et al. (New Haven: Yale University Press, 1989), 389, ll. 99–102.

of Rome is a temptation to submission for the entire world, including for the poet, so Mutabilitie is able to bring the world into her control. Such a reordering of the world in empire by both Rome and Mutabilitie takes place precisely because they are vain, earthly beings endowed with an overwhelming attractiveness. They both embody transformation, the strength of earthly desire against divine order. But also because both are transformation itself, they are destined to fail in the attempt to achieve full empire. What Rome might offer to Du Bellay and subsequently to Spenser is the model for a poetry that transforms its model and engages in a poetics of transformation that enables the progress that it promotes. The trick, of course, is not to rush toward death as quickly as Rome the model did, but rather to borrow sufficiently from its earthly beauty in order to delineate a possible way to eternity.

Heaven and Earth

Spenser is quite interested in the power of earthly beauty to point toward a more permanent condition. He raises this issue explicitly in *The Ruines of Time*, the longer poem that opens *Complaints*, through the person of Verlame, a beautiful woman who deplores the loss of all earthly glory and hence offers a lesson about such loss. He repeats this notion in a parenthetical remark in the *Mutabilitie Cantos*, when the sight of Mutabilitie turns Jove's wrath to grace: "Such sway doth beauty euen in Heauen beare" (7.6.31). Spenser acknowledges the value of indulging in earthly pleasures; they can, in the proper poetic context, be involved in contemplating the ethics and aesthetics of something more permanent than vanity. Of course, their very seductiveness suggests that they might never lead the soul to any authentic perception of the divine. In this line, Spenser even suggests a certain conciliatory capacity of the power of seduction that Mutabilitie holds. This attribute of Mutabilitie is also apparent in the above-quoted stanza 7, when she first passes through the air and then the fiery region above on her way to attempt the conquest of heaven: these regions "Made no resistance ... / But ready passage to her pleasure did prepare" (7.6.7)

Once again, the threat that Mutabilitie poses to the heavens is another version of that which Rome presented. Du Bellay and Spenser indicate as much:

> Toy qui de Rome emerveillé contemples
> L'antique orgueil, qui menassoit les cieux,
> Ces vieux palais, ces monts audacieux,
> Ces murs, ces arcs, ces thermes et ces temples ...
> > (*Antiquitez* 27, ll. 1–4)

> Thou that at *Rome* astonisht dost behold
> The antique pride, which menaced the skie,
> These haughtie heapes, these palaces of olde,
> These wals, these arcks, these baths, these temples hie ...
> > (*Ruines* 27, ll. 1–4)

That one may contemplate Rome in marvel or astonishment indicates an irony: Rome in its day was a great marvel, and Rome in ruins, because of the absence of this past glory, is at least as great a marvel. Spenser's use of *astonisht* conveys the surprise of the latter marvel more strongly. Spenser also underscores Du Bellay's favorite rhetorical figure, antithesis, to bring stronger attention to this paradox: Du Bellay's expression "monts audacieux" (which refers to Roman mounds or hills) becomes the more phonically and semantically biting "haughtie heapes"—haughty in that they can be nothing but the remnants of distant and failed hubris. Similarly, Mutabilitie, by the glory and beauty available through the capacity to transform that has already made an empire of the earth, mounts a threat to the heavens.

In the *Mutabilitie Cantos*, Spenser continues his reworking of Du Bellay's Rome as Mutabilitie by pursuing the link that such a threat suggests with the Tower of Babel. In another sonnet Du Bellay writes, "pointes du ciel voisines, / Qui de vous voir le ciel mesme estonnez"; Spenser translates this as "spyres neighbors to the skie, / That you to see doth th'heaven it selfe appall" (sonnet 7, ll. 5–6, in both cases). The temporal towers, as a result of attacking eternal towers, are left in ruin: the marvel of their destruction is material for the poetry of contemplation. But in borrowing from the audacity, vanity, haughtiness, and seductiveness of the earthly phenomenon it reports, this poetry risks a pattern of cyclical repetition. This is the prospect that Mutabilitie faces in her ascent to heaven. The response that Jove prepares also alludes to the story of Babel:

> Ye may remember since th'Earths cursed seed
> Sought to assaile the heavens eternall towers,
> And to vs all exceeding feare did breed:
> But how we then defeated all their deed … (7.6.20.2–5)

The "euer-whirling wheele"

In her plea to Nature for recognition and the restoration of her power, Mutabilitie describes just such a cyclical repetition of creation and destruction. The following stanza is a major point in her argument that, in spite of Jove's position as supreme celestial ruler, she is still in command:

> For all that from her [the Earth] springs, and is ybredde,
> How-euer fayre it flourish for a time,
> Yet see we soone decay; and, being dead,
> To turne again vnto their earthly slime:
> Yet, out of their decay and mortall crime,
> We daily see new creatures to arize;
> And of their Winter spring another Prime,
> Vnlike in forme, and chang'd by strange disguise:
> So turne they still about, and change in restlesse wise. (7.7.18)

Here she announces that creation depends on the continual movement of transformation, and that passing away and destruction are integral to creation. These cycles are the motion of the "euer-whirling wheele" with which Spenser opens the *Mutabilitie Cantos* (7.6.1). If Mutabilitie is a destructive being, she also makes the creativity of poetry possible; Spenser transposes this idea from Du Bellay's depiction of Rome. In his translation of the second quatrain of the above-quoted *Antiquitez* 27, Spenser develops the idea of time's devouring power,[24] which remains very important to him in *The Faerie Queene*:

> Juge, en voyant ces ruines si amples,
> Ce qu'à rongé le temps injurieux,
> Plus qu'aux ouvriers les plus industrieux
> Ces vieux fragmens encor servent d'exemple. (ll. 5–8)

> Judge by these ample ruines vew, the rest
> The which injurious time hath quite outworne,
> Since of all workmen helde in reckning best,
> Yet these olde fragments are for paternes borne ... (ll. 5–8)

It is evident here that the injurious, ruinous effect of time on the world is part and parcel of the dynamic of imitation that produces poetry from a model and subsequently as a model, in the second phase leaving behind the ruins of the past. In sonnet 1 of the *Songe*, Du Bellay mentions the erosion effected by time. Spenser transforms the text by writing "time's decay," perhaps for the sake of rhyme, but nonetheless in keeping with Du Bellay's tone, and also in a way that turns out to be productive in light of its recasting here and for subsequent English verse.[25]

Spenser thus borrows from Du Bellay's presentation of transformation in order to engage in it, displacing the Roman past whose passing Du Bellay at once laments and celebrates. Spenser distances his poetry from models offered by Du Bellay, France, and Rome in *The Faerie Queene* in order to present a new poetry that is necessarily implicated in transformation, but that nonetheless expresses a wish for stasis. Although his final wish in the epic is for the abolition of Mutabilitie, the dependence of his poetry on her necessitates that she be granted a place in the imperfect utopian beyond of *The Faerie Queene*. From this place she will continue to promote the generation of new poetry, on the

---

[24] A. Kent Hieatt has very adeptly shown how Shakespeare takes up and reworks the notion and vocabulary of time's devouring power in the *Sonnets*: "The Genesis of Shakespeare's *Sonnets*: Spenser's *Ruines of Rome: by Bellay*," *PMLA* 98.5 (October 1983): 800–814. See also Melehy, *The Poetics of Literary Transfer*, 75–93.

[25] Shakespeare uses variations on the expression "time's decay" five times in the *Sonnets*: 15, 16, 54, 55, and 100: *Shakespeare's Sonnets*, ed. Stephen Booth (New Haven: Yale University Press, 1971).

basis of the decay and ruin of the old that can take on life only as decay and ruin in progress. Thus, in the very gesture that he affirms the finality of canonical poetry at the end of his epic, Spenser leaves his own and, at least in theory, all of modern Western poetry subject to the transformation on which its creation depends. A reading of *The Faerie Queene* in light of Spenser's transforming incorporation of Du Bellay's notions of poetic transformation brings to light the fluid status of early modern English canonical poetry.

Chapter 4
Utopia Versus State of Power, or Pretext of the Political Discourse of Modernity: Hobbes, Reader of La Boétie?[1]

Timothy J. Reiss
Translated by Hassan Melehy

Preliminary Remarks

The title of this essay may seem slightly provocative. There is no evidence I know of that directly justifies the subtitle. By asking this question, I only wish to emphasize that the *terms* through which the European seventeenth century was able to conceive politics were furnished by predecessors, of which the name and work of Etienne de La Boétie are very precisely representative. The pretext in question is therefore that of a certain political thought that La Boétie represents; the modernity is the one that sees its beginnings around the mid-seventeenth century.[2] Whether or not Hobbes knew La Boétie's work directly (a matter of only anecdotal interest, but which would not be a surprise), we will see at the end of this

---

[1]   The earliest version of this chapter dates from 1980, from a session of a research group at the University of Montreal, "Political Discourse and Models of Rationality," sponsored by the Association France-Québec and the University of Montreal, whose principal members were Christiane Frémont, Françoise Gaillard, Pierre Gravel, Claude Lagadec, Michel Serres, and myself. In English, this version became an Eberhard L. Faber lecture at Princeton University at the invitation of Albert Sonnenfeld, and another at McGill University at the invitation of Marc Angenot and George Szanto. I thank everyone for the debates sparked by these events. Fifteen years later, I completely reconceived this study for the conference "Konfigurationen der Macht in der frühen Neuzeit" held at the Universität GS Essen in March 1996. I heartily thank Roland Galle for his invitation, his encouragement, and his generous indulgence. I also thank Alice Stroup for her later attentive and strict reading, and especially David Lee Rubin for the efficacious goodwill and careful generosity of his work as editor for the first publication of a much longer version of this essay: "Utopie versus état de pouvoir, ou prétexte du discours politique de la modernité: Hobbes, lecteur de La Boétie?" *EMF: Studies in Early Modern France, IV: Utopia 1: 16th and 17th Centuries*, ed. David Lee Rubin, co-ed. Alice Stroup (Charlottesville, VA: Rookwood Press, 1998), 31–83. For the present version, abridgement towards the goals of the current collection, and translation I am entirely and most gratefully indebted to Hassan Melehy.

[2]   The justification of this date (which is not meant to be exact) is taken less from Foucault than from two of my own books, *The Discourse of Modernism* (Ithaca and London:

study that Hobbes seems to adopt, quite exactly, certain essential terms from La Boétie's thought. I will argue that the thinkers of the sixteenth century furnished the terms that Hobbes, among others, made use of (perhaps even in a sense *could not but make use of*) in order to frame his own questions. I wish to show how their work offered the intellectual limits within which subsequent political thought was possible—or, at any rate, within which it was worked out. The intellectual air that Hobbes breathed was created by the sixteenth century; it allowed certain theoretical questions and not others, and a certain style of questions. In a precise sense, it *produced* the thought of the liberal state.[3]

La Boétie developed a social and political thought that teeters between two poles, two possibilities of state and/or social requirements and goods. Without wanting to say that he could have conceived them in this precise form or so named them, I will call them utopian and dystopian. The first rests on relations of friendship (this is, in fact, his expression), the second on relations of power. The second presents itself as the everyday reality of an authoritarian society whose functioning imposes limits on human life that are exact, unbearable, and, for La Boétie, in principle incomprehensible. I propose that one may see in them the premises of what later became (after Hobbes) liberal society. The first, utopian, pole appears very precisely as the *other* of that dystopian reality, and hangs specifically on a series of terms and concepts (given, that is, by La Boétie himself) whose subsequent "transformation" into a quite similar series furnished some of the symbolism of the French Revolution, whose precise objective was to overturn a real form of the rational "liberal" state. In La Boétie's work, this utopia of a state form that did not yet exist slips towards the divine, towards an elsewhere that, in the end, escapes the purely human. As such, this utopia represents a "failure." For it implies that social order cannot be established by human reason. Its dystopian contrary, on the other hand, following the work of the seventeenth-century thinkers, turns out to be entirely and all too practicable (hence the necessity of the subsequent Revolution).

For the needs of what follows, I will begin with the utopian pole—an association based on "entrecognoisance," "friendship," amity, *amicitia*. For I will end by suggesting that the dystopian pole leads more directly to the political thought that immediately follows. It is nonetheless important to keep in mind that La Boétie himself does not offer these two poles in that form. In his work they overlap, developing in dialectical play. I simply found that their presentation and analysis become clearer when one separates them, at the risk of ever so slightly distorting the coherence of this political thought. But in any case, before undertaking the analysis, some framing of the theoretical context is in order.

Cornell University Press, 1982) and *The Meaning of Literature* (Ithaca and London: Cornell University Press, 1992), the first of which, certainly, owes much to Foucault's work.

[3] The full demonstration of this point would doubtless require a whole book, and in certain respects what follows is only a beginning of that effort, which is slowly getting done.

La Boétie Between the Past and the Future: Contexts and Debates

Toward the end of the sixteenth century, political thinkers both Catholic and Protestant had managed to justify regicide. François Hotman, Théodore de Bèze, Philippe Duplessis-Mornay, the Catholic League a bit after that, and still later the Jesuit Juan de Mariana (most of the "blame" for which the Society as a whole nonetheless had to bear) all held that the Prince was responsible for the well-being of the people either as the outcome of a foundational "election" or by divine anointment. To lapse voluntarily and actively in that responsibility was to refuse a duty delegated by the people or imposed by God. The failure in question had doubtless to be excessive. In 1599 Mariana limited assassination to cases of the most extreme monstrosity. But he had many predecessors who believed that adherence to the "wrong" faith was sufficient proof of such excess.

Now, the widespread belief that death alone could redeem this failure, the death of a kind of scapegoat to boot, seems to signal a certain panic or anguish at the apparent insolubility of social and political conditions. One might indeed say that between the first decades of the sixteenth century and the second half of the seventeenth, Europe passed through a particularly rough and unstable period—all the more so since those seeking to explain it and sort out its conditions trusted less and less their instruments of thought.[4] This is not the place to discuss this matter, but the historical and theoretical context of these monarchomachs is important to my argument. For although it was written in 1548, La Boétie's *Discourse of Voluntary Servitude* [*Discours de la servitude volontaire*] or *Contr'un*, which forms the basis of this argument, became celebrated only after its circulation as Protestant propaganda, partially in the 1574 *Reveille matin des François*, fully in the *Mémoires de l'Estat de France, sous Charles Neufiesme* compiled in 1577 by the Genevan Huguenot Simon Goulart.[5] It was clear that one response to La Boétie's question of how to understand why thousands accept the law of a sole

---

[4]   The second question is discussed at greater length in my *Meaning of Literature*, chapters 1–3. The first has been the object of endless work by historians. For a panorama, see Harry Kamen, *The Iron Century: Social Change in Europe 1550–1660* (London: Weidenfeld and Nicolson, 1971), or its revised and expanded edition: *European Society 1500–1700* (London: Hutchinson, 1984).

[5]   The third edition of Goulart's collection printed a revised and updated version of La Boétie's text that subsequent editors have considered the second, complete, edition of the *Contr'un*: Simon Goulart, *Mémoires de l'Estat de France, sous Charles Neufiesme ...*, 3 vols (Meidelborg: Henrich Wolf, 1577). A comparison of these two texts shows however that their variants are only verbal. Even compared to the two manuscripts discovered in the nineteenth century, little more than words differ. To say, as does Pierre Léonard, even while providing the variants, that Goulart or someone else "tampered with" the text, first "partially" and then "even more," seems an exaggeration: Pierre Léonard in Etienne de La Boétie, *Le Discours de la servitude volontaire*, ed. Léonard (Paris: Payot, 1978), 100. All subsequent references to the *Discours de la servitude volontaire* will be to this edition and will be cited in the body of the text.

ruler, even a wicked one, when they could just say "no," would have been to turn this "no" into violence: an idea that many have indeed believed stems naturally from La Boétie's work.[6] In fact, such an idea was entirely foreign to it.

It has been much emphasized that the work of Machiavelli marked a moment of change in political thought, after which the human will came to the forefront and violence became an instrument, extreme no doubt but no longer a mortal sin. Published in 1531, *The Prince* immediately posed a problem. Cardinal Reginald Pole wrote in his *Apologia ad Carolum Quintum* (1539) that the text threatened the state's very existence by secularizing everything political: in reality, it justified an argument of every man for himself and made all recourse to any divine order beside the point. Doubtless this change was not immediate, but these ideas had been launched. One may certainly hold that political and economic crises were still conceived in religious terms in 1640–1641 (a third of Hobbes's *Leviathan* is dedicated to their consideration in 1651), but that is "residual" thinking. Much earlier, especially in England, writers such as Sir Thomas Smith and Francis Bacon treated the state as the creation of a purely human will.

I wish to propose that La Boétie's *Discourse* is marked by the emergence of a series of concepts aimed at the state and its formation, deployed between an idealist utopia (tending ultimately toward the divine) and a dystopian reality, which lets us grasp an essential step in Western political thought. Some of these concepts will be exactly adopted by Hobbes and thence become constitutive of later theories. At issue is not necessarily direct influence but rather the presence in a particular form of widely disseminated ideas. A century ago G.P. Gooch said of the *Discourse*, in connection with its publication by the Huguenots, that it "cannot fairly be taken as a specimen of their opinions at any time, much less at the date of its composition in 1548."[7] I would argue, rather, that it represents a widespread movement of ideas. Gooch came closer to such an argument when he added, "The political ideas to which the religious wars in France had given rise continued to circulate in England long after they were forgotten on the Continent. The writings of the Huguenots were studied and quoted by the forerunners of the great democratic thinkers of the middle of the seventeenth century, and were to become intimately known to those thinkers themselves."[8] The *Discourse* is among those writings.

In an analogous sense we recognize that it could only have been written after Machiavelli. Could La Boétie have known *The Prince* directly? In 1548, the work had not yet appeared in French. This date for the *Discourse*'s composition comes from Montaigne, the first edition of whose *Essays* (1580) said that his friend hadn't "yet reached his eighteenth year of age" ["encore atteint le dix-huitiesme an de son

---

[6]   Nannerl O. Keohane, *Philosophy and the State in France: The Renaissance to the Enlightenment* (Princeton: Princeton University Press, 1980), 96.

[7]   G.P. Gooch, *English Democratic Ideas in the Seventeenth Century* (Cambridge: Cambridge University Press, 1954), 16.

[8]   Ibid., 25.

aage"][9] when he wrote it. La Boétie was born in 1530. Did he read Italian? We don't know. He was broadly educated and cultivated, and that skill was common among his peers. But the date of 1548 is hardly trustworthy. On the one hand, Montaigne may have thought to "exculpate" on account of his youth the author of a text that had become politically suspect. The final, corrected edition of the *Essays* says simply "in his early youth"[10] ["en sa premiere jeunesse" (*Essais*, 182)], only to go on to call him "this boy of sixteen" (144) ["ce garson de seize ans" (193)]. On the other hand, explaining to his reader that he had read the *Discourse* "long before" (136) ["longue piece avant" (182)] meeting La Boétie, and that it was this very reading that instilled in him the desire to meet its author, Montaigne cannot be taking us back into a distant past. Scholars now agree that he read the text thanks to Guillaume Lur-Longa when they were both in Paris in 1553–1554.[11] A counsellor in the Parlement de Paris from 1554 to 1556, Lur-Longa had resigned in 1553 from the same post in the Parlement de Bordeaux in favor of the young La Boétie, who addresses him twice in the *Discourse*. This suggests that this version was written after January 20, 1553, the date of Longa's resignation, and before June 4, 1554, when he began his service in Paris.[12] Such a date is supported by the praise that La Boétie bestows on Joachim Du Bellay, Pierre de Ronsard, and Jean Antoine de Baïf for having renewed French poetry. As Paul Bonnefon said, such praise was hardly possible before publication of Ronsard's *Odes* of 1550 and 1552, Du Bellay's *Olive* of 1550, and Baïf's *Amours* in 1552.

But what does this tell us about the dates of the *Discourse*'s first publication? According to the historian Jacques-Auguste de Thou, La Boétie wrote it in reaction to the violent repression in 1548 by an army of Henri II commanded by the Connétable Anne de Montmorency of the people of Bordeaux and the Guyenne who were opposed to the salt tax: "more than a hundred condemnations to death or the galleys, suspension of the Parliament, suppression of the city's privileges, and so on." Here I quote Malcolm Smith, who also recalls (as do many others) that Montaigne "was witness to the event"[13] (*Essays*, 1: 24, 95–6; *Essais*, 129–30), but also that his close relatives had taken part in negotiations with the rebels, that

---

[9]   Michel de Montaigne, *Essais*, in *Oeuvres complètes*, ed. Albert Thibaudet and Maurice Rat (Paris: Gallimard, 1962), 1477, ch. 28 n. 3. All subsequent references to the *Essais* will be to this edition and will be cited in the body of the text. [Montaigne's qualification is in the endnotes of the French edition of the *Essais* and does not appear in Frame's translation of the *Essais*.—Trans.]

[10]   Michel de Montaigne, *The Complete Essays of Montaigne*, trans. Donald M. Frame (Stanford: Stanford University Press, 1958), 1:28, 135. All subsequent references to the English translation of the *Essays* will be to this edition and will be cited in the body of the text; translation occasionally altered.

[11]   Roger Trinquet, *La jeunesse de Montaigne: Ses origines familiales, son enfance et ses études* (Paris: Nizet, 1972), 612: "Montaigne."

[12]   Malcolm Smith, "Introduction," in Estienne de La Boétie, *De la servitude volontaire ou Contr'un*, ed. Smith (Geneva: Droz, 1987), 12.

[13]   Ibid., 8. [My translation of Smith's paraphrase.—Trans.]

Montaigne himself was close friends with de Thou, to whom he gave "a great deal of information."[14] From these facts, Smith concludes that it was Montaigne himself who suggested this origin of the *Discourse* to de Thou.[15] At the same time, this certainly does not mean that the *Discourse* does not refer to Plutarch's remark that "the inhabitants of Asia served one single man because they could not pronounce one single syllable, which is 'No'" ["les habitants d'Asie servoient à un seul, pour ne sçavoir prononcer un seul sillabe, qui est Non"]—which, says Montaigne, "may have given the matter and the impulsion to La Boétie for his *Voluntary Servitude*" (*Essays*, 1:26, 115) ["donna peut estre la matiere et l'occasion à La Boitie de sa *Servitude Volontaire*" (*Essais*, 156)]. This conjuncture of current event and ancient writing perfectly matched the ideals of Florentine, French, and other humanisms.

But to finish with this aspect of the question, suffice it to say that the *Discourse*, just like the *Essays*, could have been rewritten many times: after 1548 and again later, even up till 1562. There is nothing at all contradictory here. The manuscripts that we now know of were apparently drafted on the basis of another one that belonged to Montaigne from 1557 on,[16] as also on the basis of texts published by the Protestants in 1574 and 1578. These manuscripts are of a later date than the Lur-Longa copy, perhaps given to Montaigne, as some believe, by La Boétie's heirs. But it may also be that they are based on another copy given to Montaigne in 1557 to cement a friendship and show the measure of La Boétie's intelligence. We simply do not know their status—original, corrected, written expressly for informal meetings? In any case, they seem to convey thought that was taking shape over about ten years, roughly between 1548 and 1557. We know nothing about the first composition of the work other than what Montaigne and de Thou say. The central date is certainly 1553–1554.

Now, two translations of *The Prince* appeared in 1553, one by Gaspard d'Auvergne, the other by Guillaume Cappel.[17] The former, printed in Poitiers, has a royal privilege dated March 7, 1547. The latter came from the Parisian press of Charles Estienne, the Royal Printer. Both included prefatory pieces by associates and

---

[14]   Ibid., 8–9.

[15]   Smith proposes other reasons just as convincing to believe that Montaigne is the source of de Thou's information: ibid., 7–9. For de Thou, see also Louis Desgraves, "Introduction" to La Boétie, *Oeuvres complètes*, ed. Desgraves, 2 vols (n.p.: William Blake & Co., 1991), 23–4.

[16]   Léonard in La Boétie, *Discours*, 99.

[17]   Niccolò Machiavelli, *Le Prince de Nicolas Macchiavelli secretaire & citoien de Florence*, trans. Gaspard d'Auvergne (Poitiers: Enguilbert de Marnef, 1553); Machiavelli, *Le prince de Nicolas Machiauelle Secretaire et citoien de Florence*, trans. Gvillavme Cappel (Paris: Charles Estienne Imprimeur du Roy, 1553). In the copy of the d'Auvergne translation that I examined (BN Rés.p.F.39), the second "5" in the 1553 date on the title page and at the end in the colophon is crossed out and replaced by a "6" in ink in a sixteenth-century hand. The Privilège is untouched. The copy of the Cappel translation that I looked at (BN Rés.p.F.38) lacks any Privilège. In 1571, d'Auvergne republished his edition, this time preceded by a translation of the *Discorsi*.

members of the Pléiade: Jean Dorat and Marc-Antoine Muret in the first, and Muret, Etienne Jodelle, and Rémy Belleau in the second. These names, these dates, and these two editions suggest that the work of Machiavelli was well known and broadly discussed in French humanist circles—courtiers, parlementarians, educators—from at least the 1540s. It is also worth noting that since 1547, Catherine de' Medici presided over a heavily Italian-influenced court. We can be sure that someone like La Boétie was familiar with Machiavelli's ideas, if not his very text. Even if he did not know Italian, he had direct access to *The Prince* long before he met Montaigne— as therefore, sharing the same situation, did the earliest readers of the *Discours*.[18]

The Florentine had shown that the princely state *of necessity* acted as a continuous series of power grabs. La Boétie went further, showing that the prince, by the very fact of occupying the position of ruler, was always a tyrant. Machiavelli had already rejected the traditional distinction between prince and tyrant.[19] But he

---

[18]   At issue here is a question to which I still seek a clear answer. But I add (here briefly) that La Boétie may have had other, more personal access to Machiavelli's work. Sarlat in the Périgord, the city of his birth (1530), was the episcopal see to which the Florentine Niccolò Gaddi was named in 1553. Gaddi was "a relative of Catherine de Médici, … a refined intellectual, a distinguished Hellenist," a friend of members of Machiavelli's circle. The printer of the Italian edition of *The Prince* had dedicated the work to Cardinal Jean Gaddi, a relative. Niccolò Gaddi was the one who introduced the book to the French court. The bishop only came to Sarlat in 1541, and stayed just five years, resigning in 1546. Some propose a close link between the bishop and the young La Boétie. This is doubtful, but it is certain that his paternal uncle and godfather, another Etienne, himself a clergyman and a holder of several offices in and around Sarlat, took charge of his nephew's education when the latter was orphaned at ten in 1540. From a principal Sarlatian family, he had close relations with the episcopal palace (which was, moreover, very close to La Boétie's house). No less important, his maternal uncle, Jean III de Calvimont, president of the Parlement de Bordeaux, several times ambassador of France, was closely tied to, among others, Venetian and Florentine circles—banned from Bordeaux from 1542 to 1547, he also took care of his nephew during this period, lending him, notably, some of his books (which La Boétie later left to his cousin in his will—"a few on law"). An uncle by marriage published a translation of Livy's *Third Decade*. All of this suggests that the young La Boétie breathed an air of Italian humanism. See Jacques Joseph Desplat, *La Boétie: Le magistrat aux nombreux mystères* (Le Bugue: PLB, 1992), 21–4, which, for Jean Gaddi and the introduction to *The Prince*, refers to Jean Maubourget, *Sarlat et le Périgord méridional* (Périgueux: Société historique et archéologique du Périgord, 1955), 108; Paul Bonnefon, *Estienne de La Boétie: Sa vie, ses ouvrages et ses relations avec Montaigne* (1888) (Geneva: Slatkine Reprints, 1970), 5–7; for the quotation from La Boétie's will, see his *Oeuvres complètes*, ed. Paul Bonnefon (Bordeaux: G. Gounouilhou; Paris: J. Rouam, 1892), vol. 2, 259. [The translation of the quotations in French is mine.—Trans.]

[19]   About this Leo Strauss says: "the *Prince* is characterized by the deliberate indifference to the distinction between king and tyrant; the *Prince* presupposes the tacit rejection of that traditional distinction. Machiavelli was fully aware that by conceiving the view expounded in the *Prince* he was breaking away from a whole tradition of political science; or, to apply to the *Prince* an expression which he uses when speaking of his *Discourses*, that he was taking a road which had not yet been followed by anyone." Leo Strauss, *On Tyranny* (London: Collier-Macmillan, 1963), 23.

had also held that the prince, even as he set himself apart by his *virtù*, was a man and, at the start, a private person like any other. An argument like this seemed to pose a tough problem: for if such were the case, how was one to live in a society constantly ravaged by these power grabs, potentially by anyone at all, in which only the force of the last winner, subjecting the others, could bring an end to these grabs?—all the more when one now *knew* this to be the case. La Boétie found it indeed inexplicable that other such persons should accept this subjection; inexplicable because they hadn't even to be active to refuse it as he had had to be to enforce it. These persons composed a people who, in order to be free, had but to wish it, had but to withdraw their support from the prince in order to make the latter's power disappear. Why did they not whisper this entirely passive "no"? Their failure to do so justified the name of "voluntary servitude."

La Boétie himself considers his society of friendship to be utopian, "fantasist." But it is no more "imaginary" (the sixteenth-century meaning of "fantaisiste") than the one he criticizes. For people give power to a name, not a person. And this name is not mortal. It is nothing but the site of the constitution of power, a site that will *always* be fantasized by the people dominated by the power it conveys, once the name has been accepted. The question, then, remains what La Boétie considers everyone's freedom with respect to this power, and the consequent (in) explicability of the servitude voluntarily given to this fantasy: these are two sides of the same question. As a point of departure, this utopia is squarely opposed to the Machiavellian society, in which anyone at all may grab power. The *virtuoso* simply needs the means necessary to that end. There is no a priori hindrance, only the constraints of the objective situation. But this way of seeing things also gives its own kind of solution to La Boétie's problem. To his "how does one explain that …?" it simply replies: "by force," by that fear to which he reduces the many motives that Cicero offers, and by the needs of reasons of state. But since all persons have in theory been thus made "free," the observation leads to an intolerable situation: either the permanent struggle that Hobbes will describe in the guise of the state of nature before civil societies, or a society in which vicissitude, as Louis Le Roy later called it, reigns in perpetuity—since all have the same "right" to power. It was in regard to this concept and fear of permanent struggle, as well, that philosophical polemicists of the French wars of religion like Michel Hurault de l'Hôpital and Guillaume du Vair in the early 1590s would formulate what appear to be the earliest notions of an abstract *contract*, what they called a(n abstract) *lien de justice* founding civil society and uniting its members.[20]

---

[20] Timothy J. Reiss, *Mirages of the Selfe: Patterns of Personhood in Ancient and Early Modern Europe* (Stanford: Stanford University Press, 2003), 450; Michel Hurault de l'Hôpital, *Second Discours sur l'estat de France*, in *Quatre excellens discours sur l'estat present de la France* … (Paris+, 1593), 149; Guillaume du Vair, "Exhortation à la paix, adressée à ceux de la Ligue [1592–3]," in *Actions et traictez oratoires*, ed. René Radouent (Paris: Edouard Cornély, 1911), 66.

So we shall say that if on the one hand Hobbes, for example, is responding to a sort of nostalgia for origins (knowing that one cannot establish the first moment of civil society and that any "beforehand" will be only a logical construct),[21] on the other hand he is responding to the anti-state conclusions reached by such precursors as La Boétie. But he cannot say so: because his response of the contract in no way avoids, at least for those adopting these earlier theories (Robert Filmer in England, for example, or Cardin Le Bret in France), the instability and divisions that result if one accepts the primary idea of a basic equality among society's members. Their arguments must not even be shown. They must be hidden. The continuing power struggles will therefore be placed outside society: it will be established that they precede the founding of civil society, are even its cause, that they thus no longer exist and do not characterize the human being at all. In the same way, the outcome of individual conflicts *is* the contract that marks the creation of society. These conflicts are lost in the time beforehand. Conflicts and power struggles menacing the social realm are constitutive of the new concepts and practices of civil society, but for all that are not within it (in the future this way of thinking will permit other antitheses to be resolved).[22] This is doubtless what Leo Strauss meant when he spoke of the *logical* necessity for Hobbes to construct the state of nature (see note 19).

What is the thinking that makes the *Discourse of Voluntary Servitude* a work at once representative and exceptional? I will try to show that one may justly use these words to describe it, and that an important part of subsequent political theory refers to it, even while concealing certain of its consequences or inverting some of its terms in order to permit the theoretical establishment of an actual society. I will also try to show to what extent the elements of what would be, in La Boétie's eyes, an ideal society indeed form something like the *other* of Western societies that really developed on the basis of that subsequent theory—or by referring to it. It is their *other* in part precisely because this ideal is the object to which contractual thought and its attendant practices are responding. This is why I will finish this essay with a quick review of the beginning of Hobbes's *Behemoth* (written circa 1668, published in 1679). Let us remember that this text comes after the author's *The Elements of*

---

[21] "The state of nature is thus for Hobbes not an historical fact, but a necessary construction. Nevertheless, the appearance that this theory of the state of nature has an historical meaning is not entirely without foundation. It is essential to his political philosophy that it should begin with the description of the state of nature, and that it should let the State emerge from the state of nature. Proceeding thus, Hobbes does not narrate a true history, but he grasps a typical history." Leo Strauss, *The Political Philosophy of Hobbes: Its Basis and Its Genesis*, trans. Elsa M. Sinclair (Chicago and London: Chicago University Press, 1963), 104. For Rousseau, on the other hand, human life in a state of nature before the organization of society would be a historical fact. So it would be, we can say, for Locke. In this change occurring in the mid- to late seventeenth century, we perhaps see the constitution of the isolated subject of Euro-American modernity.

[22] Timothy J. Reiss, *Against Autonomy: Global Dialectics of Cultural Exchange* (Stanford: Stanford University Press, 2002), 29–67.

74 French Connections in the English Renaissance / Reiss

Law, Natural and Politic (1639–1640), after his *De Cive* (1642), and above all after *Leviathan* (1651). *Behemoth* means to be a commentary on a particular historical situation, and a kind of practical testing of the theoretical analyses that preceded it. By way of *Behemoth*, I will try to show how and why this response I speak of was made.

Liberty, Equality, Fraternity: The Utopian Face of the Future Liberal State

La Boétie builds his utopia on three terms: a fundamental "freedom [*liberté*]" of the human; a total "equality [*égalité*]" among the State's members; and a "friendship [*amitié*]" or "mutual recognition [*entrecongnoissance*]" that is the only true social bond. Of the last, Montaigne said, thinking especially of his friend La Boétie: "There is nothing to which nature seems to have inclined us more than to society. And Aristotle says that good legislators have had more care for friendship than for justice" (*Essays*, 1.28, 136) ["Il n'est rien à quoy il semble que nature nous aye plus acheminé qu'à la société. Et dit Aristote que les bons legislateurs ont plus de soing de l'amitié que de la justice" (*Essais*, 182)].[23]

As far as possible, I will analyze these terms separately, although it is difficult to dissociate them. Indeed, their mutual ambiguity signals La Boétie's inability to detach this *other* of the state from the power relations whose objective existence he sees all too clearly. This inability—impossibility—matters, because it is by seeking to deny it that La Boétie poses his question on voluntary servitude, and it is by fully accepting it, along with its consequences, that the theoreticians of the seventeenth century will operate.

The question of liberty appears at the argument's outset:

My sole aim on this occasion is to discover how it can happen that a vast number of individuals, of towns, cities and nations can allow one man to tyrannize them, a man who has no power except *the power they themselves give him*, who could do them no harm *were they not willing to suffer harm*, and who could never wrong them *were they not more ready to endure it than to stand in his way*.[24]

---

[23] In Xenophon's *Memorabilia*, Socrates also says that friendship is the most precious human possession. The idea is, of course, a commonplace from Plato to Cicero, from Seneca to Petrarch, and becomes an axiom of humanism. Gérald Allard offers a somewhat disappointing analysis of aspects of this history of friendship in the face of civil society: "Montaigne et La Boétie: Révolution, Réforme et statu quo," in Danièle Letocha, ed., *Aequitas, aequalitas, auctoritas: Raison théorique et légitimation de l'autorité dans le xvie siècle européen* (Paris: Vrin, 1992), 204–15.

[24] Etienne de La Boétie, *Slaves by Choice*, trans. Malcolm Smith (Surrey: Tunnymed, 1988), 38. All subsequent references to the English translation of the *Discours de la servitude volontaire* will be to this edition and will be cited in the body of the text; translation occasionally altered. [I have chosen to use the better-known title of *Discourse of Voluntary Servitude*, or in abbreviated form *Discourse*, for Reiss's references to the work; I mark direct quotations with the abbreviated title *Slaves* to indicate that their source is this translation.—Trans.]

> [Pour ce coup je ne voudrois sinon entendre comm'il se peut faire que tant d'hommes, tant de bourgs, tant de villes, tant de nations endurent quelque fois un tyran seul, qui n'a de puissance que *celle qu'ils luy donnent*; qui n'a de pouvoir de leur nuire, sinon *tant qu'ils ont vouloir de l'endurer*; qui ne scauroit leur faire mal aucun, sinon lors qu'*ils aiment mieulx le souffrir* que lui contredire. (*Discours*, 104–5—my emphasis)]

Let us look closely at what seems to be an immediate contradiction: if the people "*give*" the tyrant his power, how can La Boétie also speak of a "*seizure*" of power, as he has just done? Perhaps this is less a contradiction than a major ambiguity. La Boétie is speaking here of the continuation of the state rather than its beginning. Hobbes will see that the only way to avoid this ambiguity is by linking the voluntary moment to the founding of the state. But La Boétie builds his utopia from within the very state he believes himself to be living in, which he simultaneously analyzes through a series of oppositions: constraint/freedom, inequality/equality, power of one man/equal power of all (and so of no one).

La Boétie here affirms that putting one person in power *imposes* on all the others the necessity of taking unequal distance from that power. The continuation of the power of one man can only be due to a will *not to have* power on the part of those subjected and to a "common" will of the people to be treated as slaves: "not because they have had to yield to some greater force but, it seems, because they have been mesmerised by the mere name of a single man, a man they ought neither to fear (for he is just one man) nor love (as he is inhuman and barbaric towards them)" (*Slaves*, 38) ["non pas contrains par une plus grande force, mais aucunement (ce semble) enchantés et charmés par le nom seul d'un, duquel ils ne doivent ni craindre la puissance puisqu'il est seul, ny aimer les qualités puis qu'il est en leur endroit inhumain et sauvage" (*Discours*, 105)]. Once again La Boétie comments on the fact that the action of the one who makes himself "prince" singularizes him, separates him from humanity. But at the same time, people's internalization of the power that results from this action also somehow dehumanizes the other members of this society. People only need to refuse this singular power to nullify it. It would be understandable for the people to do nothing, says La Boétie, if it "cost [them] something to recover their freedom" ["lui coustait quelque chose a recouvrer sa liberté"]. Then he would say nothing—even though there is nothing "that man ought to hold more dear than *to recover his natural right*, and to become, as it were, a man rather than a beast" (*Slaves*, 41, my emphasis) ["combien qu'est-ce que l'homme doit avoir plus cher que de *se remettre en son droit naturel*, et par manière de dire de beste revenir homme" (*Discours*, 111—my emphasis)].

I will return to the problem of understanding this refusal and this will not to have power in the second part of this essay. Here, what interests me is the very concept of this lack of power and lack of freedom as constitutive of every human who dwells in the state, or at least the state built in tyranny (although, says La Boétie, there is currently no other). The human should be able to *recover* his natural right. La Boétie affirms that the freedom of each *is* his or her natural right, that the human deprived of freedom is no longer human (he or she is worse than a beast). The current state is therefore profoundly antinatural. Such an affirmation rests on the vague, but absolute and transcendent idea of a freedom that would be limited, entirely so, by the simple fact of accepting the power of one alone; by the simple fact, it is tempting to add, of living in society—if not the one of friendship advocated by La Boétie. The result is indeed that he must propose a type of society at the heart of which there would be no constraint, no power relation.

La Boétie does not have, properly speaking, a concept of freedom. For "his predecessor" Machiavelli, the problem did not truly present itself. Machiavelli aims for the effective action of the state united under a single power for the common good and unceasing expansion (without which the state decays and lets itself be grabbed by another). He surely agreed with the Greeks, for whom there was no freedom without justice, and no justice without laws: freedom was necessarily accompanied *by the recognition of power relations*. Max Horkheimer and Theodor Adorno put it as follows: "Only those who subject themselves utterly pass muster with the gods. The awakening of the subject is bought with the recognition of power as the principle of all relationships."[25]

When one looks closely at La Boétie's *other*, one is struck by two aspects. First, freedom is always defined by opposition to something else: we know what it is not, not what it is; it is never positive, always a lack. Next, La Boétie's ideal society is not, in the end, defined in terms of just any freedom, but rather as a "fantasy," a relation of "friendship" among the members of an elite. By definition, the *law* is excluded from such a relationship, and although it is not arbitrary (since it is "natural"), it is thus just as unstable as the tyranny opposed to it. This alternative is therefore really not one. The other of tyranny offers itself as a sort of Edenic anarchy—which only the elect can enjoy.

It is not surprising that Hobbes inverts all the terms that La Boétie signals. For Hobbes, the time when the human being enjoys his natural right is not when he is *more* human, but rather when he is barely human at all, when he is the beast that La Boétie places in state society. In Hobbes's eyes, as we know, the beastly, "brutish" state is the one that precedes the inception of civil society and leaves no room for any freedom but one of violence, however one defines this last word: one is not even assured of surviving. The only "right of nature" is then that of protecting oneself, saving oneself—which also gives the only possible definition of "freedom" (Hobbes is perfectly clear on the matter):

> The *Right of Nature*, which Writers commonly call *Jus Naturale*, is the Liberty each man hath, to use his own power, as he will himselfe, for the preservation of his own Nature; that is to say, of his own Life; and consequently, of doing any thing, which in his own Judgement, and Reason, hee shall conceive to be the aptest means thereunto.[26]

---

[25] Max Horkheimer and Theodor W. Adorno, *Dialectic of Enlightenment*, trans. Edmund Jephcott (Stanford: Stanford University Press, 2002), 5.

[26] Thomas Hobbes, *Leviathan*, ed. Richard Tuck (Cambridge: Cambridge University Press, 1991), 91, 1:14. Henceforth cited in the body of the text.

It is on this basis that the compromise of the contractual state turns out to be essential. For Hobbes (as for Locke, but contrary to Rousseau), there is then no question of breaking with "nature." On the contrary, the state responds *in its very constitution* to the natural. Hobbesian freedom is precise: it is simply that of surviving and doing everything necessary to that end—of which one element is the creation of the state. La Boétie never defines what freedom means. How could he? Living in state society, he has no evidence of it. But Hobbes must respond to the impossible situation described by La Boétie (and Machiavelli). He concludes that the state consecrates duties and constraints that are natural because they are the *laws of nature* that allow survival. The state thus institutionalizes two fundamental laws: the first requires that each "*ought to endeavor Peace*"; the second is

> That a man be willing, when others are so too, as farre-forth, as for Peace, and defence of himselfe he shall think it necessary, to lay down this right to all things; and be contented with so much liberty against other men, as he would allow other men against himselfe. (*Leviathan*, 92, 1:14)

It is clear that the contractual state is established on the basis of this second law, the foundation of its existence. This explains the observation in *Behemoth* according to which the only "fundamental" law is "that law of nature that binds us all to obey him, whosoever he be, whom lawfully and for our own safety, we have promised to obey."[27] The natural human condition is therefore not foreign to the state. On the contrary, the state is its fulfillment. La Boétie insists that the state negates the natural freedom of the human being, without which it is not human. Hobbes will completely invert these terms. For La Boétie, the human being must break with the state in order *once again* to place itself in its natural right and become human *once again*. And on this point we should not liken La Boétie to Rousseau, for whom the state is opposed to the human, without being any the less necessary: hence, for Rousseau, too, the need for the contract. In Rousseau, the Hobbesian inversion is offset by the ruse of the "noble savage." Man cannot get worse than a beast and Hobbesian society is therefore of necessity an improvement. Man can of course get worse than Rousseau's Edenic personage. Nonetheless, society is not responsible for his decline. It is on the contrary needed to prevent this decline from continuing. Rousseau recognizes that a ruse is at work: the noble savage is isolated. As soon as he is no longer alone, inevitable relations of force develop, requiring a society of laws. To speak of the freedom of an isolated being means nothing. For what would be the absence of freedom? Rousseau is in agreement with Hobbes, not La Boétie: as soon as there is more than one human being, freedom involves constraints.[28]

---

[27]   Thomas Hobbes, *Behemoth or The Long Parliament*, ed. Ferdinand Tönnies (Chicago and London: Chicago University Press, 1990), 68. Henceforth cited in the body of the text.

[28]   Keohane interprets the matter quite differently. In her eyes, not only does La Boétie use phrases "strikingly similar to those used by Rousseau" (95), but he also "foreshadow[s]" him (96).

It is doubtless Hegel who takes the argument of the contract to its limit, bringing together freedom and constraint, individual and state:

> Freedom in action issues ... from the fact that the rationality of the will wins actualization. This rationality the will actualizes in the life of the state. In a state which is really articulated rationally all the laws and organizations are nothing but a realization of freedom in its essential characteristics. When this is the case, the individual's reason finds in these institutions only the actuality of his own essence, and if he obeys these laws, he coincides, not with something alien to himself, but simply with what is his own.[29]

Freedom and constraint come together at the moment when the individual and the state merge. But that is the "end" of the movement of political thought that we are following. La Boétie was far from recognizing any alliance of freedom and constraint; still less its necessity. In his text, the state is rotten in its essence by the mere fact of power, and especially by that voluntary acceptance, that willed cession of the natural right of each. Precisely insofar as the consequence of this cession is no longer public benefit (what is indeed called the *res publica*, "commonwealth"), but rather that of an individual, private power—called "*in*human"—the state is fundamentally vitiated.

The difficulty that La Boétie confronts remains that of never being able to define freedom except as a sort of fantasy, as what it could have been had there never been a state. Unable to give it a positive definition, La Boétie has recourse to negative indices: the "good," freedom, is always what is not something else. Thus he writes of the wars between the Greeks and the Persians as a "victory of liberty over domination, of freedom over greed" (*Slaves*, 41) ["victoire de la liberté sur la domination, de la franchise sur la convoitise" (*Discours*, 110)]. Or he conceives this freedom as a natural desire whose fulfillment is impossible, a desire for some forever-lost transcendence:

> desire [for the good] remains [to all], as is natural. And the desire, the will, is common to the wise and the foolish, the courageous and the cowardly: they all long for what would make them happy and contented if they got it. There is just one desire which nature—I know not why—has failed to endow us with, and that is the desire for liberty. And yet liberty is such a great and pleasurable possession that if we lose it, all evils come upon us one after the other, and even those good things which we still have lose all their flavour and taste, as they are corrupted by servitude. Liberty is the one thing which men have no desire for, and it seems as though the only reason this is so is that if they desired it, they would have it. It is as though they are refusing this wonderful acquisition simply on the grounds that it costs so little effort. (*Slaves*, 42–3)

---

[29]   G.W.F. Hegel, *Aesthetics: Lectures in Fine Art*, vol. 1, trans. T.M. Knox (Oxford: Oxford University Press, 1975), 98.

[le desir de l'avoir (le bien) leur demeure (à tous) par la nature. Ce desir, ceste volonté est commune aux sages et aus indiscrets, aus courageus et aus couars, pour souhaitter toutes choses, qui estant acquises les rendroient heureus et contens. Une seule chose en est a dire en laquelle je ne scay comment nature defaut aus hommes pour la desirer, c'est la liberté qui est toutesfois un bien si grand et si plaisant quelle perdue tous les maus viennent a la file; et les biens mesme qui demeurent apres elle, perdent entierement leur goust et scaveur corrompus par la servitude. La seule liberté les hommes ne la desirent point, non pour autre raison, ce semble, sinon que s'ils la desiroient ils l'auroient, comme s'ils refusoient de faire ce bel acquest seulement par ce qu'il est trop aisé. (*Discours*, 113–14)]

Here we reach the crux of the impasse that La Boétie encounters in defining freedom. He is trying to grasp as an object of desire what he shows at the same time cannot be one. If one is "free," then one is human; but if one is not free, one cannot even have the idea of being so: less than a beast, one cannot conceive freedom. It cannot then be desired, since it is part of the definition of the human. Once lost, freedom is hard to recover since it cannot be experienced as an object of desire. At best, it becomes the obscurely-felt *other* of an intolerable condition. And every state is, properly speaking, *against nature*. Creating a sovereign power dehumanizes all those it claims to organize, without exception. Tyranny, a state where powers are ordered in a pyramid, and where all powers have been yielded to the more or less peremptory privilege of a single man, is only a little more against nature than other forms of the state—supposing, says La Boétie, that other forms may be imagined.

The tyrant is, in the strongest sense of the word, the "enemy" (*Slaves*, 43) ["ennemi" (*Discours*, 114)]: he who contradicts the ideal of friendship. "Our nature," writes La Boétie, "is such that the way we live is largely influenced by the common duties of friendship" (*Slaves*, 38) ["Nostre nature est ainsi que les communs devoirs de l'amitié emportent une bonne partie du cours de notre vie" (*Discours*, 105–6)]. The tyrant is an exception to this; and tyranny is therefore doubly unnatural. It is so firstly because this is the condition of every state: by the privation of "freedom" that it requires. It is so secondly because the tyrant is the enemy in his very being: by the complete absence of friendship. Finally, however, all power is tyrannical. Insofar as we participate in tyranny, by the mere fact of living in the state, we are complicit with the enemy, unnatural, worse than beasts: "The very beasts would not endure these humiliations if they were capable of feeling them. But you can deliver yourselves if you make the effort—not an effort to deliver yourselves, but an effort to want to do so!" (*Slaves*, 44) ["de tant d'indignités que les bestes mesmes ou ne les sentiroient pas, ou ne les endureroient pas, vous pouvés vous en delivrer si vous l'essaiés, non pas de vous en delivrer, mais seulement de le vouloir faire" (*Discours*, 116)]. Withdrawing complicity, not by any action but by a passive refusal, will be to recover the state of nature: "Resolve to be slaves no more, and you are free!" (*Slaves*, 44) ["Soiés resolus de ne servir plus, et vous voilà libres" (*Discours*, 116)]—restored to the condition of

80 *French Connections in the English Renaissance / Reiss*

natural right. But this desire cannot be activated. Once one places oneself inside the state, the latter becomes inescapable. It is no longer an arbitrary effect:

> The nature of man is certainly to be free and to desire to be free, but his nature is also such that he adopts the lifestyle that his upbringing [or "custom"] gives him.
>
> Let us say, then, that all those things which a man is brought up to do and which he becomes accustomed to, seem natural to him, but that what is proper to him is exclusively what his simple, unadulterated nature impels him to do. Thus, the first explanation for voluntary servitude is custom. (*Slaves*, 53)

> [La nature de l'homme est bien d'estre franc et de le vouloir estre; mais aussi sa nature est telle que naturellement il tient le pli que la nourriture (la "coustume") lui donne.
>
> Disons donc ainsi, qu'a l'homme toutes choses lui sont comme naturelles, a quoy il se nourrit et accoustume; mais cela seulement lui est naif, a quoi sa nature simple et non altérée l'appelle; ainsi la premiere raison de la servitude volontaire c'est la coustume. (*Discours*, 133)]

La Boétie here seems to approach the distinction we have seen Hobbes make between natural *right* and natural *law*: between the naïve and the natural. But this leaves La Boétie stuck. For on the one hand this observation implies that escape from the state is impossible. On the other, it indicates that La Boétie is admitting his inability to justify the distinction between a society without power relations and a state that depends on them. Just as in the case of the necessary harshness of the power of one man, for example, we may ask: what enables the assurance that the Venetians are more "natural" than the Turks (*Slaves*, 50; *Discours*, 127–8), the Spartans than the Persians (*Slaves*, 51–2; *Discours*, 129–31)? Quite obviously, an idea of the human outside the state, outside the society of power: so always imaginary.

His argument nonetheless reveals—and this is important—that every exception to the "upbringing," the "nurture" [nourriture]" of voluntary servitude, such as the Venetians and the Spartans, can only be conceived from within the political: not as existing somewhere before or aside from established civil societies, but as an *effect* of the political, as a (possible) "exception" produced from the very place of tyranny—and *for* tyranny. This will be so in spite of any quest La Boétie makes for something else. The impossibility of grasping, even less of instituting, *another* becomes clear: it will never be anything but a purely symbolic opposition to tyranny. Venetians and Turks, after all, are both effects of a nourishment gained in the state, by the state. These effects only prove the effectiveness of power:

> Normally, people who have kept their devotion to freedom intact despite the passage of time are unable to make each other's acquaintance, and so their zealous longing for freedom remains ineffectual, however numerous they may be. Under a tyrant, they are denied freedom to act, to speak, almost even to think, so that *they become isolated in their fantasies* [fantasies]. (*Slaves*, 54—my emphasis)

Utopia Versus State of Power

[Or communément le bon ze'e et affection de ceus, qui ont gardé maugré le temps la devotion a la franchise, pour si grand nombre qu'il y en ait, demeure sans effect pour ne s'entrecongnoistre point: la liberté leur est tout ostée sous le tiran, de faire, de parler, e: quasi de penser: *ils deviennent tous singuliers en leurs fantasies*. (*Discours*, 135—my emphasis)]

The last sentence is wonderful, referring as it does to the imaginary society. The very idea of liberty, at the heart of tyranny (or of any state), is reduced to the "fantasy" of a few individuals who have removed themselves from real practice. In a state based on a relation of master and slave, it is sufficiently clear that the very thought of a general freedom can only be reduced to a fantasy. La Boétie's situation is identical to that of the Persian in the story he cites from Herodotus. Two Spartans, sent as ambassadors to the Persians, are supposed to have conversed with the satrap Idarne. To the praises of the Persian state that he gives, they respond:

You are not in a position, Hydarnes,] to advise us on this ... You have experienced the good fortune which you are promising us but you have no knowledge of the good fortune which we at present enjoy. You have known the king's favour, but you know nothing of the sweet taste of liberty. (*Slaves*, 51)

[En cecy Iridarne tu ne scaurois donner bon conseil ..., pource que le bien que tu nous promets, tu l'as essaié; mais celui dont nous jouissons, tu ne sçais que c'est: tu as esprouvé la faveur du roy; mais de la liberté, quel goust elle a, combien elle est douce, tu n'en scais rien. (*Discours*, 130)]

Trying in this way to conceive his state, La Boétie sees himself reproved by his own Spartans. Isolated fantasies meet up with the isolation of the prince, but the first signal a withdrawal from politics, by the very fact of being conceived only as its opposite. Machiavelli did not have this problem to confront; for him a power grab is not an incomprehensible rupture, but rather an explicable and desirable moment in the dynamic of robustly healthy societies, in which the expansive virtue of the prince and continual swarming of the people (*dixit* Machiavelli) come together for the state's "advancement." La Boétie conceives the form of power in the state as permanent and always self-identical. "Freedom" then becomes indefinable, if not unthinkable, except as some vague transcendence, as an opposition to the constraints imposed by the objective system of power, as a utopian elsewhere.

La Boétie therefore offers as a "way out" the opposition between the state ruled by relations of power and a "naïve" society of equality of all and a supposed absence of power. Since he tries to conceive the state from within, not in terms of a beginning but in those of an already long-established situation, he is naturally forced to seek and find his naïve society's foundation within this establishment. He finds it in friendship, a concept apparently linked to that of equality: "friendship, which is all about equality" (*Slaves*, 68) ["l'amitié, qui a son vrai gibier en l'équalité" (*Discours*, 160)]. To speak of one is to speak of the other, so it seems.

From the start, La Boétie affirms that accepting servitude would be understandab'e, 1) if the people were forced to do so, or 2) if the very constitution of power assumed friendship toward the "great personage [grand personnage]" who will occupy the place of power, and provided only that this "friendship" were reciprocal, that the personage "ha[d] protected them by displaying great foresight, or ha[d] defended them with great bravery, or governed them with great care" (*Slaves*, 38–9) ["leur ait monstré par espreuve une grand preveoiance pour les garder, une grand hardiesse pour les defendre, un grand soing pour les gouverner" (*Discours*, 106)]. Let us note in passing that such reciprocal obedience and respect are precisely the fundamental laws of the state that Hobbes will advocate in *Behemoth*. For Hobbes, the mutual contract and *Fiat* place these laws at the very origin of the state. La Boétie, to the contrary, perhaps thinking of *The Prince*, flat out excludes them: "It is true that initially it takes force to reduce people to servitude" (*Slaves*, 49) ["il est vray qu'au commencement on sert contraint et vaincu par la force" (*Discours*, 125)]. He raises the possibility of reciprocal attentiveness, but without being able to pursue it.

We have already seen in La Boétie the apparent contradiction between the idea of a *seizure* of power and that of a *giving*. We have also seen that like the desire for freedom this need for friendship toward the "great personage" is not only excluded from the established state but is also somehow unthinkable. This need is the very mark of what the state cannot be. According to La Boétie, friendship is the sign sine qua non of the naïve condition: "In the first place, it is I think beyond doubt that if we were to live according to the rights which nature gave us and the precepts she teaches us, we would be naturally obedient to our parents, we would be the subjects of reason and we would be the serfs of nobody" (*Slaves*, 44) ["Premierement cela est, comme je croy, hors de doute que si nous vivions avec les droits que la nature nous a donné, et avec les enseignemens qu'elle nous apprend, nous serions naturellement obeissans aus parens, subjets a la raison, et serfs de personne" (*Discours*, 117)].

He even affirms that the natural difference of "talents" exists "in order to" obligate humans to be more dependent on one another, in order to "leave scope for the exercise of brotherly love" (*Slaves*, 45) ["faire place à la fraternelle affection" (*Discours*, 119)].[30] At first sight such a thought opposes most concepts of equality: this friendship is founded, he asserts, on at least one kind of *in*equality (that of talents), and this in turn seems to suppose that friendship in some way *replaces* equality. In fact, not only is equality no longer necessary, but its absence is as if required. Friendship becomes something like Charity in the sense in which this word is used in the New Testament: again we see why Protestant polemicists made use of the work.

---

[30]   People have reminded me of the praises of "debtors," "lenders," and "borrowers" in chapters 3 and 4 of Rabelais's *Tiers livre*, where just as much at issue are socially essential exchanges of goods and talents (on some historical and conceptual aspects of this, see my *Mirages* 405–8). La Boétie very likely read Rabelais, and these arguments may be related. He certainly knew Aristotle and Cicero. In both of them, reciprocity and exchange of talents and goods were fundamental (in the *Nichomachean Ethics* and *De officiis*, for example), to say nothing of Plato's *Republic* or Seneca's *De beneficiis*.

Friendship enables "a common will [une communion de nos volontés]," such that, precisely, one will no longer be "isolated [in one's] fantasy [singulier en sa fantaisie]." For nature

> has shown in everything she does that her intention was not so much to make us united as to make us one—we cannot doubt that we are by nature free, since we are companions of each other. And nobody can imagine that nature has placed anyone in a position of servitude, since she has made each of us the companion of all the others. (*Slaves*, 45)

> [a monstré en toutes choses qu'elle ne vouloit pas tant nous faire tous unis que tous uns: il ne faut pas faire doute que nous ne soions tous naturellement libres, puis que nous sommes tous compaignons; et ne peut tomber en l'entendement de personne que nature ait mis aucun en servitude nous aiant tous mis en compaignie. (*Discours*, 119)]

La Boétie's use in French of the plural "uns" for "one," which here allows him to mark "friendship," "company," "mutual recognition [*entrecongnoissance*]," is squarely opposed to the singular "one" of power, this "nom seul d'un" or name of a single man. Freedom and friendship come together, and it should not surprise us that when Montaigne weighs in on the theme of friendship, he does so in terms that reverse the ones that La Boétie makes use of here in discussing voluntary servitude:

> And then, the more they are friendships which law and natural obligation impose on us, the less of our choice and free will there is in them. And our free will has no product more properly its own than affection and friendship. (*Essays*, 1:28, 137)

> [Et puis, à mesure que ce sont amitiez que la loy et l'obligation naturelle nous commande, il y a d'autant moins de nostre chois et liberté volontaire. Et nostre liberté volontaire n'a point de production qui soit plus proprement sienne que celle de l'affection et amitié. (*Essais*, 184–5)]

In the society based on friendship, there would be no difference between nature and nurture (*nourriture*), between obligation and freedom. In this sense, this society would indeed be a bit like that of the Abbey of Thélème—though still resolutely *not* political—where a play of spontaneous sympathies bind freedom, will, and friendship by a natural necessity.[31] However, where Rabelais places this society on the side and removed from every "state" (this word in its modern sense being still somewhat anachronistic), La Boétie wishes it to be a *political* arena that could replace that of an everyday experience of tyranny: at least, until it has been understood as "fantasy." La Boétie also views the laws belonging to this naïve society as dictated by nature, required by our natural condition, our very humanity. There is nonetheless an element that may trouble us: how can one "command" friendship?

---

[31] Keohane, 90.

How can the law, however natural it may be, obligate us? Indeed we have already seen in La Boétie the observation that in the established state, this type of friendship is unthinkable, and in practice impossible. It "remains ineffectual [because people do not] know one another" (*Slaves*, 54, adjusted) ["demeure sans effet pour ne s'entrecongnoistre point" (*Discours*, 135)]: a condition that results directly from real power relations. One is inclined to relate this contradiction to that of Erasmus in the *Institutio principis christiani*, where the idea that all humans are born equal is opposed to the acknowledgement that in the hierarchical state ordained by God they are anything but.

Servitude, Power, Necessity: Towards the Liberal State

According to Hobbes, the stability of power relations in the well-constituted state permits the expansion of the "powers" of the human being into other realms: scientific wisdom, knowledge of nature, production of articles of all kinds (mercantile, artistic, technical), flourishing commerce, technological achievement, and so on. He lived indeed in a time and place where nothing of this kind seemed impossible. For La Boétie, the case was quite otherwise: then there seemed little but endless struggle, misery, brutishness, and war. Hobbes will be able to assert that such conflicts take place *before* the establishment of civil society, in a state of nature in which people only aim to keep acquiring "power after power." The creation of the state puts an end to this. Civil society will then continue on in a linear repetition of the same, once the machine, this "great engine" as Bacon called it, has been set in motion. Indeed, the founding *Fiat* with which *Leviathan* begins in all respects resembles that fillip that some complain Descartes allowed God in order to set the universe in motion—except that Hobbes's *Fiat* is purely human. This *Fiat* and the voluntary yielding of power of each (of all) to a single one— from some plural (*uns*) to one singular (*un*), said La Boétie—let Hobbes conceal certain elements of singular power while maintaining this same power.

Three ogres that La Boétie evokes are excluded in one stroke. First, the power of the prince is no longer solipsistic, proceeding uniquely from his sole authority: it has become the power of all gathered in the person of a single one. Next, this power is no longer an attack and a theft: it has been *given* by all for their mutual safe-keeping and protection. Finally, no one else has any power because all have yielded it, but *all* have power.

The Hobbesian state (and that of almost all subsequent Western political thought) is stabilized, its development and its expansion continue on as a repetitive motion without limits, a linear movement that potentially extends to infinity (provided only that there be "voids" to fill), having put an end to the stochastic chaos that preceded it. For La Boétie, the case is quite different: it is in the state itself that this quest for "power after power" is pursued (as for Machiavelli, for whom the quest must be diverted toward some "other," who is external but quite real), and it is in the state itself that its corollary servitude is found, the dominated subject's ever-increasing loss of liberty (voluntary servitude and voluntary yielding of power are, in a sense, two sides of the same coin). For La Boétie, the state is not a neutral "machine" established to make all people's lives easier. It is the property of a single one, whose action is necessarily cruel—hence his question:

> The point is this: if, to possess freedom, all you need do is desire it, if all that is required is a simple act of the will, a mere wish, is there a single nation which will still reckon the price of liberty too high? Is there a single nation which will begrudge this simple desire, which will retrieve a possession worth winning at the cost of one's blood? Any man of honor will feel the loss of such a possession so keenly as to reckon life itself as tiresome and death as salutary. A little spark can start a flame which will devour all the wood it finds, growing stronger all the time. But you do not need to pour water over it to extinguish it—if you stop supplying wood it will consume itself, since it has nothing else to consume, and will languish and die out. In the same way, the more that tyrants pillage, the more they exact and extort, the more they ruin and destroy, the more you give them, the more you subject yourself to them—so much the stronger they become, so much the readier they destroy everything. But if you give them nothing, if you withhold your obedience, then—without you having to struggle or strike a blow—they become naked, defeated, mere nonentities, nothing but the dry, dead branch of a tree whose roots have been deprived of moisture and sustenance. (*Slaves*, 42)

> [Quoi? si pour avoir liberté il ne faut que la desirer, s'il n'est besoin que d'un simple vouloir, se trouvera il nation au monde, qui l'estime ancore trop chere la pouvant gaigner d'un seul souhait et qui pleigne sa volonté a recouvrer le bien, lequel il devroit rachater au prix de son sang, et lequel perdu tous les gens d'honneur doivent estimer la vie desplaisante, et la mort salutaire? Certes comme le feu d'une petite estincelle devient grand et tousjours se renforce; et plus il trouve du bois plus il est prest d'en brusler; et sans qu'on y mette de l'eaue pour l'esteindre, seulement en ny mettant plus de bois n'aiant plus que consommer il se consomme soymesme, et vient sans force aucune, et non plus feu, pareillement les tirans plus ils pillent, plus ils exigent, plus ils ruinent et destruisent, plus on leur baille, plus on les sert, de tant plus ils se fortifient, et deviennent tousjours plus forts et plus frais pour aneantir et destruire tout; et si on ne leur baille rien, si on ne leur obeit point, sans combattre, sans fraper, ils demeurent nuds et deffaits, et ne sont plus rien, sinon que comme la racine n'aians plus d'humeur ou aliment, la branche devient seche et morte. (*Discours*, 112–13)]

The question as La Boétie poses it is one of disproportion. One may understand how one or two can accept being dominated by a single one, but not how "a million men" can accept the ill of being treated "as serf and slave" ["ce mal d'estre serf et esclave"]. One may say that the first case is one of "cowardice" ["couardise"], but the second defies words: "So what prodigious vice is this for which the term 'cowardice' is too flattering, for which there is no name vile enough, which nature herself will not admit to having created and which the tongue can find no name for?" (*Slaves*, 40) ["Doncques quel monstre de vice est cecy, qui ne merite pas ancore le tiltre de couardise, qui ne trouve point de nom asses vilain, que la nature desadvoue avoir fait, et la langue refuse de nommer?" (*Discours*, 108)]. Here we begin to get to the heart of the question.

We have seen that the state (in La Boétie's sense), the place of politics as a play of powers, is properly speaking against nature. It follows that this voluntary servitude, which alone enables the state, is directly counter to the "natural right" whose elements are liberty, equality, and friendship. Now, it is *nature* that has furnished humans with the very gift that is supposed to make possible the functioning of natural right insofar as it is composed of these three elements. Nature "has given us all the great gift of speech so that we could come to a still deeper acquaintance and brotherhood, and acquire a common will by sharing our thoughts with one another" (*Slaves*, 45) ["nous a donné a tous ce grand present de la voix et de la parolle pour nous accointer et fraterniser davantage, et faire par la commune et mutuelle declaration de nos pensées une communion de nos volontés" (*Discours*, 119)]. In this way, he continues, we are "by nature free, since we are companions of each other" ["tous naturellement libres, puis que nous sommes tous compaignons"]. The idea of servitude would literally not have entered "anyone's mind" ["l'entendement de personne"], because this "vice" cannot even be named in the language of those who share this natural condition, a language furnished by nature (*Slaves*, 42; *Discours*, 119). That potential "friends" cannot become friends in fact does not result from a particular act of the prince but from the fact that state power by definition forbids the use of this language, denies freedom "to act, to speak, almost even to think" (*Slaves*, 54) ["de faire, de parler, et quasi de penser" (*Discours*, 135)]. This state would therefore (here, for La Boétie) be the reversal of the ancient human society named by Plato or Cicero, established by right speech: transformed now into a utopian other of any space of *political* action (that of the rightly ordered *polis*).

So the State bases itself on another discourse, that discourse whose very place of authority La Boétie's successors will have to conceal: that of the subject of power—just as they will have to conceal its aggression and suppress the idea that all have the same power. This other discourse will *make use of* disproportion, even while explaining it.

After affirming that the state is established by a deliberate yielding of power, Hobbes is free to consider the state in terms, quite simply, of the continuation of its good functioning: the foundational power grab is set aside as a false problem, and henceforth established power relations may be envisaged in themselves and as though continuing without further intervention. Thus Alexandre Kojève can state: "In point of fact, governmental action within an already constituted State is purely *discursive* in its origin ...."[32] Why? And in what sense? For the simple reason that dominance and the lines of force are already established and need only reproduce themselves to infinity. The fillip has been given. The great engine is in motion. There is no more question of instauration. The *permanence* of the

---

[32] Alexandre Kojève, "Tyranny and Wisdom," in Strauss, *On Tyranny*, 157.

"instability" of the state in which power is in the hands of a single one becomes itself the guarantee of a stability that the dominated are obliged to accept, and even to pursue, were it only for their own protection. The dominated are thus obliged to speak not the "natural language" of friendship, equality, and liberty, but rather the language of state power.

It may well be that La Boétie undertook something like the analysis (which until then had not been done) of state bureaucracy. In fact, Jean Dunbabin has remarked that "the appearance and rapid development of bureaucratic administration" beginning in the twelfth century left no traces in the theorists of the age, and even that for a very long time no one gave attention to the explanation of such a phenomenon.[33] On the contrary, everyone continued to study the body politic in the image of the human or divine body, an image that continued to dominate, to be sure, for centuries (including in Hobbes). But this very general image could be applied to any group at all and never allowed thinkers to appreciate "fully the bureaucratic or administrative developments of their own time" (at least until 1450, for this study).[34] Perhaps the debates concerning the relationship between a prince and his counselors came closest—or could have come closest. But in fact they never touched on it, merely taking recourse to notions of good counsel to support the authority and the legitimate actions of the good prince.[35] The hierarchy of the dominant, as we find it here in La Boétie, is surely the missing explanation of such bureaucracies, since it sets down the idea of a hierarchy between benefactors and beneficiaries who all have their distinct share, role, and interests in the organization and administration of power

By using ideas of the contract and the necessity of this type of decreasing reproduction of powers, neoclassical, "modern," theoreticians will manage to conceal the so-called "arbitrary" side of this so-called "tyrannical" domination. This domination will no longer be a repression; it will be a benefit. Such a response will not be offered immediately. At first, it will be a matter only of opposing the thought of chaotic anarchy with the stability of a single sovereign authority à la Bodin. It is nonetheless striking how often this opposition is posited, after La Boétie, using his terms. Thus, for example, in 1576, Bernard du Haillan, at the time royal historian, composes this bit of dialogue in his *Histoire de France*:

> I will turn to you, Frankish Lords [says the speaker named Quadrek], and tell you that to live in a kingdom similar to the one in which some of our neighbors live is to live in perpetual and cruel servitude, and that to live in a Commonwealth

---

[33] Jean Dunbabin, "Government," in James Henderson Burns, ed., *The Cambridge History of Medieval Political Thought, c. 350–c. 1450* (Cambridge and New York: Cambridge University Press, 1988), 479. I owe this reference to Peter Haidu, who in his remarkable book *The Subject Medieval/Modern: Text and Governance in the Middle Ages* (Stanford: Stanford University Press, 2004) refers in passing to this theoretical gap in medieval thought (39–40).

[34] Dunbabin, 482.

[35] Ibid., 501–4.

88   *French Connections in the English Renaissance / Reiss*

[=*res publica*] is to live in full freedom. Those who can live in freedom and yet submit to servitude, you will agree, are not only fools but also deranged.

[Ie me tourneray vers vous, Seigneurs Frãcs, & vous diray que viure sous vne royauté semblable à celle sous laquelle quelques vns de nos voisins viuent, est viure en vne perpetuelle & cruelle seruitude, & que viure sous vne Chose-publique (=*res publica*), est viure en toute liberté. Ceux qui peuuent viure en liberté, & se soubsmettẽt à la servitude, vous me confesserez qu'ils sont non seulemẽt fols, mais aussi forcenez.][36]

Quadrek continues in terms that could not be closer to La Boétie's. And Charamond responds: "This is not fury or rage, Quadrek, believe me, to wish to extinguish the beginnings of a budding rage and fury, and we shouldn't term 'servitude' that condition of government without which we cannot last long" ["Ce n'est point fureur ny rage, Quadrek, (& croy m'en) de vouloir estaindre les commencemens d'vne rage & fureur naissante, & ne faut appeller seruitude ceste conditiõ de gouuernement, sans laquelle nous ne pouuons longuement nous conseruer"]. Without a sole authority, everything is discord: "a total desolation and subversion of our state, an entire ruin of our property, and an evident danger to our lives" ["vne totale desolation, & subuersion de nostre Estat, vne entiere ruine de nos biens, & vn euident dãnger de nos vies"].[37]

Since King Pharamond is then elected, we must suppose that La Boétie's vision has lost again. Later, nonetheless, the same terms turn up in Jean-Louis Guez de Balzac, who as a young man around 1615 wrote in his "Discours politique sur l'estat des provinces unies des Pays-Bas" this phrase straight out of La Boétie: "A people is free, as long as they no longer wish to serve" ["Vn peuple est libre, pourvu qu'il ne veuïlle plus servir"].[38] This does not stop him writing in his 1631 *Le Prince* a sort of Bodinian response, but even more absolutist. During the same period, contractual thought nevertheless began to take hold, again in reaction to the civil wars in France. The most interesting formulation I know of is that of Michel Hurault de l'Hôpital in 1593, nephew to the great Chancelier of France, and himself ex-Chancelier of the King of Navarre. Responding to the destruction of the country and the crumbling of society (for which he blames the Catholic League), he develops the notion of a "juridical bond [lien de justice]" which would be, precisely, a sort of contract to stabilize the political and the social. I do not think he invented the term, since Guillaume du Vair uses it in the same sense. But the interesting thing is that in the *Second discours sur l'estat de France*, Hurault conceives the "bond" as a kind of bridge between the authority of a single one who has really seized power and the chaos of the people who fight against him

---

[36]   Bernard Du Haillan, *L'Histoire de France* (Paris: Pierre l'Huillier, 1576), 9. [My translation.—Trans.]

[37]   Ibid., 10.

[38]   Jean-Louis Guez de Balzac, *Les Oeuvres* ..., ed. Valentin Conrart, vol. 2 (Paris: Louis Billaine, 1665), 482. [My translation.—Trans.]

or support him, that is to say, as a response to the very action whose absence La Boétie had discussed as incomprehensible: the fact that thousands of people did *not* rise up against singular tyranny. Now they have, and the resulting chaos has begun to extrude the solution of the contract.[39]

So while I would not say that we should read a text such as Hobbes's *Behemoth* (written around 1667–1668), with which I will end this argument, as a response specifically to La Boétie, it certainly does respond to the context of, and partly created by, the *Discourse of Voluntary Servitude*. Sometimes, though, *Behemoth* does seem to respond to La Boétie's text even seemingly word for word. This obviously does not necessarily mean that Hobbes read La Boétie. It does show that the *terms* of a text like La Boétie's have become in some way unavoidable. Hobbes takes them up indeed sufficiently specifically as to confirm certain aspects of the preceding analysis and the explicit or implicit claims made about the consequences and outcomes of La Boétie's and others' arguments.

Hobbes's first "response" is in the simple fact of anchoring his argument in a concrete situation, that of the English civil wars. But *Behemoth* is not only a history, or a "narration" of those wars, as Hobbes says: it is a debate on the constitutional crisis that provoked it, and an elaborate criticism of those who rise up against any established power: "all men are fools which pull down anything which does them good, before they have set up something better in its place" (*Behemoth*, 155). At issue here is not a call to some provisional morality along Cartesian lines—or such as Hobbes could have also found in Bacon's *Historie of the Raigne of King Henry the Seuenth*—because the state constituted rightly reproduces itself, we have seen, without limit and without anyone having to intervene: it is a machine in motion.

Behemoth presupposes the state's benevolence (in line with its author's long-established habits). Thus he had written in *De Cive* (1642) that, in a stable monarchy, the Ancients "could not entertain so strange a fancy, as not to desire the preservation of that by which they were preserved. In truth, the simplicity of those times was not yet capable of so learned a piece of folly. Wherefore it was peace and a golden age, which ended not before that, Saturn being expelled, it was thought lawful to take up arms against kings."[40] The idea of not changing society without being able to construct some new and solid building in its place was, of course, a cliché of antiquity that many of Hobbes's immediate predecessors reproduced. The cliché did not always assume benevolence.

For Hobbes, any opposition to the established state is thus not only a political aberration but also a moral wrong. And his narrative of the "causes, pretensions, justice, order, artifice, and event" of the civil wars begins with a list of seven different types of "seducers" responsible for the demolition of the benevolent state (*Behemoth*, 2–4). These seven articles allow him to examine the practical

---

[39]   Michel Hurault de l'Hôpital, *Second Discours*, 149. On this subject, see Reiss, *Meaning*, 47–56 and passim.

[40]   Thomas Hobbes, *Philosophical Rudiments Concerning Government and Society*, ed. Sir William Molesworth, *The English Works*, vol. 2 (London: John Bohn, 1841), xii–xiii.

and theoretical foundations and consequences of the constitutional crisis. The first three concern those who, under religious pretexts, affirm the prince's inability to rule: "these were the enemies which arose against his Majesty from the private interpretation of the Scripture, exposed to every man's scanning in his mother-tongue" (*Behemoth*, 3). These three articles respond directly to both the objective fact of the widespread religious malaise in England at the time and the theoretical claims of the right that God accords to all to remove a prince (by any means necessary) who supposedly transgressed divine maxims: hence Hobbes's contempt for "the private interpretation of the Scripture."

For, he asks, who is capable of furnishing the only correct reading of such divine maxims, since we are only human? All the more since the texts in question are already corrupted by translations, and are even less open to such interpretations, doubly or triply removed from the divine original language: "who can tell what is declared by the Scripture, which every man is allowed to read and interpret to himself?" (*Behemoth*, 10) Further, neither these texts nor their originals have anything to do with political skill, and preachers have no right to speak of it. "There is no plague more harmful to a kingdom than this well-spoken preacher" ["Il n'y a peste plus nuisante à un royaume que ce prédicateur bien emparlé"], said Nicolas Pasquier or his father Etienne. "He is a torrent that overflows to ravage an entire people, his tongue is much like a sword that decides the life and death of those for and against whom he employs it" ["C'est un torrent qui se desborde pour ravager tout un peuple, sa langue est proprement un glaive duquel dépend la vie et la mort de ceux, pour et contre lesquels il l'employe"].[41] In the words of Montaigne from 1580, "commonwealths that kept themselves regulated and well governed made little account of orators" ["republiques qui se sont maintenant en un estat reglé et bien policé n'ont pas faict grand compte d'orateurs"]. Their "use" of words, rather, is "pernicious" ["pernicieux"], "an instrument invented to manipulate and agitate a crowd and a disorderly populace" (*Essays*, 1:51, 222) ["un util inventé pour manier et agiter une tourbe et une commune desreiglée" (*Essais*, 292–3)].

Like his precursors, Hobbes here targets the use of speech in civil society. At issue is not simply the subversive role of a text like La Boétie's (doubtless among the preachings he condemns here), but rather speech and the right to speech. We would not be wrong to see in this, again, the Laboétian distinction between a divine language and a language of power. For Hobbes, the issue is not that the first is repressed by the princely state but rather that it properly belongs to a completely different dimension. Giving it a legitimate earthly place is to permit it to "ravage" that place. La Boétie had criticized the speech of the power opposed to that of his "utopia." But that speech belongs, says Hobbes, to the social and to those with the

---

[41] Nicolas Pasquier, *Remonstrances tres humbles à la Royne-Mère Régente en France. Pour la conservation de l'Estat pendant la minorité du Roy son fils* (1610), 48, cited in D. Thickett, "Introduction" to Etienne Pasquier, *Écrits politiques*, ed. D. Thickett (Geneva: Droz, 1966), 17–18. [My translation.—Trans.]

necessary knowledge and legitimate power. Muddling the City of God with that of humans, utopia with the real, invites everyone to claim a decision on the right to sovereignty: which was exactly what thinkers like Hotman and Bèze claimed when they redefined the sense of "usurpation."

As Hobbes put it here, questioning the legitimacy of power certainly came in part from attempts like theirs to redefine the words that applied to it and therefore the very sense of the practices that they sought to describe. And it must be said, in the case I just indicated, that the notion of usurpation could indeed be interpreted very broadly. Hotman maintained that the French monarchy had usurped the powers of the people in shrinking those of "public counsel." In the eyes of every Catholic, the English Protestant monarchy was by definition a usurping one. In 1574 Bèze could write that in a case where the magistrates did not fulfill their duty to overturn such a usurpation,

> then each private citizen should exert all his strength to defend the legitimate institutions of his country (to which, after God, each man owes his existence) and to resist an individual whose authority is not legitimate because he would usurp, or has usurped, dominion in violation of the law.

> [alors chacun particulier de tout son pouvoir s'efforce de maintenir l'estat legitime de sa patrie, à laquelle, apres Dieu, chacun se doit soi-mesmes, contre celui qui n'est point son Magistrat, puisqu'il veut usurper, ou a usurpé, telle dominion contre la loi.][42]

We can understand Hobbes's distrust.

Against such capricious and biased readings, he emphasizes, speaking of Charles I, the existence of the "right of a descent continued above six hundred years, and from a much longer descent King of Scotland, and from the time of his ancestor Henry II, King of Ireland" (*Behemoth*, 1–2). In the case of Charles I, apart from this duly consecrated and anointed descent, Hobbes rejects regicides' claims by affirming that the King was "a man that wanted no virtue, either of body or mind, nor endeavoured anything more than to discharge his duty towards God, in the well-governing of his subjects" (*Behemoth*, 2). These are the elements of a precise, term-for-term opposition to the claims advanced in order to justify regicide in general: 1) the divine right of the prince to succession, solidified by age-old custom; 2) the just and exact exercise of his "duty to God"; 3) the benevolence of his use of power, of his government; 4) his virtue. We can also see in this a response to the criticism of the power of One as La Boétie expounds it. For under these conditions, those of a benevolent, just, and legitimate power, regicide can be only an arbitrary assassination, a voluntary abuse of *power*.

---

[42] Théodore de Bèze, *Right of Magistrates*. In Julian H. Franklin, trans. and ed., *Constitutionalism and Resistance in the Sixteenth Century: Three Treatises by Hotman, Bèze, and Mornay* (New York: Pegasus, 1969), 107; Bèze, *Du droit des magistrats [sur leurs subjects]*, ed. Robert M. Kingdon (Geneva: Droz, 1970), 13.

Thus Hobbes offers the case of Atabalipe, King of Peru, assassinated by the Spanish because he refused to abdicate in favor of Charles V, to whom the Pope had given "divine" approval: "You see by this how much they [the papists] claim, when they have power to make it good" (*Behemoth*, 11). Such abuses necessarily result, said Hobbes, from utopian, mythical, and mystifying claims.

The fourth article aims more precisely at people of letters, readers of books, who have decided that "popular government," with its "glorious name of liberty," is preferable to "monarchy disgraced by the name of tyranny" (*Behemoth*, 3). In this bitter sarcasm, one readily sees a specific reply to the sort of theory expressed by La Boétie, whose terms it simply inverts. What is surprising is not the absence of revolution, Hobbes remarks, but rather the will *not* to remain in the well-regulated state: "If those soldiers had been, as they and all other of his subjects ought to have been, at his Majesty's command, the peace and happiness of the three kingdoms had continued ..." (*Behemoth*, 2). Not only is voluntary servitude not at all surprising, but on the contrary, acceptance of the prince's power is the only sure way to "peace and happiness," the only sure way to avoid the anarchy and the state of permanent war that characterize the brutal condition of humans outside civil society: "all men are fools which pull down anything which does them good ...." The ancients, we have seen him say, would never have accepted "so strange a fancy, as not to desire the preservation of that by which they are preserved." Would this not be exactly La Boétie's "fancy" of escaping voluntary servitude and "recovering" one's full utopian freedom?

The fifth article concerns the example offered to the great merchant cities of England by the prosperity of the United Provinces, achieved after the latter had rejected the yoke of the Spanish monarchy. This financial and commercial question is pursued in the following article at the level of those individuals who, says Hobbes, believed that war would shore up their own possessions. What is demonstrated here is that if, as the first four articles maintain, every claim on the basis of political or theological thought is a priori illegitimate, then revolt comes down to bringing into play only those private claims to goods and power that characterize the asocial animal: those, precisely, to which the founding *Fiat* of civil societies, the start-up "covenant" or contract, is supposed to bring an end. What is installed in place of the state's legitimate power when it has been set aside, thus says Hobbes, is not an elite group of mutually affectionate friends, but a fight to the death.

The seventh article is a sort of summary. It underscores the widespread ignorance of that "duty" of the people that is to recognize the "right" of a single one "to command him": "King, they thought, was but a title of the highest honour" (*Behemoth*, 4). If such were the case, then the people could indeed get rid of him when they wanted. It is as though the quoted sentence, and hence the article itself as a summary of all the others, were a direct reply to La Boétie's main argument: the common will to accept servitude pushes humans to let themselves be charmed to the point of believing that a mere name corresponds to true power, and that it therefore suffices to withdraw one's agreement for the prince to fall.

Hobbes indeed adds a little later: "For the power of the mighty hath no foundation but in the opinion and belief of the people" (*Behemoth*, 16).

It is a fact that in response to the question raised in his seventh article, which states that humans believed "King" to be merely a name and therefore not to signify true power, Hobbes ironically uses an expression that he could have taken almost word-for-word from La Boétie. The philosopher's interlocutor says to him about this: "In such a constitution of people, methinks, the King is already ousted of his government, so as they needed not have taken arms for it. For I cannot imagine how the King should come by any means to resist them" (*Behemoth*, 4). This is exactly La Boétie's idea:

> Now there is no need to combat this solitary tyrant, no need to defeat him: he will be automatically defeated, provided only that the nation refuses to accept slavery. There is no need to take anything from him: simply refuse to give him anything. There is no need for the nation to do anything on his behalf, so long as it refrains from doing anything against itself. It is evident, then, that people allow themselves to be dominated, or rather that they actually bring about their own domination, since merely by ceasing to serve they would be free. It is the people who enslave themselves, who cut their own throats, who, faced with a choice between servitude and freedom, abandon their liberty and accept the yoke, who consent to being harmed—or rather, seek to be harmed. (*Slaves*, 41)

> [Encores ce seul tiran, il n'est pas besoin de le combattre, il n'est pas besoin de le defaire; il est de soymesme defait, mais que le pais ne consente à sa servitude; il ne faut luy oster rien, mais ne lui donner rien; il n'est pas besoin que le pais se mette en peine de faire rien pour soy, pourveu qu'il ne face rien contre soy. Ce sont donc les peuples mesmes qui se laissent ou plutost se font gourmander, puis qu'en cessant de servir ils en seroient quittes; c'est le peuple qui s'asservit, qui se coupe la gorge, qui aiant le chois ou d'estre serf ou d'estre libre quitte sa franchise et prend le joug: qui consent a son mal ou plutost le pourchasse. (*Discours*, 110–11)]

To this Hobbes, except for the answers that we have already seen, can only reply: "There was indeed very great difficulty in the business" (*Behemoth*, 4). But he insists that acceptance is very far from an incomprehensible act, that it is on the contrary *necessary*—and then he asserts that the only solution to this "difficulty" is to be found in the analysis of the real, or at least in the "narration" of this real as a historical process (*Behemoth*, 4). Saying this, he announces *Behemoth*'s project, one founded on the theoretical preparation furnished by *The Elements of Law, Natural and Politic*, *De Cive*, and *Leviathan*. It was perhaps in the course of this preparation that Laboétian *friendship* (but that is a very familiar commonplace) became the Hobbesian *contract*, thus transformed from a moralizing and "imaginary" relation into a logical and legal demand. In such ways, Hobbes's work responded to a historical crisis in practice and action (which the civil wars underscored) and to a theoretical problematic, one of whose faces was brought to light by Machiavelli, the other by La Boétie.

Chapter 5
Milton and the Huguenot Revolution

Catherine Gimelli Martin

Scholars have paid scant attention to Milton's "French Connections" for a variety of legitimate reasons. These range from the poet/politician's diatribes against the corrupt French queen and court of Charles I in *Eikonoklastes*, to his anonymous early biographer's remark that Milton had no admiration for "the manners and genius" of France, where he "made small stay, nor contracted any acquaintance" aside from Hugo Grotius, the Dutch natural law theorist (Hughes, 1039).[1] While Milton certainly spent less time in Paris than in the Italian cities where he undoubtedly felt more at home, these remarks obscure as much as they reveal about Milton's political debts to France. Not just his too often neglected *Commonplace Book* but his major political defenses of tyrannicide demonstrate a surprisingly serious and close engagement with French resistance theorists and historians, a connection long obscured by the tendency of Whig historians to focus tightly on the native sources of the "Puritan Revolution." In its way, this focus on the English as opposed to the Huguenot revolution is also legitimate, since as Milton's diatribes suggest, one of the well-known causes of the English civil wars was anti-French sentiment. Many of the King's opponents suspected him and his Queen, Henrietta Maria, of attempting to import French-style absolutism into England, and this threat rallied them around Britain's "ancient constitution," its native traditions of limited monarchy. When these revolutionaries looked abroad, they pointed to the classical republican ideals of mixed and representative government preserved in the free Italian states, not to the sad example of Bourbon France. After the 1649 execution of Charles I, England's most radical revolutionaries justified their egalitarianism by claiming that their demands would merely restore the native liberties lost after the Norman conquest.

The mature Milton became as fully anti-monarchical as these revolutionaries, but he never adopted the "Norman Yoke" theories advanced by the Leveller and Digger factions. He preferred instead to argue from a classical republican perspective significantly supplemented by treatises circulated by the French Huguenots a generation earlier. Since this tactic was not only unusual in itself but also in light of an "anti-French" disposition still seen as integral to Milton's thought, his reasons for taking this course will form the substance of this essay.

---

[1]   Milton's early biographies and poetry (cited hereafter by abbreviated title, book, and line number) are taken from Merritt Y. Hughes, *John Milton, Complete Poems and Major Prose* (New York: Odyssey Press, 1957).

Some of those reasons will necessarily remain conjectural, but as a whole, this strategy seems to form part of a larger anti-Calvinist subtext too often overlooked in Milton studies.[2] One reason for this oversight is that much like the Scots and English revolutionaries, the Huguenots were generally Protestant Calvinists imbued with similar theological and ideological assumptions. This general similarity nevertheless obscures an important difference: unlike the Scots but like the more secular partisans among the English, the Huguenots did not defend their religious rights on strictly Calvinist or, indeed, on any narrow theological grounds. Drawing broadly upon both classical and Catholic Conciliarist sources, they defended their theories of limited government with historical precedents broadly synthesized from Roman, Hebrew, Italian, and "Gothic" or Franco-German example.[3] Scots and English Puritans (as most British Calvinists were) employed many of the same precedents but couched their resistance theory in a decidedly more theocratic mode. As the latest of the Lord's chosen people, God's Englishmen would fulfill their divine mandate by restoring pure worship to a nation "polluted" by Charles I, his queen, and his "papist" prelates. Milton made many famous pronouncements defending this course, but a closer look at his equally famous defenses of the English people confirms the pattern outlined above: time after time, he slights the major Scots Calvinist resistance theorists (John Knox, George Buchanan, and Samuel Rutherford) in favor of the more secular arguments of the Huguenot "monarchomachs," or king killers.[4]

The term "monarchomach" is now generally applied to anyone arguing for the execution of tyrannical kings—whether usurpers or legally installed betrayers of the nation's laws; it was originally a term of opprobrium coined by William Barclay in a lengthy response (1600) to George Buchanan, the Scottish exponent of similar ideas. Barclay was not alone: even Puritan "martyrs" such as William Prynne opposed any form of regicide, while more radical Puritans often preferred some version of Knox's religiously inspired resistance theory to the concepts advanced by the more secular "king killers." Like Prynne, Englishmen who joined the

---

[2] Milton's reliance on the French resistance theorists has nevertheless not gone unremarked. Merritt Hughes mentions it in his edition of the *Complete Prose Works of John Milton*, gen. ed. Don M. Wolfe (New Haven: Yale University Press, 1953–1982, hereafter cited as *CPW* by volume and page number), and Ernest Sirluck notes it in "Milton's Political Thought: The First Cycle," *Modern Theology* 61 (1964): 211–12, 219, 223. More recent discussions include Martin Dzelzainis in *John Milton: Political Writings* (Cambridge: Cambridge University Press, 1991), xii–xix, and John Sanderson, *"But the People's Creatures": The Philosophical Basis of the English Civil War* (Manchester: Manchester University Press, 1989), 131–5.

[3] See Quentin Skinner, "Humanism, scholasticism and popular sovereignty" in *Visions of Politics*, 3 vols (Cambridge: Cambridge University Press, 2002), 2: 245–63.

[4] For a more thorough analysis of this problem in Milton scholarship, see my book chapter, "Unediting Milton: Historical Myth and Editorial Misconstruction in the Yale Prose Edition," in *Milton, Rights and Liberties*, ed. Christophe Tournu and Neil Forsyth (Bern: Peter Lang, 2006), 113–30.

Parliamentary cause against the king for wholly secular reasons did not necessarily reject monarchy altogether, which makes Milton's early monarchomachism and republicanism doubly unusual.[5] Equally unusual is his bold pan-European approach to issues on which he strongly differs not only from conservative Puritans like Prynne but also from the radicals who embraced the "Norman Yoke" rationale for the regicide and also for more thorough political reform. As Martin Dzelzainis observes, Milton's infrequent allusions to the Levellers rhetorically but not seriously or substantively supports their cause.[6] Some scholars explain this hesitation as class-based (Milton and his family were property-holders with more to lose from radical reform than most of the Levellers), but it also seems to be philosophical. Based on his own post-graduate studies, he knew that locating the origins of English liberty in the Anglo-Saxon institutions of pre-Norman Britain ran up against the "awkward fact" noted by a modern scholar: Anglo-Saxon rule was itself based on a "violent and treacherous act of conquest."[7] The same studies directed him instead to the earlier and "purer" examples of limited, legal monarchy established by the pre-imperial Romans and Franco-Germans. He recorded this information in his *Commonplace Book* and used it in his published regicide tracts, which further reveal his debts to the Huguenot theorists.

François Hotman and Philippe Duplessis-Mornay are generally regarded as the greatest of these theorists; the latter with his friend Hubert Languet (either as co-author or compiler) most probably composed the anonymous—and notorious—*Vindiciae contra Tyrannos*.[8] Like Hotman, these friends were staunch Calvinists, although their approach to government is less stringently faith-based than that of their close contemporary Théodore Beza (or de Bèze, 1519–1605), the ministerial leader of the French Protestant churches and Calvin's successor in Geneva. Milton incorrectly attributes the *Vindiciae* to Beza but strangely ignores a renowned defense against tyrants that he actually did write, *Du Droit des Magistrats*. His neglect of the latter work makes more sense, however, when we consider how deeply he disagreed with the "real" Beza's position on a number of important issues, primarily his support for ministerial above lay authority and for Calvin's sanction of the death penalty for heresy. Milton's campaign against both principles

---

[5]   On Barclay, see Skinner, *Visions of Politics*, 2: 396; on the contrast between Knox and the French monarchomachs, see 2: 247; on Milton's early rejection of monarchy and embrace of republicanism, 2: 303; and on the monarchomachs broader importance to the early phases of the English civil wars and to Milton, see 2: 297–8.

[6]   See Christopher Hill, "The Norman Yoke," in *Puritanism and Revolution* (London: Secker & Warburg, 1958), 46–111, and Martin Dzelzainis, "History and Ideology: Milton, the Levellers, and the Council of State in 1649," in *The Uses of History in Early Modern England*, ed. Paulina Kewes (San Marino: Huntington Library, 2006), 265–83.

[7]   Philip Schwyzer, *Archaeologies of English Renaissance Literature* (Oxford: Oxford University Press, 2007), 192.

[8]   On the authorship question, see Julian H. Franklin, *Constitutionalism and Resistance in the Sixteenth Century: Three Treatises by Hotman, Beza, and Mornay* (New York: Pegasus, 1969), 138–40.

informs the entire span of his prose publications. He began this campaign in his anti-prelatical tracts against the English bishops (1641–1642), specifically defended individual liberty of conscience in *Areopagitica* (1644)—a position repeated near the end of his life in *Of True Religion* (1673)—and argued for the disestablishment of all state-supported Protestantism, including tithes, penalties, or mandatory confessions of faith, in *Of Civil Power* and *The Likeliest Means to Remove Hirelings from the Church* (1659). In short, Milton pointedly disapproved of the combined spiritual-civil power of magistrates defended by Beza in works such as *De Haereticis* (1554) and *Du Droit des Magistrats* (1574), which assume a Calvinist and theocratic rationale for the commonwealth as a whole.[9] In the latter, Beza declares that "the true end of all rightly ordered government is not tranquility in this life, as certain pagan philosophers have thought, but the glory of God, to which all of our present life should be directed."[10] In *Eikonoklastes*, Milton's definition of ordered government is closer to that of the "pagan philosophers":

> every Common-wealth is in general defin'd, a societie sufficient of it self, in all things conducible to well being and commodious life. Any of which requisite things if it cannot have without the gift and favour of a single person, or without leave of his privat reason, or his conscience, it cannot be thought sufficient of it self, and by consequence no Common-wealth, nor free; but a multitude of Vassalls in the Possession and domaine of one absolute Lord; and wholly obnoxious to his will. (*Eikonoklastes, CPW* 3: 458)

In other words, Beza's Christian commonwealth is a vehicle of divine grace and glory, while Milton's secular commonwealth is simply "the nurse of all great wits." These are not simply secular "wits," since their role—the role of free subjects—is to "rarify" and "enlighten … our spirits like the influence of heav'n"; but their overall function is more intellectual or educative than strictly religious: to "enfranchise," "enlarge," and "lift … up our apprehensions degrees above themselves" (*CPW* 2: 559).

Milton's more secular understanding of the commonwealth also seems to explain why he favors Hotman's arguments for limited monarchy over those of Duplessis-Mornay, who actually stresses his nation's covenant with God more than Beza. Granting collective rights of resistance either to the whole populace or to individual representatives of this covenant, Duplessis-Mornay often approaches the position of the Scots Calvinist on many points consistently rejected by Milton in *Eikonoklastes, The Tenure of Kings and Magistrates*, and even his late tragedy, *Samson Agonistes*.[11] All three of these works deny the right of "private persons" unilaterally to serve the will of God by overthrowing established authorities,

---

[9]   See Franklin, *Constitutionalism and Resistance*, 98–9.

[10]   Theodore Beza, *The Right of Magistrates*, in Franklin (ed. and trans.), *Constitutionalism and Resistance*, 133.

[11]   Franklin, *Constitutionalism and Resistance*, 39–44; on the similar covenantal emphasis of John Knox, Christopher Goodman, and John Ponet, see Franklin, 31.

whether parliamentary, kingly, or tribal. Personal conscience or conviction is not enough; legal or other public testimony and confirmation are required to justify active resistance. On other points, however, Milton's disagreement with the *Vindiciae* is less sweeping, and its method of arguing from examples broadly taken from the Old Testament, Egyptian, Greek, Roman, Persian, and northern European accounts essentially agrees with his own.[12] He also agrees with many if not all of its key principles: 1) kings may be corrected by their own people (although Duplessis-Mornay also grants this right to prophets and "saints," not just to magistrates, judges, or assemblies); 2) they were created by and for the people for their greater good; 3) in all civilized nations royal power is subject to law; 4) if checks on this power fall into abeyance, they must be restored; 5) even a legally installed or "legitimate" tyrant may be deposed; 6) "lawful" tyrannicides should be regarded as deliverers of their people; and last but hardly least, 7) "to obey a king without the law or against the law is the same as to be subject to a beast. Absolute power is virtual tyranny, since no human being can exercise it properly."[13] Based on essentially the same neo-Roman principles, Milton argues that the subjects of a tyrant are the same as "slaves and arrant beasts; not fitt for that liberty which they cri'd out and bellow'd for" (*Eikonoklastes*, *CPW* 3: 581).

As a whole, however, Milton's case for resistance is closest to Hotman's legal reasoning, which provides the basis for the seven-point position articulated in the *Vindiciae* and briefly summarized above.[14] After the St. Bartholomew's Day massacre, Hotman's systematic, thorough, and legally informed constitutional reasoning in fact became the bulwark of most Huguenot resistance theory. To these arguments Duplessis-Mornay mainly added his own eloquence and populist rhetoric.[15] Much the same may be said of Milton, but as Quentin Skinner adds, "This is not to say that Milton inertly recapitulates these earlier lines of thought"; "he is at once more individualistic in his premises than a writer like Henry Parker and at the same time more broadly concerned with popular sovereignty than merely with the right of resistance."[16] Parker was an early and influential champion of Parliament who led the way in using the French monarchomachs

---

[12] On Milton's rejection of resistance by exclusively private persons, see my article "The Phoenix and the Crocodile: Milton's Natural Law Debate with Hobbes Retried in the Tragic Forum of *Samson Agonistes*," in *The English Civil Wars in the Literary Imagination*, ed. Claude Summers and Ted Pebworth (Columbia: University of Missouri Press, 1999), 242–70.

[13] Philippe Duplessis-Mornay, *Vindiciae contra tyrannos*, cited in Franklin, *Constitutionalism and Resistances*, 148–9, 155–6, 161, 163, 169–70, 177, 181, 189.

[14] For a succinct but useful summary of Hotman's sophisticated intellectual lineage, see Richard Tuck, *Natural Rights Theories: Their Origin and Development* (Cambridge: Cambridge University Press, 1979), 41–2.

[15] Franklin, *Constitutionalism and Resistance*, 29. Hotman's *Francogallia* (1573) is the earliest of the three treatises translated and reproduced by Franklin. Beza's *Right of Magistrates* was composed shortly afterward, in consultation with Hoffman (30), while the *Vindiciae* (probably composed 1574–1575) was published in 1579 (39).

[16] Skinner, *Visions of Politics*, 2: 298.

against the king, but Milton does not "inertly" follow him either. Rather than merely recapitulating Parker, his case for popular sovereignty and his scrupulous demonstration that both pre-imperial Rome and post-imperial Gaul achieved their highest degree of social and political perfection through limited, elective monarchies returns directly to their common source, Hotman. Milton also extends Hotman's argument(s) by showing that Britain imported limited monarchy when it adopted the institution of the king's council, or parliament, from France. He concedes that these traditions were ignored by barbaric and corrupt despots, but proves the rest of his points by referring to Hotman's *Francogallia*, chapter 10, "The form in which the kingdom of Francogallia was constituted." This central chapter shows first that the "common law among all peoples and nations who practise regal rather than tyrannical government [is] ... that 'THE WELFARE OF THE PEOPLE WAS THE SUPREME LAW.'" Second, it shows the "liberty of holding a common council is a part of the law of nations," and third, that "kings who oppress that sacred liberty with their evil arts, as if they were violators of this international law and beings set apart from human society, should not be regarded as kings but rather as tyrants."[17] Skinner views Milton's skillful synthesis of these neo-Roman principles with French as well as Roman condemnations of the sloth, servility, and degeneration encouraged by tyrants (and later, by all monarchs) as the basis of his immense persuasive power and authority.[18]

Milton's Political Development: A Brief Outline

The poet's early correspondence shows that he first undertook his pan-European study of liberty with much the same rigor displayed in Hotman's "virtuoso scholarship."[19] His efforts began in earnest with private, post-graduate studies of history, which culminated in his grand tour of France and Italy. Scholars such as Leo Miller plausibly trace Milton's interest in political liberty even farther back to his undergraduate days, when he encountered Isaac Dorislaus's classical republican lectures on "Junius Brutus" at Cambridge.[20] Whether or not Miller is right, Milton's historical studies were certainly well underway by 1637, when he informs Charles Diodati that he has been recently examining "the affairs of the

---

[17] Francois Hotman, *Francogallia*, trans. J.H.M. Salmon (Cambridge: Cambridge University Press, 1972), 317. Significantly, this same chapter traces the transference of limited monarchy and parliamentary government (on the authority of Polydore Virgil) from France to England; see 305–7.

[18] Skinner, *Visions of Politics*, 2: 302. Here and in what follows, I emphasize the "French connections" in Milton's intellectual armory not only for the purposes of this volume but also because Skinner so thoroughly covers his Greco-Roman sources. This is not to say that he utterly ignores his French sources or that I in any way disagree with his views on the neo-Roman influences at work in Milton's classical republicanism.

[19] On Hotman's scholarship, see Franklin, *Constitutionalism and Resistance*, 29.

[20] Leo Miller, "Milton's Clash with Chappell: A Suggested Reconstruction," *MQ* 14 (1980): 77–87.

Milton and the Huguenot Revolution 101

Greeks to the time when they ceased to be Greeks," and then proceeded to "the obscure history of the Italians under the Longobards, Franks, and Germans, to the time when liberty was granted them." He adds that he strives to understand "what each State did by its own Effort" to gain or recover liberty, and that wherever he finds "anyone who, despising the warped judgment of the public, dares to feel and speak and be that which the greatest wisdom throughout all ages has taught to be best, I shall cling to him immediately from a kind of necessity." Even if "by nature or by my fate" he fails truly to emulate their example, "neither men nor God [can] forbid me to reverence and honor those who have attained that glory or who are successfully aspiring to it" (*CPW* 1: 326–7). These lines suggest the emergence of a scholar more deeply imbued with the ideology of classical republican *vertu* than with Puritan piety, which accords with recent findings that Milton's own family was broadly Protestant, even Arminian, rather than Puritan; the elder Milton was a church warden of the chapel at Hammersmith, a Laudian foundation dominated by Laudian enthusiasts, and both father and son were interred in an Anglican church.[21]

At any rate, the intellectual influences on Milton were truly pan-European, and he never hesitated to credit the Italian Catholic thinkers he met in Florence and perhaps Venice with shaping his resistance to the "tyranny" of pre-publication censorship. They agreed that such censorship produced intellectual and cultural decline rather than true morality or religion, and Milton used the example of the great Galileo to warn his countrymen what can happen when narrow-minded zealots like his "Franciscan and Dominican licencers" take over (*CPW* 2: 538). *Areopagitica* instead urges England to live up to its own reputation among his Italian friends, when as a contributor to their Academies, he was

> counted happy to be born in such a place of *Philosophic* freedom, as they suppos'd England was, while themselves did nothing but bemoan the servile condition into which lerning amongst them was brought; that this was it which had dampt the glory of Italian wits; that nothing had bin there writt'n now these many years but flattery and fustian. (*CPW* 2: 537–8)

By then his studies had taught him that the states suffering most from the repressive policies of the Inquisition and Counter-Reformation had once flourished under Roman republican and native "Gothic" traditions of freedom later corrupted by European princes and popes, a line of thought his Latin defenses later expanded in pleading the cause of the English regicides abroad. His principal opponent in the debate was not a Catholic but a French Protestant, Claude de Saumaise: this circumstance is another factor (but, as we will see, not the only one) that made the French Huguenots such useful sources of support for his arguments.[22]

---

[21] See Gordon Campbell and Thomas N. Corns, *John Milton: Life, Work, and Thought* (Oxford: Oxford University Press, 2008), 67–8, 379.

[22] Milton's *Commonplace Book* is not dated, but his 1637 letter to Diodati makes it clear that he studied French history and politics long before he published *Defensio pro populo Anglicano* against Salmasius (1651).

Milton's reputation as a patriot has led too many of his admirers to forget that he never departed from this broad international outlook, never penned a national epic or heroic poem, and never composed a tribute to any English martyr. Aside from a famous digression in *Lycidas*, the only truly politico-religious elegy he ever penned laments the slaughter of the Waldenses of northern France and Italy, although "On the Late Massacre at Piedmont" arguably asks for justice not just for these Reformers but also for like-minded Christians all over Europe.[23] Near the end of the Protectorate period, he again turned to a European audience to defend himself and his political principles. His *Defensio Secunda* of 1654 broadly praises the Germans' hostility to slavery, the courage of the Spaniards, and the "generous ardor of the Franks, worthy of their name" (free). He singles out Italian magnanimity because to him it epitomizes the pan-European spirit thriving "wherever liberal sentiment, wherever freedom, or wherever magnanimity either prudently conceals or openly proclaims itself." This spirit encourages him to believe that "from the Pillars of Hercules all the way to the farthest boundaries of Father Liber, I seem to be bringing home again everywhere in the world, after a vast space of time, Liberty herself, so long expelled and exiled" (*CPW* 4.1: 555–7). Like his first *Defensio pro populo Anglicano*, this work also confirms the strong Huguenot contribution to his thought. He ranks their legal and historical masterpieces alongside Aristotle's *Politics*, Cicero's republican writings, and Richard Hooker's *Laws of Ecclesiastical Polity*, although as J.W. Gough points out, it was *principally* from the French monarchomachs, Protestant and Catholic alike, that Milton drew his proto-Rousseauian conception of a social contract in which "the king [is] the mere servant of the people, dismissible at will."[24] Merritt Hughes, the Yale editor of Milton's central defense of tyrannicide, *The Tenure of Kings and Magistrates*, similarly concedes that it was through them rather than through Scots resistance theorists like "Buchanan, or even ... [Puritan] Parliamentary spokesmen like [Samuel] Rutherford or Levellers like Lilburne" that he became (in Gough's phrase) "one of the first Englishmen to use contractarian phraseology" (*CPW* 3: 116).[25]

Yet Hughes's commitment to the "Puritan Revolution" thesis is apparently such that he immediately qualifies this statement, adding that Milton's argument is nevertheless based upon Augustinian and Calvinist tenets incompatible with the classical natural law tradition followed by both Hooker, the great English theologian, and the French monarchomachs. Strangely misconstruing an important passage in *The Tenure*, he tells us that Milton regarded government as a punishment for original sin, a view contemporarily in favor with Puritan theocrats and later with

---

[23]   Milton's *Commonplace Book* also amply records his deep admiration of and interest in the Waldenses, an independent society of proto-Protestants who only partly separated from the Roman Church.

[24]   See J.W. Gough, *The Social Contract: A Critical Study of Its Development* (Oxford: Clarendon Press, 1957), 38, 62, 101.

[25]   Gough, *The Social Contract*, 72; here Gough also credits Hooker's influence on Locke as well as Milton.

the more radical Fifth Monarchists.[26] Yet this Augustinian conception of government is ultimately incompatible with legally constituted Parliaments since it justifies all forms of human rule, including either monarchic or theocratic absolutism. Milton instead favored the exclusively secular and originally French tradition of Parliamentarianism, which he actually sought to strengthen. Recommending an ongoing *"parlie"* or discussion between both branches of government, princely and parliamentary, his *Readie and Easie Way* resists subjecting it to the pleasure, whim, or literal "calling" of a restored *"Norman* king." This failed attempt to forestall the Restoration also resists any strongly centralized government by calling for a permanent Senate and executive council to carry on national affairs while delegating local rule to the provinces. While far from ideal, his proposal was partly aimed at preventing theocrats "pretending to a fifth monarchie of saints" from trying to dissolve Parliaments or subjecting them "to thir own tyrannical designs" (*CPW* 7: 373, 380), and partly at preventing either a restored king or Lord Protector from wielding exclusive executive authority. If successful, he hoped that his compromise solution might help the French "fatherland" to restore a free commonwealth at home, a hope contemporarily justified by the Parisian Fronde (1648–49) and the Ormée movement at Bordeaux (1652–1653) (*CPW* 7: 356). Historically, it was also justified by the strong commonwealth tradition that France had bequeathed to England.

Milton's study of this history led him to believe that this bequest was made possible by the Anglo-Saxons' own insistence on accepting "a king rather than endure a conquering tyrant." They were thus willing to swear "to William ... while he swore to them" to govern according to law, but when he failed to keep his oath, they took up arms and caused him to "swear anew on the Gospels to keep the ancient laws." Not only was this second vow kept, but a "most reliable volume of Caen shows" that William never appointed any "heir to the realm of England." He thereby set the precedent for elective, limited monarchy later traced in "Hotman's *Franco-Gallia*" and also by "Gerard, the historian of France," who together prove not only that the "'King's Parliament' ... is [rightly] ... called the *king's bridle*" (*CPW* 4.1: 480–81), but also that a king who commits illegal acts against his own nation loses "the title of king." Contra Saumaise, the "very Glanville" he cites proves that "high treason may be committed against the kingdom as well as the king" (*CPW* 4.1: 526), who if he betrays his nation may be rightfully resisted. Even before he crossed swords with Saumaise in his first *Defensio*, Milton formulates the same essentially secular and (*pace* Hughes) non-Augustinian justification for limited government in his *Tenure of Kings and Magistrates*. Relying on solidly French humanist rather than Calvinist sources, the *Tenure* does concede that government is one result of Adam's fall, but regards it as a remedy rather than as a punishment for human sin. In fact, government is not even a *direct* consequence of the lapse. Silently quoting Cicero, Milton here proclaims that

---

[26] On Augustine's view of sin as a justification even for repressive government, see especially Elaine Pagels, *Adam, Eve, and the Serpent* (New York: Random House, 1988), especially 113, 134, 145, 105–6, 147.

> No man who knows ought, can be so stupid to deny that all men naturally were borne free, being the image and resemblance of God himself, and were by privilege above all the creatures, born to command and not to obey: *and that they liv'd so*. Till from the *root* of *Adam's* transgression, falling among themselves to doe wrong and foreseeing that such courses must needs tend to the destruction of them all, they agreed by common league to bind each other from mutual injury, and jointly to defend themselves against any that gave disturbance or opposition to such agreement. (*CPW* 3: 198–9, emphasis added)

According to this view, humans lived in freedom for an unspecified length of time until the "root" of Adam's sin began to bear too much bad social fruit. Then the predatory and destructive behavior of their fellows led wiser men to use their God-given reason to circumscribe it by providing laws against mutual aggression and pacts for common defense. These laws and leagues ultimately may be the result of sin, but they are also rational remedies and social restoratives of the public peace, not punishments.

Such restoratives naturally would not have been needed without Adam's fall, as *Paradise Lost* explains through an angelic intermediary (PL 11.342–6), but the biblical epic also concludes with a portrait of postlapsarian history and government which is far more Aristotelian than Augustinian. As in the *Tenure*, fallen humans enjoyed at least a semi-stable state of fraternal peace until their growing numbers, rivalry, and lack of a single paternal or other authority required them to make formal covenants and laws. In the epic, this fraternal state clearly continued among the "sons of Seth" (*PL* 11.577–80) before the Flood and endured long after it, when Noah's sons still managed to dwell "Long time in peace by Families and Tribes / Under paternal rule." Only when greed and pride taught some to despise "fair equality, fraternal state" did kings arise to "dispossess / Concord and law of Nature from the Earth" (*PL* 12.23–4, 26, 28–9). As a result, monarchical misgovernment, not all forms of government, are punishments for the supreme Miltonic sin of ignoring "Rational Liberty," which "always with Right reason dwells / Twinn'd, and from her hath no dividual being" (*PL* 12.83–5). Without it, inner tyranny leads to outer servitude, as "Reason in man obscur'd, or not obey'd, / Immediately [causes] inordinate desires / And upstart Passions [to] catch the Government / From Reason, and to servitude reduce / Man till then free" (*PL* 12.86–90). This state of ignorant enslavement is not permanent, however; liberty is not lost once for all time, but perpetually lost and again recovered. After their Egyptian bondage, the Hebrews recover "true Liberty" in the wilderness, where "thir Senate choose / Through the twelve Tribes, to rule by Laws ordain'd" (*PL* 12.225–6). God of course ordains "republican" laws for the Jews, but nowhere in the epic does he institute government itself, which humans spontaneously invent long before. Even the Jews' mild, republicanized form of theocracy "fortunately" gives way to a more universal historical principle, the rule of Christian liberty or self-determination (*PL* 12.525–6), although this principle is perpetually threatened by superstition and tradition, its common enemies (*PL* 12.512).

Milton's Anti-Calvinist, Humanistic Principles

Both Hughes and Annabel Patterson have traced Milton's political lineage to Scots rather than Huguenot resistance theorists, in Patterson's case mainly through the work of the Calvinist Buchanan. In some ways this makes eminent good sense because Buchanan is widely recognized as a humanist rather than strictly theocratic thinker along the lines of Knox or Rutherford.[27] Yet oddly enough, even Hughes concedes Buchanan's lack of influence on Milton's politics even though they share many common assumptions. The written record clearly supports this view: Milton uses Buchanan only to establish some fairly minor anti-monarchist points or in some instances actually to comment sarcastically on the national character of the Scots (*CPW* 3: 110). As in his preference for Hotman over Duplessis-Mornay or Beza, the most compelling reason for this treatment seems to be Milton's general discomfort with Calvinist or "neo-Augustinian" theories of government. Buchanan clearly supports such theories by claiming that after Noah's flood government was directly established by divine intervention, not human reason. Richard Tuck considers this claim an obvious concession to his Calvinism, an example of "someone deeply imbued with humanism adjusting it to fit his religious sensibilities." Without God's guidance, sinful humans prove incapable of leaving the state of nature on their own: no Ciceronian orators, no Aristotelian or Hebrew patriarchs, nor any Machiavellian law-givers influence them, but only the Almighty's direct command. Buchanan's most important political treatise, *De Iure Regni apud Scotos* (1579), additionally "denies that men construct political institutions for their own benefit" because their own political life is never fully natural to them. This line of thought remained "a fundamental feature of Calvinist political thinking" from Buchanan to the greatest "of the seventeenth-century British Calvinists such as Rutherford," although Tuck duly notes that Buchanan's "juridical humanism" places him in a much more liberal lineage than Knox, Christopher Goodman, or John Ponet, whose work is "derived stylistically from the sermon rather than the legal treatise." The latter resistance theorists mainly exhort "an oppressed people to rise against an heretical tyrant, and treat him as the Israelites had treated their oppressors," an approach generally avoided by Buchanan. Yet despite his useful and novel discussion of constitutional remedies for tyranny, Buchanan failed to make any true contribution to natural rights theory simply because he saw human rights as God-given rather than natural.[28]

In contrast, Milton plainly insists on natural rights in his *Tenure*, *Eikonoklastes*, in both of his defenses of the English people, *The Readie and Easie Way*, and even in *Paradise Lost*, where as we have seen, freedom from both civil and religious oppression are described as universal rights bestowed in Eden and retained by all of Adam's heirs unless they succumb to an irrationality alien to their original condition. He also departs from both Aristotle and Augustine

---

[27] Annabel Patterson, "The Good Old Cause," in *Reading between the Lines* (Madison: University of Wisconsin Press, 1993).

[28] Tuck, *Natural Rights Theories*, 43.

by making slavery an intrinsically unnatural result of tyranny. In Skinner's view, these advances explain why Milton became not only "incomparably the greatest writer to speak out in defense of the regicide," but also one of the first to transcend the common lawyers' narrow defenses of fundamental *English*, as opposed to more universal *human*, liberties.[29] Tuck traces this universalist approach to pre-Calvinist, mainly Italian humanist thinkers who profoundly influenced the Huguenots and their successors. He credits two of the earliest and most important, Andrea Alciato and Mario Salamonio, with developing the idea that legal social compacts were so essential to civilized society that no one, including "any prince who stepped outside the agreed law," could be allowed to endanger them. Such princes should be considered tyrants who could be honorably killed by their fellow citizens, an idea later taken up by the Calvinist resistance theorists but with a predictable difference: they emphasized "the omnipotence of God and his part in human affairs," a consideration completely absent in Alciato or Salamonio.[30] This difference stems partly from Calvinist theology itself, which stressed God's divine omnipotence and inscrutability rather than his rational accountability, and partly from the Italians' greater familiarity with Roman law and its Greco-Roman lineage. As experts on the *lex regia* of Justinian's *Digest*, they viewed the emperor's authority as derived from the community, not the deity, which meant that the community and not an act of God either bestowed or revoked it. Much as in private contracts, in their social contract the people are the principals and the emperor an agent or representative who can be dismissed at will. If he proved reliable, he retained a full prerogative over their "business," although some Italian theorists even held that the people retained a right to legislative power. Similar conclusions could be reached by those who took Aristotle's *Politics* rather than Roman law as a starting point, the most radical of whom is generally considered the early Italian republican, Marsilius of Padua. Through these and related sources, Julian Franklin shows that the post-feudal or high Middle Ages witnessed a gradual expansion of the natural restraints and limits on royal prerogative. Estates assemblies gained power across the continent and also in England, where John Fortescue developed an important forerunner of constitutional thought.[31]

Tuck emphasizes other phases and aspects of these developments than those that interest either Skinner or Franklin, but all agree that a combination of Italian humanism and late scholasticism effectively revived Aristotle's account of natural as opposed to divinely instituted human government across Europe. Protestant Aristotelians tended to be more faithful to the historical Aristotle than Catholic theorists such as Louis Le Roy, who inconsistently combined Aristotle's natural "political animals" with Cicero's naturally asocial humans.[32] These inconsistencies notwithstanding, across Europe "divine right" theories of kingship began to give way to various versions of social contract theory wherein citizens retained the legal right to remove sovereigns or to require them to serve chiefly as agents of their

---

[29] Skinner, "John Milton and the Politics of Slavery," in *Visions of Politics* 2: 287.

[30] Tuck, *Natural Rights Theories*, 35–40, 43, cited, 38, 43.

[31] Franklin, *Constitutionalism and Resistance*, 12–13.

[32] Tuck, *Natural Rights Theories*, 44–5.

Milton and the Huguenot Revolution 107

collective interests. Late scholasticism contributed to these developments through the Conciliarists, the early sixteenth-century schoolmen who used the nominalist philosophy of William of Ockham to limit the power of the pope.[33] Their fourteenth-century antecedents prominently included Jean Gerson and his followers, who at the time of the Great Schism "adopted the Roman Law theory of corporations in such a way as to defend a thesis of popular sovereignty in the church." As Skinner adds, they stopped short of granting "popular sovereignty" to individuals but contributed to constitutional thought in three ways: by vesting sovereignty in the Church's "general council as the representative assembly of the faithful," by giving this council greater coercive power than the pope, and by permitting it to remove him from office.[34] Gerson never spelled out the implications of his corporate theory for political communities, yet to some extent these were obvious: once transferred to the civil sphere, these bodies could only conclude "that the highest authority to make laws must remain lodged with the people or their representatives at all times." With the assistance of Jacques Almain and John Mair, Ockham's and Gerson's heirs at the University of Paris soon developed civil applications of the theory in order to confirm King Louis XII's claim that the church as a body possesses greater authority than the pope. A final corollary Almain and Mair bequeathed to the Reformation is that "no rulers placed in power by a free people can ever possess absolute sovereignty, since they must originally have been installed on agreed terms to serve as delegates or 'ministers' of the community that appointed them." This idea effectively revives the patristic view that (as with the Jews) "Very many kings ... must then have been introduced by the consent of the people, and were able justly to maintain their government only by popular consent."[35]

These principles came to play a central role in both Huguenot and Miltonic thought, as did Mair's and Gerson's belief that originally "Adam enjoyed a paternal but not a political form of dominion, since there was no need for coercive authority in a sinless world."[36] By instead focusing on how man's "total depravity" after the

---

[33] On Ockham, see Francis Oakley's seminal article, "Medieval Theories of Natural Law: William of Oakham and the Significance of the Voluntarist Tradition," reprinted in *Natural Law, Conciliarism and Consent in the Late Middle Edges: Studies in Ecclesiastical and Intellectual History* (London: Variorum Reprints, 1984), chapter 15.

[34] Skinner, *Visions of Politics*, 2: 254–6.

[35] All citations in this paragraph are from Skinner, *Visions of Politics*, 2: 257, who in the final citation translates and quotes John Mair [Major], *In Quartum Sententiarum Quaestiones Utilissimae* (Paris. 1519), fo. ciiir.

[36] Milton's own beliefs are famously expressed by Adam, who dissociates himself from the first monarch and thus from any form of monarchy by declaring his

> Authority usurpt, from God not given:
> He gave us only over Beast, Fish, Fowl
> Dominion absolute; that right we hold
> By his donation; but Man over men
> He made not Lord; such title to himself
> Reserving, human left from human free. (*PL* 12: 66–71)

fall ruptured any connection with Adam's unfallen condition, the Scots resistance theorists—including, as we have seen, the humanistic Buchanan—avoided such confident assertions of universal rights. Reserving them only for the Calvinist "Elect"—God's ministers, magistrates, or chosen people—they continued to deny that the "mere" natural man could be capable of self-government at all. Like Knox, they affirmed the inherent right of God's chosen to oppose or depose governments that either failed to restrain sin or actually encouraged it, but this affirmation should not be confused (as it often has been) with populist sentiment.[37] In times of crisis it may have been possible to identify "the people" as a whole as the Elect and its godless rulers with the reprobate, but the key Calvinist distinction between the multitude of "goats" and the small class of "sheep" always reasserted itself. Calvin's dim view of the capacity and morality of the masses was also echoed by English Puritans such as Robert Bolton, who preached that without the coercive power of kings and magistrates the world would be literally flooded with crime:

> Men would become cut-throats and cannibals one unto another. Murder, adulteries, incests, rapes, robberies, perjuries, witchcrafts, blasphemies, all kinds of villanies, outrages, and savage cruelty, would overflow all Countries. We should have a very hell upon earth, and the face of it covered with blood, as it was once with water.[38]

After the more radical Puritans of the revolutionary period rejected the rule of godly princes or magistrates, they vested it not in popular consent but either in the authority of "visible Saints" or the promised "Fifth Monarchy" of God.[39] The same holds true even for the most humanistic of the post-Dispersion Huguenots, whose "dislike for the masses" took on renewed rigor under exile.[40]

This disciplinary, at times even reactionary aspect of godly politics has led Tuck, Skinner, and most other modern historians to overturn earlier "Whiggish" or Marxist identifications of Puritanism with liberty, including the idea that revolutionary Calvinism in England or elsewhere should be credited with the rise of proto-democratic theories of natural rights and contracts. Building on foundational studies such as Guy Dodge's exploration of Huguenot political theory, they show that Calvinism was neither inherently revolutionary nor inherently democratic. Although it sometimes defended itself or attempted to ward off persecution by borrowing populist rhetoric, the resolution of political conflict in favor either

---

[37] See Quentin Skinner, *The Foundations of Modern Political Thought*, 2 vols (Cambridge: Cambridge University Press, 1978), 1: 50, 2: 339.

[38] Cited in C.H. and Katherine George, *The Protestant Mind of the English Reformation 1570–1640* (Princeton: Princeton University Press, 1961), 217. Bolton was one of the favorite divines of the "moderate" Puritan Richard Baxter.

[39] William Lamont, *Godly Rule: Politics and Religion 1603–1660* (New York: Macmillan, 1969).

[40] Guy Howard Dodge, *The Political Theory of the Huguenots of the Dispersion* (New York: Columbia University Press, 1947), 19.

of the godly or of their enemies soon revealed an authoritarian and elitist (if not necessarily classist) bias.[41] Skinner also objects to historians like Franklin and Michael Walzer who assume that contractual theories of government were solely religious in origin. Although Calvinists indeed led the attempted *"coups d'etat* in Scotland and England in the 1550s as well as ... the upheavals in Holland and France in the 1570s," the rights of communities or citizen-representatives "to assert their sovereignty by overthrowing tyrannical governments" was not always their battle cry. Even when it was, they viewed "the lawfulness of forcible resistance not as a moral right but as an aspect of the people's religious duty to uphold the law of God." Buchanan's *De Iure Regni apud Scotos* partly countered Knox's *Appellation* of 1558 by holding that political societies are not *directly* ordained by God, but rather by citizens concerned with improving their welfare, security, and civil rights. Yet as we have seen, even Buchanan concedes that these concerns were originally instilled less by right reason than by natural feelings of sociability mercifully implanted by God. This position at once fails to define the actual basis of a legally delegated power or collective agency and promotes an unbalanced view of government where power is almost entirely reserved for "the people," an abstract and poorly defined collective entity. Skinner thus complains that Buchanan's "almost anarchistic view of the right of forcible resistance" extends beyond the people's representatives and theoretically resides in "each individual citizen as well." The leaders of the English revolution fortunately averted these unwieldy claims because they associated them with radical Jesuit arguments mounted at the Sorbonne over a half century before and widely anathematized in the aftermath of the papal pronouncements against Elizabeth I and the Catholic Gunpowder Plot against James I.[42]

As theorists who needed to appeal to a non-Calvinist audience, the Huguenots had the advantage of necessarily relying on the Italian humanist and Conciliarist sources outlined above. This situation especially prevailed after the St. Bartholomew's Day massacre of 1572, when they sought the support of their more liberal Catholic brethren by denying that the right of resistance remains either in the people as a whole or in a godly "remnant," and by stressing the role of duly delegated authorities in defending the commonwealth and its individual citizens once a sovereign betrays his promise of just rule.[43] For as a minority in a still largely Catholic nation-state, the Huguenots *had* to rely on legal representatives and laws to protect them from the very sort of self-righteous religious majority

---

[41] Dodge, *The Political Theory of the Huguenots of the Dispersion*, 93, 23, ff; on the Arminian use of similar tactics in England, see Peter Lake, "Anti-popery: the structure of a prejudice," in *The English Civil War*, ed. Richard Cust and Ann Hughes (London: Arnold, 1997), 181–210.

[42] Skinner, *Visions of Politics*, 2: 245–50, 262. For Walzer's very different views, see *The Revolution of the Saints: A Study in the Origin of Radical Politics* (Cambridge, MA: Harvard University Press, 1965).

[43] Skinner, *Visions of Politics*, 2: 247; *Vindiciae contra Tyrannos*, ed. and trans. George Garnett (Cambridge: Cambridge University Press, 1994), 129–37, 155–8, 169–72.

privileged by the Scots theorists. Milton and his allies ironically found themselves in much the same position. As a minority in a nation wracked by religious upheaval, divided over the regicide, and ruled by either an unpopular Rump or "purged" Parliament or an equally controversial Protectorate, they similarly needed to appeal to reason and constitutional tradition rather than to any narrowly "faith-based" convictions. Milton's brilliance consisted in almost uniquely understanding this situation, although (again ironically) it made his writing more popular abroad than at home. Of course, he also understood that his case for tyrannicide was too precarious *not* to make some use of Buchanan, Knox, Goodman, Calvin, and even Luther, who was generally hostile to revolution (*CPW* 3: 243–51). Yet in citing these authorities he is usually perfunctory; he warms to his theme mainly in referring to the French monarchomachs or their Italian humanist antecedents. His lack of enthusiasm for the rest can be partly explained by his bitter personal and political experience with the "backsliding" Scots and English Presbyterians, whose covenant ultimately caused them to balk at king killing. He also frequently complains of Scottish inconsistency, which he mentions in an otherwise approving reference to Buchanan. Despite the fact that Buchanan's *History of Scotland* amply "bore witness that regal power was nothing else but a mutuall Covnant or stipulation between King and people. *Buch. Hist.*, l. 20.[,]" "these Scotchmen and Presbyterians … [now] think such liberty less beseeming us then themselves." Deviating from their own contractural tradition, they now make "a Maister" of a monarch "whom thir law scarce allows to be thir own equal" (*CPW* 3: 226).

Hughes inexplicably forgets these complaints in noting with some amazement that "nowhere in *The Tenure* does Milton refer to Samuel Rutherford," the Presbyterian author of *Rex, Lex*, who had recently claimed that "wars waged by subjects were lawful" (*CPW* 3: 226, n. 128). Hughes also seems to forget that Milton's poem "On The New Forcers of Conscience" openly scorns Scots Presbyterians who dared to seize "the Civil Sword / To force our Consciences that Christ set free, / And ride us with a classic Hierarchy / Taught … by mere A.S and Rotherford, /… By shallow *Edwards* and Scotch what d'ye call?" (5–8, 12). In a related poem on the Presbyterian response to his divorce tracts, Milton sneers that Scottish names are so harsh that they are not worth pronouncing, and he fails to include Scotland in the list of the nations he was studying to see how they achieved or lost liberty (*CPW* 1.327). At about the same time, Milton's *Commonplace Book* records highly detailed citations from the French historians and their glowing portraits "of a primitive free France" (*CPW* 3.177). Only Aristotle and Machiavelli prove as pertinent or are cited as often. Even when he delights in deriding Saumaise as "a cheap French mountebank" and as a "crackbrained, moneygrabbing Frenchman" paid off to support a "penniless king and his huge voiceless train of scholars and priests" (*CPW* 4.1.527), he also implicitly taunts him as a French Protestant "backslider" or defector from this glorious tradition. By betraying the naturally "lively and generous ardor of the Franks, worthy of their [free] name" (*CPW* 4.1: 555), his enemy is at once an unworthy opponent and a failed or unnatural Frenchman.

Milton's Real French Connections

Milton's Yale editors Whiggishly suspect his compliment to the Franks of insincerity, thereby creating a false conundrum as to why "Milton is so eager to have French Protestant support for his views that he cites" Duplessis-Mornay's *Vindiciae contra Tyrannos* "without concern for the correctness of its ascription" (*CPW* 4.1: 659, n. 463). This question clearly overlooks the fact that the anonymous tract's authorship was long in doubt (and to some extent—given Languet's contribution—still is), and that its exact source—Beza or otherwise—is not central to Milton's point. In any case, the sincerity of Milton's compliment to the Franks can hardly be cast in doubt due to its larger context. He here clearly alludes to the first chapter of Hotman's *Francogallia*, which opens with the announcement that pre-Roman Gaul was "termed free," and that the word "frank" retains this secondary meaning in both French and English to this day. The same compliment is moreover repeated by Milton's nephew John Phillips in a defense at least partly co-written with his uncle.[44] Here Phillips warmly attests that

> The French to a man boast that they are free men—in this sense indeed "frank"—that from time immemorial they have had the power to elect or reject their kings for the welfare of all. Everyone knows that the command of Gaul was conferred upon Pepin by this procedure and similarly after him upon others. In the present age also the people of many other cities, but especially the people of Bordeaux, have demonstrated by their deeds a similar opinion, in vigorously repelling by strength of arms the "absolute power" and tyranny of their king or his deputies. (*CPW* 4.2: 948–9)

Phillips also summarizes the principles that his uncle's major defenses glean from the writings of Hotman, Bernard de Girard, Seigneur du Haillan, and Claude de Seyssel on "free" French history. Even the dense Saumaise recognizes these preferences when he remarks that Milton's *Defensio pro populo Anglicano* cites only one Scot (Knox), but Milton wittily retorts that Knox's widely reviled teachings were ultimately derived from a Frenchman, Jean Calvin (*CPW* 4.1: 661).

Finally, then, it should begin to seem obvious that not Milton but only his editors are inconsistent when they complain that his "readiness to deny primacy to the English in such matters" conflicts with his stated belief that "God speaks first to his Englishmen" (*CPW* 4.1: 658, n. 459). They base this opinion on a well-known passage in *Areopagitica*, which has been further popularized by Christopher Hill's famous book title, *God's Englishman*.[45] Yet as Peter Lake observes, the concept of the "'elect nation'" was actually "theological nonsense for Protestants," who knew that until the end "it was still an open question whether England would

---

[44]   Hotman, *Francogallia*, trans. Salmon, 147.

[45]   Christopher Hill's *God's Englishman: Oliver Cromwell and the English Revolution* (New York: Dial Press, 1970), obviously focuses on Cromwell rather than Milton, but the identification in the popular or non-specialist mind has been strong.

triumph with Christ or be destroyed with Antichrist."[46] Lake's assessment closely accords with what *Areopagitica* actually says, which is *not* that God speaks for or through the English nation. Its argument is far more complex than that: just as the Sermon on the Mount proclaims that the last shall be first, so it *may be* that the English, the last northern nation to take up the cause of Reformation, will be the first to complete it. Yet the only real certainty is that until now they have been in last place. Although Wycliffe and Hus earlier "offer'd to have made us" the foremost teachers and leaders of the Reformation, the English neglected that offer and remained "the latest and the backwardest Schollers" until God graciously saw fit "to begin some new and great period in his Church." Not long afterward England indeed became the first European nation to depose a tyrannous king who threatened the "reforming of Reformation itself" (*CPW* 2: 553), but the glorious new "period" belongs to a universal God, not to England, whom he merely uses to prove the hidden strength of the weak, the wayward, and the downtrodden. Yet as Milton frankly admits to Saumaise, "if you search out the records all the way from the Waldensians" of Piedmont and Lyons and from "the people of Toulouse to the famine of Rochelle, we shall certainly be found the last of all churches to have taken arms against tyrants. But we are the first to have condemned them to death ... because we were the first to whom this course was possible." Milton's French and Italian precedents further establish the pan-European nature of the English cause, as he is well aware: "a tyrant is not our enemy alone, but the public enemy of virtually the entire human race." Nor is England's leadership any great claim to glory, for "the French too would have don [the same], if the same opportunity had been granted them." In fact, the "doctrine [behind it] belongs no more to us than to" them, and the French can perhaps claim the principal share, since "from what source, except from France, comes that *Franco-gallia*" of Hotman's, the *Vindiciae contra Tyrannos*, "or the other books which Thuanus" [or de Thou] "mentions?" (*CPW* 4.1.658–9). This line of argument may not constitute outright Franco-philia, but it is very far from Franco-phobia.

Of course, as Hughes rightly cautions, France provides the primary touchstone of Milton's resistance theory partly due to external circumstances of which he is not in control. He details the full range of these circumstances as follows:

> The link between the France of Charles IX and Henry III, the France of the Holy League, and Milton's England of the Civil War, was not of his making. In what was rapidly becoming an accepted historical pattern, ... comparisons of ... English Grand Remonstrances with the protests of the French *parlements* against some of the policies of Henry III ... [in] De Thou and several other French historians ... support[ed] ... his distrust of monarchy and faith in parliaments. Just before De Thou's account of Poncet [who unjustly proposed "a plain Turkish Tyranny" to Charles IX] he found a defense of the doctrine of elective monarchy in France, and a bibliography of some of the famous anti-monarchical works of the Huguenot pamphleteers: Hotman's *Franco-Gallia*,

---

[46] Lake, "Anti-popery: the structure of a prejudice," 190.

Milton and the Huguenot Revolution

the anonymous *Junius Brutus* or *Vindiciae contra Tyrannos*, and others, notably Simon Goulart's *Memoires de l'Estat de France sous Charles IX*, which includes the *Dialogue Politique sur la Puissance, l'authorité, & Dévor des Princes, & sur la Liberté du Peuple* In Hotman's *Franco-Gallia*, which is twice quoted in the *Doctrine and Discipline of Divorce*, Milton could find the great picture of a primitive free France[, which,] "according to Caesar, Polybius, Strabo, and Ammeanus" [was] never a "*whole* under the Government of a *single Person*; … "but all Gaul so divided into *Commonwealths*, that the most part were Govern'd by the *Advice* of the *Nobles;* and these were called *Free*." (*CPW* 3: 176–7)

Yet we should not forget that Milton's later decision in *The Readie and Easie Way* to attempt to save the English republic by recommending a federated system much like the one described by Hotman lay very much *within* his own power.[47] So, too, did his citation of the many French sources collected in his *Commonplace Book*, only some of which appear in his published prose. The common scholarly neglect of this citation index is another important reason for overlooking his large debts to France.

The *Commonplace Book*'s three closely related headings on "state," "king," and "subject" cover a broad range of ideas that may be grouped into ten basic political principles, which, aside from the classical sources surveyed by Skinner and Tuck, derive largely from the Conciliarists, French Catholic historians, and the Huguenot theorists who applied the political precedents they established. Logically enough, the first and most general principle is taken not from them but from Sulpicius Severus (c.365–c.425 A.D.), an early church historian who contended (contra Constantine) that "the name of kings has always been hateful to free peoples," "condemns the action of the Hebrews in choosing to exchange their freedom for servitude," and argues "that the church must be independent of and above the state" (*CPW* 1: 440; 415, n. 1). Earlier, Milton notes that even Constantine the Great calls his subjects "by no other name than 'brothers,'" *CPW* 1: 433, the same course Duplessis-Mornay had recommended to wise kings.[48] In an era when even Francis Bacon tended to identify "primitive" with "pure" knowledge, both Severus's early date and Christian credentials usefully support Milton's anti-monarchical views. The fact that the entries are undated makes it difficult to calculate by how much they precede his extremely anti-monarchical and federalist *Readie and Easie Way*, but it is clear that Milton's second and most consistently held principle regarding limited kingship already looked toward early France. This principle holds that

---

[47]   On the federalism of *The Readie and Easie Way*, see Blair Hoxby's excellent account in *Mammon's Music: Literature and Economics in the Age of Milton* (New Haven: Yale University Press, 2002), 62, 77–90. In contrast, Franklin points out that in the *Vindiciae* "the participation of localities in the covenant with God is not to be equated with a federalist conception of the people. Federalism is latent here and there in the *Vindiciae*, but the idea of formation of the people by a contract, real or virtual, is neither stated nor supposed," not even in the sections that deal with resistance on secular grounds; see *Constitutionalism and Resistance*, 43.

[48]   Duplessis-Mornay, *Vindiciae contra Tyrannos*, the "Third Question," in Franklin, *Constitutionalism and Resistance*, 171, 177.

European monarchs were not traditionally absolute, nor should become so, as partly shown by the ancient kings of Aragon (*CPW* 1: 442–3). Third, the king does not own his kingdom, but as de Thou shows, he "is merely the usufructurary of the property of the realm in his possession" (*CPW* 1: 441). Fourth, the people have a right to depose an unfit prince despite their sworn oaths to support him, and a deposed king may not return: "From Chilperic Pope Zacharias takes away his kingdom because of his idleness, thus freeing the Franks from the obligation of their oath of allegiance," a point also confirmed by de Thou (*CPW* 1: 444–5). Fifth, Charles Martel set the precedent for elective and representative monarchy in 730 by convening a Parliament composed of three estates to choose their prince, which made France "an elective kingdom either to choose or to depose." On this point Milton reminds himself to "see the book entitled *Franco-gallia*" and to "read also the excellent speech of an embassador from ye french ... shewing reason why they had rejected ... the right heir to ye crown, & chosen Hugh Capet. Girard." De Thou adds that Commons participated in this process by informing the knights and burgesses of their wishes (*CPW* 1: 445–6, 461–2).

Milton's sixth point, however, is fully English: "to say that the lives and goods of the subject are in the hands of the K.[ing] and at his deposition is ... most tyrannous and unprincely" [Holinshed, Magna Carta] (*CPW* 1: 444–6). The seventh adds that Charlemagne unjustly introduced tenures of Fief or Feud in place of the more noble Roman agrarian laws. According to Girard, his barons should have been considered servants or ministers rather than lords (*CPW* 1: 450). Eighth, if a king intends to appoint his son as his successor, he should make sure that he receives the realm "not as inherited spoils, but as the reward of worth" [Gregoras] (*CPW* 1: 434). Ninth, the crowning of kings is "not admitted till thire oath receav'd of justice to be administerd, according to the laws. Stow & Holinsh. William conqueror. And other Ks." Moreover, these laws are why the "King of France considers it necessary ... to submit to the decrees of his general parliament, which Sesellius calls the 'bridle' of the King in his de repub. Gallor." [*De Republica Galliae*] (*CPW* 1: 435, 458). This is a reference to de Seissel (c.1450–1520) most likely gleaned from Hotman, who stresses the royal "bridle" near the beginning of the first chapter of *Francogallia*.[49] Tenth, "A commonwealth is preferable to a monarchy" not only "'because more excellent men come from a commonwealth than from a kingdom; [but] because in the former virtue is honored most of the time and is not feared as in the kingdom,' &c. Macchiavel. arte di Guerra. Book 2. P.63" (*CPW* 1: 421). This important tenth and final point is obviously taken from Machiavelli, who in turn took it from the Roman historians discussed by Skinner. Yet Hotman (who cites Cicero) similarly supposes that commonwealths flourish best without a king for most of the same reasons Milton cites here and later in *The Readie and Easie Way*.[50]

---

[49]   Hotman, *Francogallia*, 155.

[50]   Hotman, *Francogallia*, 401–5. These include the king's mortality, tendency to debauchery, and the unfortunate accidents of heredity which are no guarantee of either virtue or ability.

This ten-point list conveniently condenses the *Commonplace Book*'s overall descent from general anti-monarchical points to specific principles of limited kingship, from which it then turns to general pro-commonwealth arguments. As a whole, the list helps us to appreciate the variety and depth of Milton's debts to earlier scholars. It also shows that his most general principles are mainly adopted from early church historians and from Machiavelli, the great reviver of classical republicanism and its Greco-Roman defenders. For more specific principles of limited kingship and resistance to tyranny however, he is mainly indebted to the traditions surrounding William the Conqueror, Magna Carta (usually cited in Holinshed), and the broad French bibliography cited by Hughes above. Why do French authors dominate these sections? Probably because they provided a respectably "primitive" Francogallic tradition that sidesteps the troubled history of the Anglo Saxons and Celts of England. According to Milton's own *History of Britain*, these early Englishmen had always been liable to what the first *Defensio* terms "the two great evils in human life, the most fatal to virtue, namely tyranny and superstition" (*Defensio pro populo Anglicano*, *CPW* 4.1: 535). As a result, he needed generously to credit the French for bringing elective or limited monarchy to England. Yet another, perhaps equally important reason seems to be Milton's anti-Calvinism, which his Yale editors so zealously overlook. Like Knox but unlike the Huguenots, even the humanistic Buchanan based his resistance theory on an "organic" and "voluntarist" or God-given rather than representative view of the people and their rights, which did little to combat the anarchic tendencies inherent in the Calvinist theology of grace. As Milton was only too well aware, this voluntarist theology and the anointed Saints who proclaimed it continually disrupted the fledgling Commonwealth of England.[51] Much like Knox, the Saints called directly on "the nobles as inferior magistrates to mount a Calvinist revolution"; hearing the voice of God in their hearts, they urged their brethren to "'promote to the uttermost of your powers his true religion' and 'defend your brethren and subjects.'" As Skinner adds, there is thus much "truth in the assertion that [Knox's] … theory of resistance is not strictly speaking a *political* theory at all, since [it] … is couched entirely in terms of … alleged religious obligations."[52] The same cannot be said of Buchanan's theory, which broadly focuses on individual rights, not just religious duties; but by replacing an Aristotelian with a Stoic account of how our fallen, apolitical, and "savage" human nature must be "saved" by God, Buchanan was forced to give the right to resist tyrants to all the saved, apparently the whole godly people, and therefore failed to protect the minority rights of the reprobate. This approach to revolution would frighten any minority attuned to the potential for assassination and massacre inherent in such doctrines, a fear which rightly made the French Huguenots "anxious to repudiate

---

[51]   With Skinner, I am assuming that anarchism is not truly progressive; not all (and probably not Walzer) might agree.

[52]   Skinner, *The Foundations of Modern Political Thought*, 2: 211; he cites Knox's most radical text, *The Appellation*, 495.

as far as possible any populist or insurrection elements in the heritage of Calvinist political thought," and instead eager "to broaden the basis of their non-sectarian support" by guaranteeing broad religious toleration for all. In the process, they came to defend the Aristotelian teaching that the universal purpose of government was to improve the general welfare, not to fulfill a divine mandate. Political historians therefore credit them with making the "epoch-making move" from a religious covenant to a genuinely political theory of contract in which rulers may be resisted when they fail to keep their promise to pursue the general welfare of the people. This movement not only anticipates Locke but clearly aided Milton in developing a proto-constitutionalist theory of natural rights and universal precedents.[53] Benefiting from Erasmus's revival of pre-Augustinian thought, all of the above began to see that in religion as in politics, "A king, if he wishes to do his duty, is not truly a king but a steward of the people" (*CPW* 1: 439).[54] If not—if he "regardeth not the wealth of the commons, but the advancement of himselfe, his faction, and his kindred"—he is a tyrant who may be overthrown (*CPW* 1: 443).

From a fully modern perspective, however, the most radical and foresighted part of this readjustment involves the separation of church and state, which as the early Huguenots realized, was centrally important to defusing disruptive factions. Against the precedent of Elizabeth and her Stuart heirs who believed that "Separation between religion and state cannot be," Milton strongly agreed with "Hospital, the very wise chancellor of France," once again as cited in de Thou, that established religion is both harmful and wrong. He thus reaffirms L'Hôpital's startlingly modern belief that "Many can be citizens who are by no means Christians, and he who is far from the bosom of the Church does not cease to be a loyal citizen, and we can live peacefully with those who do not reverence the same religious rites as we do" (*CPW* 1: 421). Thus at a time when many Catholics and Protestants could not consider each other fellow Christians much less fellow citizens, Milton, like the pre-exilic Huguenots, argued for a state governed by secular law and secular freedom, not by religion or religious revolutionaries. On this point, at least, his personal stake in the argument could hardly be clearer: according to his earliest biographers, Milton attended no religious services, state or sectarian, but worshipped privately at home. The biographer who knew him most intimately, Edward Phillips, the nephew he partly raised as a son, attests that his private and public accomplishments and fame were nevertheless such that had he lived in the time of de Thou, "he had justly merited from that great historian, an eulogy not inferior to the highest by him given to all the learned and ingenious that lived within the compass of his history" (Hughes, 1025). Given Milton's own opinion of the Frenchman's sound learning and political principles, he would have basked in the warmth of Phillips's praise had he only lived to hear it.

---

[53] Skinner, *Foundations*, 2: 344–5, 305, 310, 329–31, 315, 339, 335, 270, 321.

[54] On Duplessis-Mornay's role in anticipating this liberal theology, see D.P. Walker, *The Decline of Hell* (Chicago: University of Chicago Press 1964), 16.

PART 3
Translation and the
Transnational Context

Chapter 6
Cross-Cultural Adaptation and the Novella: Bandello's Albanian Knight in France, England, and Spain

Dorothea Heitsch

J'écris en langue maternelle
Et tâche de la mettre en valeur,
Afin de la rendre éternelle
Comme les vieux ont fait la leur.[1]

Shall I apologize translation? Why but some hold (as for their freehold) that such conversion is the subversion of universities. God hold with them, and withhold them from impeach or impair. It were an ill turn, the turning of books should be the overturning of libraries.[2]

Introduction

In 1554, the first three volumes of Matteo Bandello's *Novelle* were published in Lucca.[3] Four years later, an adaptation as *Histoires tragiques*, begun by Pierre Boaistuau and continued by François de Belleforest, was brought out in France. In 1567, Geoffrey Fenton's *Certain Tragical Discourses of Bandello* appeared in London, and, in 1589, Juan de Millis issued *Historias trágicas ejemplares* in Salamanca. The latter two translations are not based on the Italian originals, but on Belleforest's French collection. By looking at the migration of one particular novella, the story of the Albanian knight, I propose to compare notions of style and to trace the concepts of exotic, tragic, and moral from the Italian text first to the French translation and then to Fenton's English and Millis's Spanish renderings. It should be stated clearly that I use the term "exotic" in the sense of barbaric, as in the dichotomy of barbaric and civilized, which is a key element of all four versions and relevant to my discussion of cultural specificity.[4] I have chosen the story of

---

[1]   Jacques Peletier du Mans, "A un poète qui n'écrivait qu'en latin," in Claude Longeon (ed.), *Premiers combats pour la langue française* (Paris: Livre de Poche, 1989), 128.

[2]   John Florio, "To the Courteous Reader," in Douglas Robinson (ed.), *Western Translation Theory from Herodotus to Nietzsche* (Manchester, UK and Northampton, MA: St. Jerome Publishing, 2002), 133.

[3]   The fourth part was published in Lyon in 1573.

[4]   What is meant by "tragic" and "moral" will depend on the texts discussed.

the Albanian knight because of its dual connection to historical personages and to an exotic setting, being fully aware that many such tales, some of which with moralizing glosses by their adapters, circulate in the Renaissance.[5] Yet only a small selection of Bandello's novellas can be traced to Belleforest as well as to Fenton and Millis; therefore, those that were translated by all three authors would have been of particular interest to translators and readers alike.

My points of analysis are important for the novella at the time, because one theoretician of the genre, Francesco Bonciani, in 1574 is unable to accept the tragic novella with its mixed registers.[6] As it is the nature of novellas to travel across national boundaries, I take up the story of my choice in its four versions, instead of only in French and English. I hope to show, by tracing the extensions, transformations, and "improvements" to be found in the transferred texts, that this cross-cultural adaptation not only illustrates the history of the novella but also the reception of Italian culture in Europe and, what is more, the formation of a literary heritage through competition in France, England, and Spain. Moreover, by examining certain early modern notions of literary translation and genre in this prime example, I hope to draw some conclusions concerning the relationship between the early modern novella and national identity or politics.

Bandello's Novella: Truthful History or Marvelous Exoticism

Matteo Bandello's novella is entitled "Il cavalier Spada per gelosia ammazza se stesso e anco la moglie perché non restasse viva dopo lui" (I.51) [The knight Spada kills himself and his wife out of jealousy so that she might not live after him] and is found in the first of the three volumes published in 1554.[7] It takes place in Mantua and presents the murder of Pietro Barza's widow Regina, called "the Greek Helen," by her second husband, the Albanian Spada who commits suicide after killing his wife. This contemporary event dates back to 1516–1518, is known to two witnesses named by Bandello,[8] and was told by Giovanna Trotti, wife of the banker Carlo

---

[5]   One instance of such a circulation is discussed by Emma Campbell, "Sexual Poetics and the Politics of Translation in the Tale of Griselda," *Comparative Literature* 55.3 (2003), 191–216.

[6]   Francesco Bonciani, "Lezione sopra il comporre delle novelle," in Nuccio Ordine, ed., *Traités sur la nouvelle à la Renaissance* (Torino: Aragno, Paris: Vrin, 2002), 117–81.

[7]   Bandello was born at Castelnuovo in 1480, 1484, or 1485 and died at Agen in 1561. For his life, see Fiorato's "Notice Biographique," in *Nouvelles*, ed. Charles Adelin Fiorato et al. (Paris: Imprimerie Nationale, 2002), 85–7 and the "Introduction" to Geoffrey Fenton's *Certain Tragical Discourses of Bandello* (New York: AMS Press, 1967). All translations are mine unless otherwise indicated.

[8]   It happens "questi dì": Matteo Bandello, *La prima parte delle novelle* (Alessandria: Edizioni dell'Orso, 1992), 471. The date given is roughly "17 years ago," from the time of its telling as we assume (ibid., 471, n. 8; 473, n. 19). The two witnesses are Mario Equicola and Giovan Giacomo Calandra, according to Bandello's dedicatory letter to the novella.

Ghisi, in order to amuse Isabella d'Este as well as the "lieta brigata" (including Bandello) around her in Diporto.[9] The briskly narrated story is first dedicated to her as well as then, by Bandello, to Sigismondo Fanzino de la Torre[10] in a letter that relates it as a strange but true case. Indeed, according to recent research, the plot is based on a news item that occurred in Mantua on November 3, 1518.[11]

The plot structure has a historical frame concerning Bayazid's war against Venice on Greek territory, in Modoni (Methoni) on the Peloponnesus (also called Morea in early modern times), from where the protagonist immigrates with her first husband and her brother to Mantua, Italy.[12] Here the Albanian Spada falls violently in love with the quickly widowed Regina/Helena and becomes inconceivably and incomprehensibly jealous of her soon after their marriage. Upon hearing that his mentor Giangiacomo Trivulzio supposedly has died in disgrace, Spada suffers from an increasing imbalance of the humors, which aggravates his melancholic jealousy to the point that he desires death and prepares for the catastrophe. In a moment of delay, his wife attempts to prevent him from committing suicide, but he ends by stabbing first her and then himself. The victim survives long enough to tell her story and the novella ends with the narrator's comments as well as with a poem. Evidently, Bandello's tale unfolds according to the classical movements of tragedy. Despite some interesting suspense, I concentrate on what is told—the marvelous, exotic plot—as well as on those aspects of the author's style that make this plot plausible enough to pass for historically true.[13]

Verisimilar Representation

How Bandello intertwines reality and the marvelous is one striking aspect of this text, which thus satisfies the most basic modern definition of the "novella" as a brief account of a recent, often bizarre event narrated in realistic terms.[14]

---

[9] Carlo Godi, *Bandello. Narratori e dedicatori della prima parte delle Novelle* (Roma: Bulzoni Editore, 1996), 278, 281. The "brigata" is a merry group of like-minded humanists whose conversations often result in a collaborative work or in a new poetic movement.

[10] A public figure in Mantua (Godi, 277).

[11] It is taken from Marino Sanuto's *Diarii* (Bologna: Forni Editore, 1969) vol. XXVI, 196–7. See also Godi, 279–80.

[12] Bayazid lived from 1446 to 1512. His war with Venice lasted from 1499 to 1503.

[13] For my analysis of Bandello's novella, I have adapted the terminology proposed by Mario J. Valdés, *World-Making. The Literary Truth-Claim and the Interpretation of Texts* (Toronto: University of Toronto Press, 1992), 20–21, 38–77.

[14] "Une nouvelle est le récit, le plus souvent bref, d'une aventure en général récente et présentée comme réelle." Roger Dubuis, *La Nouvelle et l'art du récit au XVe siècle en France* (Lyon: Presses Universitaires de Lyon, 1998), 22. For a more elaborate definition, see Robert J. Clements and Joseph Gibaldi, *Anatomy of the Novella* (New York: New York University Press, 1977), 3–7.

Thus, brevity of structure, elements of surprise, and a particular rhetoric are defining traits of this genre. In the dedicatory letter we find both an affirmation of the truth of this historical news item and the author's wish to astound us by recounting it as a truly extraordinary case:

> Mirabili nel vero son tutti quei casi che fuor de l'ordinario corso del nostro modo di vivere a la giornata accadeno, e spesso quando gli leggiamo ci inducono a meraviglia, ancora che talvolta molti uomini, non avendo riguardo a la santità de l'istoria che deve esser con verità scritta, come leggono una cosa che abbia del mirabile o che lor paia che non deverebbe esser di quel modo fatta, dicono: – Forse non avvenne così, ma chi questo fatto scrisse l'ha voluto a modo suo adornare.[15]

> [Marvelous and true are all those cases that happen outside the ordinary course of our daily life, and often amaze us when we read them, so that sometimes many men, who do not have respect for the holiness of the story that should be told truthfully, say when they read something that is miraculous or that seems to them as if it should be made differently: – Maybe it did not happen just so, but whoever described this event wanted to adorn it in his own way.][16]

This twofold intention of presenting wonderful cases as if they could be true is confirmed as the story develops: the jealous husband, a literary archetype or stock character, is here transformed into a lifelike personage by transferring him to a historical context and by giving explanations, reasons, and motivations for his actions. The crime is quickly discovered by a series of witnesses who ultimately serve to lend credibility to the narrator of the novella.[17] The deed may be motivated by the supposed death of a seemingly disgraced mentor who cannot help an Albanian immigrant with a Greek wife in his Italian career any longer and who may even have disgraced his protégé. In a paradoxical twist, the archetypal figure or situation is turned into a believable *persona* or setting by embellishing it with even more detailed archetypal traits. These specific sets of circumstances that correspond to a strong "as-if position" have "logical" consequences:[18] the atrocity of Spada's crime is heightened first by the fact that Regina/Helena is not only immensely beautiful but also extremely virtuous and therefore entirely innocent.[19] In several instances, this exemplary woman attempts to mitigate her husband's unmotivated jealousy, another verisimilar key concept. It leads Bandello to mention the theory of the humors and significantly is repeated twice in a short

---

[15] *La prima parte*, 471.

[16] Translations are mine unless otherwise indicated.

[17] Ibid., 474–5: "fante di casa," "vicini," "cirurgico," "sacerdote," "Francesco I marchese di Mantova," "Sigismondo Fanzino."

[18] Valdés, 21.

[19] "[G]iovane di tanta e sì incredibil bellezza dotata che da tutti era detta la 'greca Elena'. Era poi oltra l'estrema beltà in modo costumata e gentile e di tanta onestà di quanta altra donna si ritrovasse" (*La prima parte*, 472).

Cross-Cultural Adaptation and the Novella 123

novella in which, due to the author's laconic and "objective" style, we find more than one information gap:

> Veggendola adunque bellissima e d'ogni mosca che per l'aria volava temendo, egli oltra ogni credenza geloso di lei divenne, di tal sorte che pensava ch'ognora gli fosse da le braccia rapita. Né altra cagione a ciò lo sospingeva se non che com'egli molto l'amava e molto bella la vedeva e conosceva che ella con tutto il suo studio s'ingegnava di piacerli, così da malinconico umore avvelenato, s'immaginava che ciascuno l'amasse e che ella ad ogni uomo piacesse, e ancora che così cercasse di piacer altrui come a lui faceva.[20]

> [Seeing her therefore so very beautiful and fearing every fly that flew through the air, he became jealous of her beyond all belief, such that he thought she would be taken from his arms at any time. There was no other reason that drove him on than this: as he loved her a lot and saw how beautiful she was and realized that she with all her will tried to please him, so he imagined, poisoned with melancholy, that everyone loved her and that she pleased every man, and even that she tried to please others the way she pleased him.]

In addition, the narrator reiterates the Albanian's jealousy as well as his awareness of Regina's beauty, underlining the male protagonist's fixation. Such jealousy, although caused by a disarray of the humors, may also be inherent in national character and, as the narrator insists, may be typical of Albanians: "Io non credo che sia nazione al mondo più sospettosa de l'albanese; onde il cavaliero Spada ingelosiva ogni ora molto più e pareva che d'ogni cosa avesse paura, e non sapeva dir di che"[21] ["I do not think there is a nation in the world that is more distrustful than the Albanians; thus the knight Spada became each hour more jealous and it seemed as if he was afraid of everything and could not tell of what"]. Evidently, Albanians can outdo Italians with violent love, as proverbial Italian jealousy is here transferred to a supposedly barbaric contemporary.[22]

Spada's jealousy thus becomes not only a quasi-realistic trait of the novella, but also one of the exotic elements (jealousy linked to supposed Albanian mentality) as well as tragic elements (character determines destiny) of the text together with its exotic beginning in the south of Greece under Turkish rule. Exoticism in this case would mean Albanian customs or behavior patterns that are presented as different from Italian ones and that rise to the surface under adverse circumstances as jealousy, credulity, and cruelty, thus enabling the narrator to emphasize the contrast between Albanian-barbaric and Italian-civilized. In addition, this

---

[20]   Ibid., 472.

[21]   Ibid., 473.

[22]   It should be noted that melancholic behavior caused by an excess of love is not exclusively linked to foreigners, for Bandello describes it in several novellas: Galeazzo (I.20), Francesco Totto (I.43), Malatesta (I.50), Niccolò Sanese (II.58), and Teodoro Zizimo (III.37) are some examples. For elaborate definitions of melancholy we may consult the dedicatory letters of II.40, 356, and II.47, 456.

paragraph is one of two places in the novella where we find a narrator's comment. The other passage is at the very end where the narrator evaluates Spada's character as that of a cruel monster ("fiero mostro") whose love was rage ("furore") and whose conjugal benevolence was a strange and barbaric frenzy ("rabbia strana e Barbara"). He concludes in a devout wish that jealous husbands are cursed and beastly ("mariti maledetti e bestiali") and should be sent to Paradise before they can harm anyone. At the end of the novella, then, the novelistic stock character's excessive love has become an Albanian national trait. And though this character is out of the ordinary and, as it were, fictitious, he still claims authenticity through the narrator's use of general experiential premises that form semantic coherence and enable the projection of the figurative imagination into a pattern of causality and action.[23]

Historical Truth Claim

What is known about Spada, the Albanian? Bandello presents him as a man who is well enough esteemed among his countrymen ("uomo tra la nazion sua assai stimato"),[24] which indicates that he comes from a prominent Albanian family. Barza, Regina's first husband, and Spada are both "stradiotti," knights from Greece, Albania, or Dalmatia who were introduced to Italy in the fifteenth century.[25] He therefore has a cultural background and position similar to Regina's first husband and initially worked together with her brother, who appreciates him as a good colleague and later esteems him a good husband for his sister. Yet Spada unexpectedly will give in to rumor and he will commit the final crime on the basis of his unfathomable jealousy.

Among the Albanian immigrants living in Italy in Bandello's time, there is the Spata family, a family of high importance in Albanian history.[26] If we assume that Spata is a clan name[27] and if we accept a sound change from Spata to Spada together with an Italianization, Bandello's claim of historical veracity is proven once more. Regina's family comes from the Morea: at the time, Methoni and the neighboring fortress Koroni were called the "eyes of Venice," because in 1209, the Franks had ceded both fortresses to the Venetians for whom they had become

---

[23]   Valdés, 59.

[24]   *La prima parte*, 472.

[25]   Paolo Petta, *Stradioti. Soldati albanesi in Italia (sec. XV-XIX)* (Lecce: Argo, 1996), 17. Marino Sanuto describes their arms as "scudo," "spada," "lancia," "mazzocca di ferro" (ibid., 45). The name of Regina's husband ("sword") is thus a pars pro toto. The "stradioti" are known for their courage and their good horses, both of which figure in Bandello's novella I.47 about Costantino Boccali.

[26]   Paolo Petta, *Despoti d'Epiro e principi di Macedonia* (Lecce: Argo, 2000), 18, 137. See also Giuseppe Schirò, "La genealogia degli Spata tra il XIV e XV sec. e due Bua sconosciuti," *Rivista di studi bizantini e neoellenici* 8–9 (1971–1972), 67–86.

[27]   Petta, 18.

defense and trade centers. In 1500, the Ottoman army under Bayazid II besieged Methoni and captured Koroni, which was an enormous loss for Venice because the sea route to the Levant was not protected any longer by outposts. It is in this context that Regina's family leaves home: the Ottoman invasion of Albania is exploited by the Republic of Venice, which plans to capture the prosperous cities along the coast of Albania, before they have to surrender to the new rulers. Therefore the senate of Venice promises rewards to the nobility if they give up these cities.[28] This also means that Italy is a likely place of refuge for Albanians once the Ottoman army has carried the day. Bandello's novella thus straddles Greek, Albanian, Ottoman, and Italian history in a configuration that is both historically plausible and, possibly, historically accurate.

Textual Authority

Like Boccaccio's *Decamerone* that originates in the dialogic exchange of a group of interlocutors, Bandello's novellas may be said to uphold the fiction of oral transmission. In their pretense to imitate oral expression, they favor a style that is uneven, disjointed, non-exemplary, and as incongruous as their view of fate. In the preface to the first volume of the *Novelle*, Bandello says:

> Io non voglio dire come disse il gentile ed eloquentissimo Boccaccio, che queste mie novelle siano scritte in fiorentin volgare, perché direi manifesta bugia, non essendo io né fiorentino né toscano, ma lombardo. E se bene io non ho stile, ché il confesso, mi sono assicurato a scriver esse novelle, dandomi a credere che l'istoria e cotesta sorte di novelle possa dilettare in qualunque lingua ella sia scritta.[29]

> [I do not want to say, as says the amiable and most eloquent Boccaccio, that these novellas are written in Florentine vulgar, because I would tell an outright lie being born neither Florentine nor Tuscan, but Lombard. And even though I have no style, which I confess, I have succeeded in writing these novellas, which leads me to think that the story and this kind of novellas can delight in whichever language it is written.]

In spite of this disclaimer, Bandello's style is conceived to imitate oral presentations for a select group of elegant and refined interlocutors, as can be seen in the elaborate rhetorical means that are all the more striking due to the brevity of the tale of the Albanian knight. This imitation of orality creates a level of discourse that appeals to the intended audience and it solidifies the fictive construct of the story through an interesting variety of rhetorical means.

---

[28]   Kristo Frasheri, *The History of Albania* (Tirana, 1964), 57.

[29]   See also *La prima parte*, 4 and *La terza parte de le novelle* (Alessandria: Edizioni dell'Orso, 1995), 1, 7.

The most conspicuous oral features are the exclamations ("Ma che!" 473) and the adjective accumulations ("misera e disgraziata donna," 474; "perfido e disleal marito," 474), which in one instance appear as four binaries in one single sentence: "il crudelissimo e scelerato albanese," "si solenne e nefandissima pazzia" "la bella e gentilissima greca," "le sue bellezze e leggiadri costumi" (475). We also find redundancies, such as the coupling of "bellezza" and "beltà" (472), or verb accumulations in "seppe tanto dir e far e persuaderla" (472) and "l'amava" / "l'amasse" as well as "piacesse" / "piacer" (472–3). There is the changing rhythm of the narration in which we sometimes see unusually short sentences that serve as cadenzas in the narrative: "Né guari stette che messer Pietro morì" (472); "Ma il totto era indarno" (473); "Ma cosa che ella li dicesse, niente gli giovava" (473); "Veramente egli non l'amava" (475). But we also see elaborate constructions more akin to written style, such as the present participle sequences in moments of suspense in a series of three sentences: "Onde essendo ... Avvenne che non essendo ... E veggendo che cosa ..." (472); or, then again, three participles in one sentence: "A la fine veggendo ella ... non mangiando nè dormendo ..." (473). In addition, there is the tense change from the past tense of the narration to the present tense of the narrator's comments. Evidently, the novella is presented in refined style that gives the impression of being oral, unpredictable, and varied, which is typical of a genre that hovers between the conversation and the court manual. Such features are not only carefully selected, thus creating a strong and reliable enunciating voice, but also clearly arranged with a view to constructing a coherent textual world through rhetorical means.

Representation of an Empirically Verifiable World

In the novella I.51, which tells the story of the Albanian knight, Bandello develops a tragic plot with a deadly ending due to barbaric jealousy as an unheard-of case within a historical setting. Human actions in this tale are not motivated, for they surprise the protagonists whose character traits, which are explained in privileged narratorial comments, seem to determine their destiny over which they have no influence. If we accept that Bandello is both a *novelliere* and a chronicler, telling his tales both laconically and objectively, such a plot would mirror the destiny of Italy and historical events during Bandello's lifetime, as he indicates in the dedicatory letter to III.62: "E se mai fu età ove si vedessero di mirabili e differenti cose, credo io che la nostra età sia una di quelle ne la quale, molto piú che nessun'altra, cose degne di stupore, di compassione e di biasimo accadono" (285) ["And if ever there was a time when wonderful and different things were seen, I believe that ours is one of those times in which more than at any other moment occur things worthy of wonderment, compassion, and reproach"]. Though marvelous, the tale of the Albanian knight is still verifiable for Bandello's readers through an appeal to their empirical experience of the world.

From the Novella to the *Histoire Tragique*: Belleforest and Translation as Passage

François de Belleforest takes up the story of the Albanian knight in his French translation of the *Novelle*.[30] He continues the work begun by Pierre Boaistuau who already had translated six Bandellian stories.[31] Both authors' texts are published in 1559, Boaistuau's in the spring and Belleforest's in September of that year. In his new title, "De la cruauté barbare d'un chevalier Albanois, lequel sur la fin de ses iours occit sa femme, pour crainte qu'un autre apres son decez ne iouist de l'extreme beauté d'icelle, & lequel se tua quant & sa femme"[32] ["Of the barbarous cruelty of an Albanian knight who at the end of his days slew his wife for fear that another after his death might enjoy her extreme beauty and who killed himself and his wife"], Belleforest emphasizes the barbaric element and the fact that the event happens at the end of the Albanian's life, staging a sacrificial custom unheard of in Europe as an indirect explanation for the murder. Thus, the novella about the Albanian knight lends itself to shaping French national morality and ideology, because Belleforest can distance himself from the so-called negative aspects of the Italian/Albanian context as well as depict a colonial setting with all its inconsistencies and problems. In this way, the translator, in playing on the Greek and Albanian frame which he decides to keep, engages in a discussion of exotic regions, whereby his strategic location is that of a mediator.[33]

In Belleforest's French version, the time frame as well as the structure of the story remain the same, but the names are slightly frenchified as Pierre Barze, Royne, or Trivulze. The catastrophe is discovered by the chambermaid and the neighbors as before (237v), but the other witnesses that serve to lend credibility to Bandello's narration are omitted. Several significant changes are noted by A.C. Fiorato, who offers a list of formal modifications that concern the destruction of the frame, de-Italianization, an emphasis on the tragic and the sentimental, the defense of the French language, and some moral and ideological changes.[34]

---

[30] Belleforest was born in 1530 and died in 1583.

[31] Therefore the novella I am reading is sometimes counted as I.4, sometimes as I.10. For the problem of the numerous varied editions of the *Histoires tragiques*, see Donald Stone, "Belleforest's Bandello: A Bibliographical Study," *BHR* XXXIV (1972), 489–99 and A.P. Stabler, "A Further Note on Belleforest Bibliography," *BHR* XXXV (1973), 541–2.

[32] I quote from *Histoires tragiques, extraictes des oeuvres italiennes de Bandel, & mises en langue française. Les six premières, par Pierre Boisteau, surnommé Launay, natif de Bretaigne. Les douze suivans par Franc. de Belle Forest, Comingeois.* A Turin: par Cesar Farine, MDLXX.

[33] For such a position, see Edward W. Said, *Orientalism* (New York: Vintage, 1979), 20.

[34] Adelin Charles Fiorato, "Le 'Bandel' ou la moralisation d'un conteur de la Renaissance italienne en France" in Mariella Colin (ed.), *Heurs et malheurs de la littérature italienne en France* (Caën: Université de Caën, 1995), 113. See also Thierry Pech, *Conter le crime. Droit et littérature sous la Contre-Réforme: Les histoires tragiques (1559–1644)* (Paris: Champion, 2000), 80–83.

Among the latter are the summaries. In the summary that precedes this tenth novella, Belleforest professes to present for once not female jealousy, but the crime of a jealous man whom no one can support after hearing the case ("executé par un homme sans occasion quelconque en la ialousie causee par un mespris," 226v), thus suggesting how his readers should respond toward an illness that seems to be associated with the female rather than the male sex. Similarly, he inserts an exhortation to his intended lady readers: "Oyez, mes dames, l'acte le plus effroiable, iniuste & detestable que (peut-estre) vous ouïstes iamais raconter, & qui onc avint, ce croy-ie, entre mary & femme, veu que l'occasion ne s'y offroit pour ce faire" (236v) ["Hear, my ladies, the most terrible, unjust, and detestable act that maybe you ever heard and that ever occurred, I think, between man and wife, given that there was no reason to do it"]. In addition, Belleforest expands the two original narrator's interventions (231r, 232r) by the initial comments that emphasize story telling as theatrical edification and by embellishments such as classical allusions or similes from natural history that fill the information gaps we find in Bandello with explanations of the protagonists' motivations. It is made clear in the introduction, for example, that Spada lacks motivation for his jealousy; the translator thus emphasizes the barbaric nature of the knight's final act. Moreover, he disregards the theories of the humors mentioned by Bandello in favor of a personified jealousy as "diable ministre."

These particular changes serve to enable a theatrical set-up that will be typical of the "histoire tragique," to the point that a later representative of the genre, Jean-Pierre Camus, will call one of his collections *L'Amphithéâtre Sanglant*. Indeed, the play-like structure of the plot is mentioned from the beginning by Belleforest ("qui servira d'un theatre sanglant, où lon presente les personnes ne iouans que furieuses & mortelles tragedies," 227r), a trait that the French translator develops in his version as follows: he elaborates on the married bliss of Pierre Barze and his wife (227v–228); he adds a long passage on the goddess Fortune, who is a determining influence in most of his other adaptations (228r–v); he comments on Spada's excessive feelings ("devint estrangement amoureux" 228v; "Luy à la fin vaincu d'amour & impatience, ne pouvant autrement remedier à sa passion, & amortir le feu qui luy brusloit incessamment les entrailles" 229r; "effroy & esbahissement à mes sens" 229v); he adds a dialogue between Regina's brother and Spada (229v–230r) and another one between Regina and her brother concerning her marriage to the Albanian (230r–231r) that ends with: "Il fit et dit tant, qu'à la fin sa soeur condescendit, quoy qu'à regret, à ce que son frere luy demandoit" ["He said and did so much that at the end his sister agreed, though regretfully, to what her brother asked of her"].

Equally noteworthy in this context are the amplifications, a frequent rhetorical means according to translation theories of the time and that is here used to emphasize theatricality.[35] Belleforest adds a passage on Spada's love,

---

[35]   Michel Ballard, *De Cicéron à Benjamin. Traducteurs, traductions, réflexions* (Lille: Presses Universitaires de Lille, 1992), 101.

which he compares to that of a she-ape toward her offspring who crushes their bones with her caresses ("ainsi ceste grande vehemente, & trop excessive amour du mari vers sa femme causa une rage q estoit semblable à l'amour de la singesse à l'endroit de ses faons, laquelle les caresse si lourdement, que de belle force d'embrassmens elle leur fait craquer les os encor tendres, & les suffoque, leur pensant faire quelque grand faveur & advancement" [232r]). Moreover, the translator comments on Spada's perturbed mind: "la nourriture de la fantaisie du malheureux, lequel aimoit en elle ce qu'il y haïssoit le plus & souhaitoit ce qu'encor le plus il detestoit" (233v). He adds a long conversation between Spada and Regina (234v–236r) in which the latter admonishes her husband that, in order to honor the dead, one should not sacrifice oneself on their tombs as formerly did the barbarians and still do some nations (235v). In this adaptation, Regina's murder becomes an act of exemplary cruelty committed by a man "plus furieux que tigre, lion, ou liepart, que jamais l'Aphrique (nourricière de monstres) ait veu par ses deserts" (237r) In fact, one distant source of the "histoire tragique" is the "exemplum" that corresponds to Counter-Reformation ethics and imagery,[36] yet Belleforest narrows it down and at the same time dampens the variety and color of the world as it is seen by Bandello.

The Reception of Aristotle's *Poetics*: Tragic Style as Moral Style

Bandello's style is one of the elements that did not find favor with François de Belleforest: he considered the author's Lombard dialect as rough and vulgar, but, echoing some of Bandello's own remarks, thought well enough of the invention and truth of the stories that young French readers might benefit from them.[37] He justifies the changes that he makes to Bandello's text as follows:

> [J]e l'ay enrichy de sentences, d'adoption d'histoires, harangues, & epistres, selon que j'ay veu que le cas le requeroit [..]. Et encore, pour mieux embellir l'histoire, [...] j'ay fait le sommaire de chaque narration, & la fin selon le subject, y accommodant les sentences qui me sembluient faire pour l'institution de la vie, & formation des bonnes moeurs. Cest embellissement donq (je ne l'appelleray plus traduction) pourra servir d'enseigne vainqueresse sur le fort de mon autheur, afin qu'il se resente mieux poly en nostre langue, qu'il n'estoit rude & grossier en son Lombard.[38]

---

[36] See Michel Simonin, *Vivre de sa plume au XVIe siècle ou la carrière de François de Belleforest* (Geneva: Droz, 1992), 18 and Pech, *Conter le crime*, 65.

[37] René Sturel, *Bandello en France au XVIe siècle* (Geneva: Slatkine Reprints, 1970), 1 and Adelin Charles Fiorato, *Bandello entre l'histoire et l'écriture* (Firenze: Olschki, 1979), 623.

[38] Belleforest is quoted in the introduction by Richard Carr to Pierre Boaistuau, *Histoires tragiques* (Paris: Champion, 1977), XLVIII n. 49.

[I have enriched it with sentences, adopted stories, harangues, and letters according to what the case required (…). And then, to better embellish the story, (…) I have made a summary of each narration at the beginning as well as at the end, according to the subject, including the sentences that seemed to me to contribute to the institution of life and the formation of good manners. This embellishment then (which I would not call translation any more) will serve as a banner of victory on the fortress of my author so that he would feel more polished in our language, than he was rough and heavy in his Lombard.]

Belleforest's choice of style in its turn was early compared unfavorably to Boaistuau's, his predecessor in translating the *Novelle*,[39] because the former uses a great deal of direct discourse with aphorisms, moral commonplaces, or sentences, and because his style is in general much less direct, less simple, and less unadorned than Bandello's.

J'ay basty ces discours, […] non pour chatouiller les désirs à suyvre les inclinations du sensuel, mais à fin que la jeunesse Françoise, comme elle a l'esprit gentil et bon, voye et juge de la bonté et du vice, et prenne esgard à la fin de l'un et de l'autre; que si le pire emporte le meilleur en bonheur, et félicité, je suis d'advis qu'elle le suyve, et s'y adonne; mais si, au contraire, c'est la vertu qui véritablement bienheure les hommes, et rend leur mémoire glorieuse, je suis d'advis que ces discours et hystoires soyent visitées pour le seul esgard et respect de ce qui est bon, et qui rend louable le nom des hommes.[40]

[I have construed these discourses, (…) not to tickle the desires to follow the inclinations of the sensual, but so that young French people, who have good and nice minds, see and judge goodness and vice, and take note of the one and the other; so that if the worse beats the better in happiness and felicity, I think they should follow it and give in to it, but if on the contrary it is virtue that really makes men happy, and makes for glorious remembrance, I think that these discourses and stories should be read for the exclusive attention to what is good and what makes praiseworthy the name of men.]

Belleforest declares, in his *Continuation des Histoires Tragiques*, that the end bestows a moral on a work and that culpable passions may be depicted if they are punished by misfortune. Both Boaistuau and Belleforest are conscious of creating something new and of not being imitators but innovators, as Boaistuau explains in his note to the reader:

Te priant au reste ne trouver mauvais si je ne me suis assubjecty au stile de Bandel, car sa phrase m'a semblé tant rude, ses termes impropres, ses propos tant mal liez et ses sentences tant maigres, que j'ay eu plus cher la refondre *tout de neuf* et la remettre en *nouvelle forme* que me rendre si superstitieux imitateur,

---

[39] See *Les Bibliothèques françaises de La Croix du Maine et de Du Verdier*, ed. Rigoley de Juvigny (Paris, 1772) t.II, 254.

[40] Belleforest is quoted in Sturel, 53.

n'ayant seulement pris de luy que le subject de l'histoire, comme tu pourras aisément descouvrir si tu es curieux de conferer mon stile avec le sien.[41]

[Asking you not to find fault if I did not submit to Bandello's style, for his phrases seemed rough to me, his terms improper, his comments badly linked and his sentences so meager that I found it better to recast them totally new and reform them than to make myself into a superstitious imitator, having not only taken from him the theme of history, as you will easily see if you are curious to compare my style to his.]

The French translators' stylistic choice is thus extremely important, because it is this element that determines the new genre of the "histoire tragique." It is more than likely that this choice is influenced by Aristotle's *Poetics*, a work that enjoyed a renewed reception at the end of the 1540s in Europe and that occasioned the writing of a number of *Artes poeticae*.[42] With regard to the imitation or representation ("mimesis") of actions Aristotle proposes "praxis," "dianoia," "ethos," that is, "actio," "sententia," and "mores" (49b–50a).[43] This is why, for Belleforest, style is tied to morals.

For his translation of the entire collection, Belleforest adopts the title from Boaistuau. By calling it a collection of tragic stories, which no one before him had done,[44] Boaistuau was looking for a new form. As tragedy was enjoying high popularity at the time, its conventions seemed a natural extension of many novellas' plots, such as that of the Albanian knight (I.51), which has a brief exposition, a transition toward a climax with a turning point, a moment of delay, and a tragic conclusion. Boaistuau explains in his "Advertissement au lecteur" that he has entitled this book tragic although there may be found some stories that do not correspond entirely to conventions of tragic plays ("intitulé ce livre de tiltre Tragique, encor que / peut estre / il se puisse trouver quelque histoire, laquelle ne respondra en tout à ce qui est requis en la tragedie").[45] Yet the dramatic structure of the novella clearly corresponds to the dramatic form that was at the time enjoying a renewed interest and that would be perfected, among others, by the English dramatists. Whereas he could have chosen "nouvelle," because the word existed, for example, in the collection of the *Cent nouvelles nouvelles*,[46] he chose "histoires tragiques," which attests to the pedagogical value he saw in the stories as well

------

[41]   Pierre Boaistuau, *Histoires tragiques*, 7 ("Advertissement au lecteur").

[42]   Bernard Weinberg, *A History of Literary Criticism in the Italian Renaissance* (Chicago: University of Chicago Press, 1961), vol. I, p. 349.

[43]   Aristote, *La Poétique. Le texte grec avec une traduction et des notes de lecture* (Paris: Du Seuil, 1980).

[44]   Boaistuau, *Histoires tragiques*, XLVIII.

[45]   Boaistuau, *Histoires tragiques*, 7.

[46]   In the title of the collection as well as in the novella 57, where it is used in the sense of original, bizarre, or out of the ordinary in order to describe the actions of a nobleman (*Cent nouvelles nouvelles* [Geneva: Droz, 1966], 361).

as to the intellectual climate in France. Though "tragique," a consciously chosen polysemous adjective, may imply a depiction of the miseries of man, a tragic ending that could be Christian, classical, or simply dramatic, the important trait of the new genre is tragic style, that is, elevated style. As it has been stated, "le choix de l'épithète 'tragique,' […] ne fonctionnne pas tant par référence à la poétique des genres dramatiques, que dans l'opposition digne/vulgaire."[47]

Translation as Configuration of Meaning

The new title, "histoire tragique," also hints at the freedom of a translator who does not feel obliged to furnish a faithful or word-for-word translation. In this context it is useful to remember what translation might constitute for Belleforest and his contemporaries: above all, it means the text's transfer to and appropriation for a different cultural context. In France, the word "traduire" had been used for the first time by Robert Estienne in 1539 and a year later, Etienne Dolet added "traduction" and "traducteur."[48] It was highly considered by Sébillet who thought that the translator naturally and properly said things that already had been expressed well in another language before and that he therefore should be praised like a poet. Peletier even considered it the best kind of imitation. Yet Du Bellay in his defense of the French language maintained that though translations were important, they cannot sufficiently perfect the French language "pour ce qu'il est impossible de le rendre avecques la mesme grace dont l'autheur en a usé: d'autant que chacune langue a je ne sçay quoy propre seulement à elle, dont si vous efforcez exprimer le naïf en une autre langue, observant la loy de traduyre, qui est n'espacier point hors des limites de l'autheur, vostre diction sera contrainte, froide, et de mauvaise grace"[49] ["for it is impossible to render a work with the same grace the author put into it, inasmuch as each language has an indescribable something that belongs to it alone so that if you strive to express its inborn qualities in another language, abiding by the law of translation, which is never to stray beyond the bounds of the author, your diction will be constrained, cold, and graceless"].[50] As the translated texts are appropriated for "localized needs in the other culture," they end up not being interchangeable with their originals.[51] In this way, Belleforest's translation constitutes a reading of Bandello that results in a configuration of meaning for a different time and context.

---

[47] Pech, 69.

[48] Ballard, 101.

[49] I would like to thank Hassan Melehy for this suggestion. Joachim Du Bellay, *The regrets; with, The "Antiquities of Rome," Three Latin Elegies, and "The Defense and Enrichment of the French Language,"* trans. and ed. Richard Helgerson (Philadelphia: University of Pennsylvania Press, 2006), 335.

[50] Ibid., 334.

[51] Renate Blumenfeld-Kosinski, Luise von Flotow, Daniel Russell, eds, *The Politics of Translation in the Middle Ages and the Renaissance* (Ottawa: University of Ottawa Press, 2001), 34.

Forming Cultural and Linguistic Sensibility through Translation

Scholars have reflected on the possible motivations for Belleforest's numerous changes. One reason might be the intended reader, that is, the French bourgeoisie that prefers reading to conversation[52] and that at the time is developing an ethics of domesticity.[53] This may be why the hero of the "histoire tragique" comes to be a neither entirely vicious nor entirely virtuous member of the lesser nobility.[54] The bourgeois preference might also explain Belleforest's choice of stories, because, according to some critics, the author selects those that expound the tragic in love in order to extirpate excessive passions in his readers, as would a good doctor in his patients.[55] Another reason might be Belleforest's strongly Catholic outlook at the end of the Italian wars.[56] This may be coupled with intensified censorship between the end of the Council of Trent, which will impose an ecclesiastical and cultural discipline (the Index will be published in 1559 and books such as the *Decameron* will be purged), and the beginning of the wars of Religion, which create a climate of instability in France.[57] In a mood of moral severity and intransigence, violation of social order and royal justice must be punished.[58] Yet another reason that has been offered is Marguerite de Navarre's Neo-Platonism that may have influenced Belleforest's view of Fortune and of the life of man who is obliged to strive for salvation but not guaranteed it.[59] Let us remember here that Belleforest would have had access to Marguerite's novellas at a time when these were distributed in manuscript form.[60]

I would add that the immense success of the new genre in France may have been due partly to the sensational topic, that is, accounts of scandals and criminal activities, and partly to the happy choice of a title pandering to a new reading public. By translating and adapting an author as conscious of Italy's misfortunes as Bandello was, Belleforest consciously engages in the creation of a French national literature: the battles of Agnadello in 1509, of Marignano in 1515, of Pavia in

---

[52]   Matteo Bandello, *The French Bandello*, ed. Frank S. Hook (Columbia: University of Missouri Press, 1948), 11.

[53]   Erich Auerbach, *Zur Technik der Frührenaissancenovelle in Italien und Frankreich* (Heidelberg: Winter, 1921), 11.

[54]   Pech, 26.

[55]   Sturel, 54 and Fiorato, "Le 'Bandel' ou la moralisation," 114.

[56]   Sturel, 50.

[57]   Fiorato, "Le 'Bandel' ou la moralisation," 109–10 and 120–21.

[58]   Pech, 15.

[59]   Walter Pabst, *Novellentheorie und Novellendichtung* (Hamburg: Cram, de Gruyter, 1953), 198–203 gives quotes and establishes textual connections that could be elaborated. See also Kelver Hartley, *Bandello and the Heptameron* (Melbourne University Press, 1960) and Pierre Jourda, *Marguerite d'Angoûleme* (Paris: Champion, 1930, vol. II), 708.

[60]   Hervé Campangne provides a recent discussion of this connection in "Marguerite de Navarre and the Invention of the *Histoire Tragique*" in *Approaches to Teaching Marguerite de Navarre's* Heptameron, ed. Colette Winn (New York: The Modern Language Association of America, 2007), 91–6.

1525, and the sack of Rome in 1527 are milestones of defeat; France should and can do better. According to Belleforest, this would be a matter of rectitude, of passions tamed, and of virtue followed. Thus, the choices made by him in his adaptation of Bandello's tale seem to be as much politically and morally motivated as provoked by his pride in creative translation. Translating, and therefore reading, Bandello for Belleforest's own time and context results in an appeal to the reading self's sense of order. The latter, an internal reference, can and should be shared so as to be assimilated by Belleforest's readers into an external reference, into an external physical configuration of the world, that is, empirical authority.[61]

Theatrical Distance: The Morality of Fenton's *Tragical Discourses*

In spite of its title, "Certain Tragical Discourses of Bandello translated into English by Geffraie Fenton" is not based on the Italian original, but entirely on the Belleforest translation.[62] The French version thus may be regarded as a Renaissance go-between.[63] By acknowledging to force "certeyne Tragicall Discourses oute of theyr Frenche tearmes into our Englishe phrase,"[64] Fenton becomes independent of Bandello's authority, free to add or to adapt, and he is aware of the mass and referential power that Belleforest's text has acquired. In the fourth story of the *Tragical Discourses*, the translator makes Regina into Helene of Grece (166), slightly Italianizes some men's names to Pierro Barzo or Don Spado (175), keeps the timeframe as that of the present ("in our tyme," 165), and dedicates his adaptation to readers looking for moral edification by changing Bandello's plot about a specific Albanian to a general story about fault in men.

Yet Fenton overemphasizes the exotic context of the tale, making Morea in Greece into a city of the "Mores," an obvious allusion to North African Moors,[65] and he traces Bayazid's genealogy to Sultan Soliman who is the current cruel ruler of the Ottoman Empire. Both details together serve to highlight a fictitious background of religious difference. Likewise, Fenton underlines the exotic nature of Spado's behavior in the description of a "barbarian" sacrifice that is reminiscent of widow burning in India (184–5). This behavior is illustrated by Spado's bizarre

---

[61] Valdés, 20–21.

[62] Fenton was born in Nottinghamshire in 1539 and died in Dublin in 1608.

[63] Andreas Höfele, Werner von Koppenfels, eds., *Renaissance Go-Betweens* (Berlin, New York: de Gruyter, 2005), 1–14.

[64] *Certain Tragical Discourses of Bandello translated into English by Geffraie Fenton.* 2 vols (New York: AMS Press, 1967), vol. I, XXXII.

[65] See also Constance C. Relihan, "'Dissordinate Desire' and the Construction of Geographic Otherness in the Early Modern Novella," *Prose Fiction and Early Modern Sexualities in England, 1570–1640*, ed. Constance C. Relihan and Goran V. Stanivukovic (New York: Palgrave Macmillan, 2004), 51.

Cross-Cultural Adaptation and the Novella

reactions (187) and his fiendish laugh (189).[66] The translator adopts and even elaborates on the digression concerning the ape's love toward her offspring, which had been added by Belleforest:

> But as in every thing excesse is hurtful, bringinge with it a doble discomoditie–I meane both a sourfet to the stomake by the pleasure we delite in, and a jelouse loathing of the thing we chiefly love and hold most dere–so the extreme and superfluitye of hoate love of this fonde husbande towards his wife, began, within the very month of the mariage, to converte itselfe into a contrary disposition not much unlike the loving rage of the she ape towards her yonge ones; who as the poetes do affirme, doth use to chuse among her whelpes one whom she loves best, and keping it alwaies in her armes doth cherish and loll it in such rude sorte that, or she is ware, she treketh the boanes and smothereth it to death killing by this meanes with overmuch love the thing which yet wold live if it were not for th'excesse of her affecticn. (176)[67]

Fenton clearly emphasizes his lack of sympathy for the protagonist: "Whereof I have here presented you a litle proofe in the picture and person of this selly Albanoyse," but also qualifies Regina as "selly," because she does not rise to her self-defense when her patience is tried (179). He may have had in mind Chaucer's high expectations of women in the epilogue to the Griselda story.

Like Belleforest, the English translator emphasizes the play-like structure of his text that might be effective on stage. While shortening the couple's death (189), he several times emphasizes the role of Fortune ("Fortune beareth the greates swaighe ..." 166).[68] He gives ample information about the Albanian protagonist's psychological motivations[69] and he volunteers numerous narrator's comments, such as "I appeale to th'opinions of those who earst have changed their miserable

---

[66] René Pruvost speaks of a "deepening of the sombre colours of the Italian original" (*Matteo Bandello and Elizabethan Fiction* [Paris: Champion, 1937], 116).

[67] Fenton's digressions have been commented (Pruvost, 122; *The French Bandello*, 13–17).

[68] "And Fortune, who is alwayes jelouse of the ease of man, and not content to let us lyve longe in quiet ..." (168); "geving Fortune also her peculiar thankes, that had kepte this good torne in store for him, ..." (176).

[69] "[B]eing unhappelye espied [...] of an Albanoys captaine" (169); "Neyther had he the face eftesones to attempte her of hymselfe, and muche lesse to desyste from the purseute of hys desyere" (170); "... the one to his lodging with a thousand hammors in his heade till he sawe the effecte of his dryfte" (172); "But nowe this Albanoys enjoyeng thus the frutes of his desier, colde not so wel brydel his present pleasure, nor conceile the singuler contentment he conceived by the encounter of his new mystres, but, in publike show, began to prate of his present felicitye" (175); "But as in every thing excesse is hurtful, bringinge with it a doble discomoditie [...] so the extreme and superfluitye of hoate love of this fonde husbande towards his wife, began, within the very month of the mariage, to converte itselfe into a contrary disposition" (176); "Which was one of the greatest faltes in this valyante Albanoyse" (178).

condicion, or state of adversytie, with the benefyt and goodnes of the lyke fortune" (167); "I leave it to the judgement of that smal number of happy men" (167); "Albeit, afore I procede to the ceremonies of her unfortunat mariage, I thoughte good to tel unto you in this place th'oppynion of mine author …" (175); "But nowe to our pourpose" (175); "But nowe to the place of our historie" (181). As in Bandello, there are two turning points introduced by "But nowe …" (175, 181), yet Fenton inserts numerous direct discourses (170–74, 182, 184) that differ from Belleforest's in length and content, and he lists the stations of the plot as well as the moral gist of the story as notes in the margins.[70] Dialogue and stage directions are added to intensify the theatricality of the story and all these devices serve to elicit a particular reader response.

Above all, the English translator forecasts the catastrophe in the initial description of the lady's virtuous life, the captain's strange and bizarre personality,[71] and in the sister's answer to her brother's request that she remarry, which contains forebodings of her end.[72] In his depiction of the Albanian's tragic and exotic traits[73] and of his madness, Fenton goes so far as to make Spado's jealousy typical of the Italian: "Wherin he suffered himselfe to be so much subject and overcome with the rage of this follie, that, according to the jelowse humor of *th'Ytalian*, he thoughte every man that loked in her face, wente aboute to grafte hornes in his forehed" (176).[74] This removes his English adaptation even further from the Italian original. At the same time, it testifies to the translator's Protestantism while tying in with a certain anti-Italianism or Italophobia of the time.[75] The latter is proposed in John Lyly's *Euphues* from 1578 or in Roger Ascham's *Scholemaster* from 1570 that warns against Italianate Englishmen.[76]

---

[70] For example: "Death hath no power but over our bodye" (191).

[71] "[N]ever beinge seene abrode but of holye and great festivall dayes, when she wente in devoute maner to the churche to here the divine service of God; beinge unhappelye espied […] of an Albanoys captaine" (169).

[72] "[M]y hart, devininge diverslye of the successe of this mariage, threatneth a further mischiefe to fall upon me …" (173); "Wherwith he so muche prevailed over his obedyent syster, that she, beinge unhappely overcom with his vehement importunyties, condissended very willinly to his unfortunat request" (174).

[73] "[D]oating without discrecion uppon the desyer of his newe lady, and rather drowned beastely in the superfluitie of her love" (176); "raging the more (as it seamed) by the incredible constancye he noted in this mirror of modestie, obedience, wisedome, and chastetie" (180).

[74] Emphasis mine.

[75] For examples, see Robin Kirkpatrick, *English and Italian Literature from Dante to Shakespeare* (London and New York: Longman, 1995), 224–53.

[76] See in this context also Pruvost, Charlotte Pressler, "Intertextual Transformations: The Novella as Mediator Between Italian and English Renaissance Drama," in *Shakespeare and Intertextuality. The Transition of Cultures Between Italy and England in the Early Modern Period*, ed. Michele Marrapodi (Roma: Bulzoni, 2000), 135–48, and Pamela Brown, "*Othello* and Italophobia," *Shakespeare and Intertextuality*, 179–92.

Forming English Language and Morals

Fenton's style has been described as mannerist, and euphuist. According to one critic, Belleforest's already elaborate prose becomes even more so in English; therefore Fenton's pleonasms, balanced periods, and alliterations make him a "Euphuist before Euphues." The descriptions and actions that Fenton adds turn many passages not necessarily into more lifelike, but rather into more elaborate ones.[77] A good example of this style is found at the end of the novella:

> The worthie ende of this wicked wretche argueth the juste rewarde of the evill disposed and suche as are unhappelie dropped out of the favor of God, the ordenarye successe of those enterprises that are begon without the consente of wisedome or raison, but chiefly th'effectes and fortune of such as (blinded with the vaile of their owne wil and dymned with the myste of follye) do reapose so muche for theim selves in the opinion of their owne witte, that, detestinge good councell and advise of the wise, doo credit onlye the conceite of their owne fancie, whiche (as a blinde guide) doth leade them into infynit miseries and laborinth of endles annoye, where there is no dispense of their follie, but losse of libertie, perpetual infamie, and sometime punishemente by untimely deathe. (190)

In this *sententia* or universalizing proposition of consensus morality, with its alliterations and parallelisms, Fenton conveys his moral concerning man in general, tragically blinded by folly, not the Albanian knight any longer who suffered from melancholy and jealousy.[78] Regina's story thus becomes a timeless example, one that should not be followed by contemporary English women, but for which alternatives need to be found. Since both masculine authority and feminine submission are rejected by the author, he may be influenced by Protestant ethics.[79]

Fidelity to the text evidently is not Fenton's concern. He therefore is not a dictionary-conscious translator in the way of Mary Sidney, for example, the translator of Duplessis-Mornay's *Discourse of Life and Death*[80] and the dedicatee of the *Tragic Discourses* to whom he explains: "Whyche, also, moved me to speciall discrecion in coollynge oute suche examples as beste aggreed wyth the

---

[77] *Certain Tragical Discourses*, liv, lv. Euphuism, introduced in John Lyly's *Euphues: The Anatomy of Wit* (1578), is a style marked by excessive use of antithesis in connection with alliteration and of allusions to historical and mythological personages and natural history. *The Oxford Companion to English Literature*, ed. Sir Paul Harvey (Oxford: Clarendon Press, 1975).

[78] For a definition of "sententia" or "adage," see Pressler, "Intertextual Transformations," 144 and Rosalie Colie, *The Resources of Kind. Genre-Theory in the Renaissance* (Berkeley: University of California Press, 1973), 33–6.

[79] The new emphasis placed on mutual love and spirituality by the Church of England in the wake of the Reformation. For information about the role of wives in Protestant England, see Marilyn Yalom, *A History of the Wife* (New York: Harper Collins, 2001), 97–145.

[80] I would like to thank Roger Kuin for this suggestion.

138 *French Connections in the English Renaissance / Heitsch*

condicion of the tyme, and also were of most freshe and familyar memorye; to the ende that, wyth the delyte in readynge my dedication, I maye also leave, to all degrees, an appetitt and honeste dsyeere to honor vertue and holde vice in due detestation" (8). Don Spado, who is portrayed as a demonic infidel by Fenton, poses a clearly recognizable social and psychological threat. Moreover, like his colleagues John Florio with Montaigne's *Essais* and Joshua Sylvester with Du Bartas's *Sepmaine*, the translator explores the linguistic potential of the English language and educates the English reader in the values of a new age.

Exemplary Tragic Tales by Vicente de Millis

Unlike Fenton's English adaptation that is based on the French version of Bandello's novella about the Albanian knight, the Spanish text is quite close to the French "histoire tragique." It is adapted, as indicated on the title page, from Boaistuau's and Belleforest's version and the Spanish translator, like Fenton in his dedication to Mary Sidney, is concerned with not offending in what he terms *Historias trágicas ejemplares*.[81] The collection was approved by the Spanish royal council in 1584, a year before the outbreak of the Anglo-Spanish war, but only after censorship as it appears from the *Aprobación*: "muchos y muy buenos ejemplos y moralidad, fuera de algunas maneras de hablar algo desenvueltas, que en la lengua francesa (donde está más extendido) deben permitirse y en la nuestra no suenan bien, y así las he testado y enmendado otras"[82] ("many and very good examples and moralities, except some manners of speaking a bit indecorous that in the French language [where this is more widespread] can be permitted and that in ours don't sound good, and therefore I eliminated them and emended others"). Vicente de Millis alludes to having been mindful of censors by affirming that Bandello collected his stories from trustworthy people and authentic writings and that he did not describe anything he had not seen ("no dice cosa que no la haya visto").[83] The translation was published in 1589, a year after the defeat of the Spanish Armada,

---

[81] Juan de Millis Godínez published 14 of Bandello's novellas in Spanish (see Marcelino Menendez y Pelayo, *Orígenes de la novella* [Madrid: Consejo Superior de Investigaciones Cientificas, 1943], vol. 3, 34–7). The translator of this Spanish version is his father Vicente, as indicated in the letter to the royal council, and the typographical mark and frame of the title page stem from Guillermo de Millis, Vicente's father and Juan's grandfather. For information about the Millis family, see Cristóbal Pérez Paster, *La imprenta en Medina del campo* (Madrid: Sucesores de Rivadeneyra, 1895), 484, 488–9. There also is a Spanish edition of the *Historias tragicas exemplares* published in Valladolid in 1603 by Lorenzo de Ayala that is preserved in the National Library in Madrid.

[82] Matteo Bandello, *Historias trágicas* (Madrid: Atlas, 1943), 6. Matteo Bandello, *Historias trágicas exemplares, sacadas de las obras del Bandello Verones* (Salamanca: Pedro Lasso, a costa de Juan Millis Godinez, 1589), 2v.

[83] *Historias trágicas*, 7. *Historias trágicas exemplares*, 5r.

during a climate of renewed national pride in Spain, when Drake's invasion with the English Armada had failed and the Spanish navy was being rebuilt.

A comparison of the French and Spanish texts clearly shows their close affinities. These affinities only cease when the translator decides to shorten occasional lengthy descriptions: "añadiendo o quitando cosas superfluas, y que en el español no son tan honestas como debieran, atento que la francesa tiene algunas solturas que acá no suenan bien"[84] ("adding or removing things that are not as honest as they should be in Spanish, given that the French language has some turns that here do not sound good"). At the same time, and contrary to Fenton's English version, Millis produces a much more formal text, for the Spanish translator divides his tenth novella on the Albanian, which Belleforest had extended before him, into two chapters so that the reader, as he puts it, does not get fatigued ("porque la lectura larga non canse").[85] The first chapter introduces the protagonists and gives an account of the Albanian knight's love that results in his marriage to Regina due to her brother's intervention. The second chapter retells the cruel murder of the unhappy wife. In this way, the original novelistic event is moved off-center and is not necessarily predictable any longer, because the intricacy of intrigue diverts the reader from the astonishing event. In keeping with the thus created tension, Millis does not turn the stories into tragical discourses with moral commentary like Fenton. Instead, he keeps *Historias trágicas* close to his French model and adds "exemplary" to the title of his collection. Although the term "novela" had arrived in Spain during the first half of the sixteenth century through a series of translations of Boccaccio's "novelle,"[86] Millis avoids it. The creation of "novelas ejemplares" will later be attributed to Cervantes. Indeed, the latter will insist on his originality in the prologue to his *Novelas exemplares* (1613).

Conclusion

Having followed the story of the Albanian knight from its Italian version to its French, English, and Spanish adaptations, we can draw a series of conclusions from this multi-sited gathering. Bandello's novellas have a simple, laconically narrated plot, and are restricted to one single, unheard-of event that often mirrors the protagonists' entire life in one hour of crisis. The stories do not provide an all embracing view of the world; instead, a detail of one particular life reflects life in general with its interaction of character and destiny. In the novella I.51, the Italian author combines a genre and an event (the news item) so as to shift the reputation of jealousy from Italians to an exotic context, thus improving Italian reputation and status in Europe. The model for such a national project may be Della Casa's *Galateo*.[87]

---

[84] Ibid.

[85] Ibid.

[86] Mariano Baquero Goyanes, *Qué es la novela. Qué es el cuento* (Murcia: Universidad de Murcia, 1988), 101.

[87] I would like to thank Konrad Eisenbichler for this suggestion.

Bandello's novella then migrates to France with Belleforest, to Spain with Millis, and to England with Fenton in a double transformation of genre and scope. While the Italian original I.51 contains approximately 2,250 words, Fenton's discourse IV has roughly 10,870 words.[88] In all extended versions the author appears as narrator and mediator in order to present a moralizing adaptation of the original. On the one hand, this may be regarded as an expression of national character, both in the sense of Greenblatt's self-fashioned individual and Anderson's imagined community.[89] On the other hand, the adaptations have a pedagogical purpose such as it is described by Norbert Elias, because the development of a super-ego, that is, moral distance enabled by theatricality, edification, and judgment, can be seen as part of the process of civilization.[90] At the same time, all translations offer an appeal to the moral self as a means to social and linguistic conditioning.

All three translators bring out the exotic element in their cross-cultural adaptations: the unhappy ending implicitly condemns acts of transgression such as Regina's marriage to a foreigner whose non-Christian traits they underline, although this is not played up in Bandello's version. Belleforest, Millis, and Fenton stress the element of story, "fabula," or confabulation in their adaptations, whereas novellas, for Bandello, are "vere istorie," emphasize verisimilitude, not necessarily in order to avoid censorship, but because the gist of these stories truly may be based on historic occurrences. Accordingly, we see a transformation from the historical to the exotic, from a news item describing the change in the fortunes of specific protagonists to a story or narration offering a universal morality. Fenton thus shifts furthest away from the original novella's bizarre surprise, its inexplicable and original elements, toward the calculable and the explicable. Rather than reading this as a move from fact to fiction or from the real to the ideal, I would see it as an example of localized world-making.[91]

The new genre may be called tragic by the French, Spanish, and English translators in order to avoid a combination of low laughter and refined tears. Removing the confusion of register (within one novella) and ensuring instead that the reader knows what to expect facilitates a reading free of (moral) ambiguities,

---

[88]   Clements and Gibaldi, 219.

[89]   Stephen Greenblatt, *Renaissance Self-Fashioning. From More to Shakespeare* (Chicago, London: Chicago University Press, 1980), 4; Benedict Anderson, *Imagined Communities. Reflections on the Origin and Spread of Nationalism* (London, New York: Verso, 2003 [1983]), 37–46.

[90]   Norbert Elias, *The Civilizing Process: Sociogenetic and Psychogenetic Investigations* (1939), trans. Edmund Jephcott (Oxford and Cambridge, MA: Blackwell, 2000).

[91]   William Nelson, *Fact or Fiction. The Dilemma of the Renaissance Storyteller* (Cambridge, MA: Harvard University Press, 1973); Yvonne Rodax, *The Real and the Ideal in the Novella of Italy, France and England* (Chapel Hill: University of North Carolina Press, 1968). For the construction of different versions of the world through composition and decomposition, weighting, ordering, deletion and supplementation, deformation, and degrees of truth, see Nelson Goodman, *Ways of Worldmaking* (Hassocks, Sussex: Harvester Press, 1978), 4–19 as well as Valdés, *World-Making*.

which at the same time allows for a teleological plot development. Abandoning the mixture of genres, which in its Bandellian form combines tragic, comic, and exotic elements, is regarded as an improvement by all the translators, French, Spanish, and English. As a result, the novella of the Albanian knight experiences an elevation in style and genre by rising through the ranks of its later adaptations. In this way, Belleforest, Millis, and Fenton each produce what may be called "assimilative translations."[92] Each translator engages in a cross-national competition that involves showing off the national language to advantage, as Peletier du Mans indicates in the first quote at the beginning of this essay. The turning of books thus becomes, in John Floric's words, the symbolical overturning of other nations in favor of one's own.

---

[92] "A term used by foreignist translation theorists to describe what they consider the worst kind of translation, translation that assimilates the foreign text to target-cultural and target-linguistic values" (Douglas Robinson, *Translation and Empire* [Manchester, UK and Northampton, MA: St. Jerome Publishing, 1997], 114).

Chapter 7
Life, Death, and the Daughter of Time: Philip and Mary Sidney's Translations of Duplessis-Mornay

Roger Kuin

It was John Florio who said that all translations are defective and thus "reputed femalls."[1] Whether, as sometimes alleged, this makes translation suitable for women, or the translator a harmless drudge, is moot; perhaps it would be better to think of him as a Lear: a father of daughters as perverse as they are unpredictable. He is also, say the Italians, a traitor: "traduttore traditore," he betrays both the original text and the expectations of his linguistically challenged readership. Yet, toiling to till this thorny soil, he is also a lover: every translation begins with an *inamoramento*, a falling-in-love with a text, with all that that entails of the irresistible urge to communicate a beauty and a truth, to persuade a whole world into sharing one's wonderment. Each translation, then, finds its *energia* between the poles of love and betrayal, between treason and Trewnesse. To the efficient and the vulgar, of course, it is simply to be consumed for the matter, cited or dismissed as a foreign *auctoritas*; but for the discerning, to tread between the poles, to experience and to investigate the energy, is a scrupulous and intimate delight.

The following brief sketch of such an examination concerns two Sidneian translations, their *inamoramento*, their making, and their eventual escape into print and posterity. Philip and Mary Sidney's versions of French texts by their friend Philippe de Mornay du Plessis (usually known as Duplessis-Mornay)[2] constitute an unusually controlled environment, and a look at them may lead us to an understanding of their value to readers then and now.

Chronologically, Philip's Mornay translation came first, and its current of *energia* is curiously conflicted. Mornay, I have argued elsewhere,[3] was not only Philip Sidney's friend but his model of a statesman; and both A.C. Hamilton and

---

[1] *The essayes or morall, politicke and millitarie discourses of Lo: Michaell de Montaigne ... now done into English by ... Iohn Florio* (London: Edward Blount, 1603), sig. A2.

[2] His full name is Philippe de Mornay, sieur du Plessis-Marly: Mornay is the family name, du Plessis-Marly the *nom de terre*. But the hybrid form Duplessis-Mornay was used as early as the seventeenth century.

[3] Roger Kuin, "Sir Philip Sidney's Model of the Statesman," *Reformation*, vol. 4 (1999), 93–117.

144   *French Connections in the English Renaissance / Kuin*

Anne Lake Prescott have suggested that if not he, then someone very like him may have been the true adversary-addressee of the *Defence of Poesy*.[4] Be that as it may, one of Sidney's four last literary labors was the translation of Mornay's *Vérité de la religion chrestienne*. Of this *inamoramento* we may usefully look at the Why, the Who, and the How.

The two men did not often have occasion to meet. Their principal time together was in the years 1577–1578, when Mornay with his family spent 18 months in London,[5] and which, in retrospect, represented Sidney's finest hour as a courtier. His correspondence shows that he was very much in favor at this time, having fulfilled his embassy to the new Emperor Rudolph II with both glamour and efficiency. Mornay, five years older than his friend, had been sent to solicit funds from the queen for the French Huguenots, and remained as Henri de Navarre's representative. His wife, of whom more presently, later recalled this English intermezzo as a halcyon time. She gave birth to a daughter, who was christened Elisabeth in the French church in Threadneedle Street on June 1 of 1578, and whose godfather was Philip Sidney.

When the Mornays went back to Antwerp in 1579, Philippe was plunged at once into the complex and dangerous affairs of the Netherlands; but with his usual frenetic and indomitable energy he also began work on what was to become the most influential of his books. This major work, which in spite of business and a serious illness he finished in the record time of nine months, he dedicated to Henri de Navarre:

> In this wretched time Sir, wherein ungodlinesse [the French calls it *impiété*] (which was woont but to whisper men in the eare, and to mumble between the teeth) hath bin so bold as to step into the pulpit, and to belk out blasphemies against Gospel: I take upon me ... to convince hir, even by hir own principles and peculiar records, that if I cannot make hir to come backe againe to a better mind, I may at leastwise yet make her hold hir peace for shame, and keepe close hir venim in hir hart.[6]

---

[4]   A.C. Hamilton, *The Structure of Allegory in the Faerie Queene* (Oxford: Clarendon Press, 1961), 124–7, 223–4; Anne Lake Prescott, *French Poets and the English Renaissance* (New Haven and London: Yale University Press, 1978), 178–9. Both are thinking in the first instance of Du Bartas. Huguenots did not write "poesy" in Sidney's sense of fiction.

[5]   The best modern study of Mornay's life and work is Hugues Daussy, *Les Huguenots et le roi: le combat politique de Philippe Duplessis-Mornay (1572–1600)* (Geneva: Droz, 2002); but the earlier biography by Raoul Patry (*Philippe Du Plessis-Mornay: un Huguenot homme d'état 1549–1623*; Paris: Fischbacher, 1933) is still valuable, as is the first biography by Mornay's secretary David de Licques, *Histoire de la vie de Messire Philippes de Mornay, seigneur du Plessis Marly &c* (Leiden: Elsevier, 1647).

[6]   *A vvoorke concerning the trewnesse of the Christian religion, written in French: against atheists, Epicures, Paynims, Iewes, Mahumetists, and other infidels. By Philip of Mornay Lord of Plessie Marlie. Begunne to be translated into English by Sir Philip Sidney Knight, and at his request finished by Arthur Golding* (London: Thomas Cadman, 1587), sig. **

He called it *De la vérité de la religion chrestienne*, and the subtitle shows it to be (as the English version puts it) "written ... against Atheists, Epicures, Paynims, Jewes, Mahumetists, and other Infidels." As his secretary and first biographer David de Licques shows, he wrote it "to oppose the Atheism which not only crept but entered barefaced almost everywhere."[7] When it was done, in 1580, and printed by Christophe Plantin, he showed it to his mentor and spiritual father Hubert Languet, then living a few streets away and in poor health. The old bachelor said he had never thought that the subject could be treated in such a sound and solid manner, and urged him to translate it into Latin, doubtless to make it internationally available. Mornay at once obeyed, and even though he was constantly on the move during this time, completed the Latin version less than two years later. Languet had died during this time, cared for by Madame de Mornay, and had asked her to have her husband put a memorial to their friendship in his next published work. And so it was that when Plantin's son-in-law Raphelengius printed the *De veritate religionis christianæ* in 1583, it appeared with a touching and dignified tribute to the man she said they looked upon as a father. (It was to become something of a best seller: the great Hugo Grotius copied its title in 1618 with acknowledgement; Cardinal Vincenzo Gotti did so, complete with subtitle—*Contra Atheos, Polytheos, Idololatras, Mahometanos, & Judaeos*—but without acknowledgement, in 1737; and a Kantian Catholic, Patriz Zimmer, did so one more time, in 1789.)[8]

Philip Sidney, meanwhile, had turned author in a different kind. In 1578 he had composed *The Lady of May*, a courtly entertainment for the queen's visit to Wanstead; the following year he had been persuaded by his uncle Leicester and his future father-in-law Walsingham to write an open letter to Her Majesty urging her not to marry Anjou. Exactly how this was received is not certain; but around this time he also fell into a bitter quarrel with the odious but very grand Edward de Vere, seventeenth Earl of Oxford, and when it became clear that the Earl was plotting his murder, he left the Court to spend a year with his sister Mary at Wilton House in Somerset. Here, in the rains and ruins of a wet and windy winter, for someone who disliked hunting there was little to do but write. Moreover, Mary shared and perhaps even exceeded his taste for letters: Daniel Rogers, in a New Year's tribute to Philip, suggested that it was she who would make him a poet.[9] At Wilton, then, he seems to have written the *Defence of Poesy* and the first version of the *Arcadia*, and possibly begun also his quirky revitalization of the Petrarchan "songs and sonnets" form with what was to become *Astrophil and Stella*.

---

[7] De Licques, p. 55.

[8] Hugo Grotius, *De veritate religionis christianæ* (Leiden: Elzevier, 1632), subsequently translated by Edward Pocock into English, Arabic, Persian, and Chinese; Vincenzo Gotti, *Veritas Religionis Christianae et librorum quibus innititur contra Atheos, Polytheos, Idolatros, Mahometanos et Judaeos demonstrata*, 7 vols (Rome: Rocco Bernabò, 1735–1740); Patricius Benedictus Zimmer, *Veritas christianae religionis, seu Theologiae christianae dogmaticae sectio I* (Augsburg: Rieger, 1789–1790).

[9] Roger Kuin and Anne Lake Prescott, "Versifying Connections: Daniel Rogers and the Sidneys," *Sidney Journal* vol. 18, no. 2 (Winter 2000), 27–8.

When, and why, did he turn to the *Vérité*? The first, French, printed version was not available till the summer of 1581; by 1583 he was joint Master of the Ordnance, and by the autumn of 1585 he left for the Netherlands. The year 1581–1582 was the low point of Sidney's life: his career as a courtier was not advancing, yet no alternative seemed to be in the offing.[10] Hubert Languet, who more than anyone had believed in his high calling and urged him to virtue and godliness, died just before Philip's 27th birthday. It seems not unlikely that all these influences combined at this time to turn his mind toward a kind of writing even more serious than he had been practicing hitherto. In the next two or three years, we know, the literary work he undertook consisted of revision and translation: revision of the *Arcadia*, his "toyfull book," into something more responsible and more concerned with governance; a complex effort to transform the Psalms into what I suspect were lute songs; and translation of two works from the French: the Huguenot Guillaume de Salluste du Bartas's long poem on the first Week of God's Creation, *La Sepmaine*, and Mornay's *Vérité*.

The fact that the result is not more celebrated is due to a still-unresolved problem of authorship, or rather of translatorship. The title page reads: *A Woorke concerning the trewnesse of the Christian Religion ... Begunne to be translated into English by Sir Philip Sidney Knight, and at his request finished by Arthur Golding. Imprinted at London for Thomas Cadman, 1587.* A certain amount of ink has been spent in attempts to determine the exact meaning of this. Even the simplest theory— that Cadman and Golding are telling the truth—involves difficulties, since neither they nor anyone else have thought to tell us how much of the *Vérité*'s translation Sidney had completed before he was himself translated to a higher calling. And the problem is complicated by what we might call the advent of Attitude. In 1973, for example, Jan van Dorsten and Katherine Duncan-Jones prudently and cautiously declined to incorporate any of the *Trewnesse* in Sidney's *Miscellaneous Prose*, as his contribution could not reliably be separated from Golding's.[11] By 1991, Duncan-Jones puts this differently. Quoting Fulke Greville's letter to Walsingham about the publication of the *Arcadia*, she boldly states:

> The 'mercenary book' was Arthur Golding's translation of *De la vérité*, entered in the Stationers' Register within days of the news of Sidney's death, and published early in 1587, which he claimed was completed at Sidney's request. However, it does not appear to retain any of Sidney's wording, being written with an avoidance of Latinisms which is not at all like Sidney, and Golding's close association with the Earl of Oxford (he was his uncle by marriage and had been his tutor) makes it probable that the project was, as Greville said, 'mercenary'.[12]

---

[10]   Cf. his letters to Burghley and Hatton in October and November 1581.

[11]   Katherine Duncan-Jones and Jan van Dorsten, eds., *Miscellaneous Prose of Sir Philip Sidney* (Oxford: Clarendon Press, 1973), v.

[12]   Katherine Duncan-Jones, *Sir Philip Sidney: Courtier Poet* (New Haven and London: Yale University Press, 1991), 251–2. The first to suggest that none of the surviving *Trewnesse* might be by Sidney, however, was D.P. Walker, in "Ways of Dealing with

Life, Death, and the Daughter of Time

The theory behind this new interpretation is that either Golding revised the translation so completely as to leave nothing of Sidney's, or that Sidney wrote another, complete translation since lost. As this is now in danger of becoming, by default, the reigning orthodoxy it is worth a brief refutation. In the first place, Duncan-Jones ignores the fact that both Ronald Rebholz and Joan Rees in their studies of Greville consider, to my mind rightly, that Greville is here defending Ponsonby and that the "mercenary book" is the proposed *Arcadia* edition he wants stopped.[13] The case is excellently summed up by F.J. Sypher in the introduction to the *Trewnesse*'s 1976 facsimile edition.[14]

Two arguments need particular attention. The whole position of Arthur Golding, first, has generally received far too little, and too cursory, attention.[15] It is true that his half-sister Margery married John de Vere, the amorous and slightly dim-witted sixteenth Earl of Oxford (1516–62). What is rarely mentioned is that this *mésalliance*—the Goldings were upwardly mobile landed gentry, scarcely a match for one of the oldest houses in England—followed a ruthless blackmail operation by Protector Somerset and his client, Margery's eldest brother Thomas Golding, to strip the collateral heirs of the Earl's possessions. Somerset fell; but Golding moved confidently ahead and achieved his sister's advantageous marriage.

Although Arthur—Margery's younger half-brother, the scholar of the family— seems to have been on good terms with Edward de Vere during the seventeenth Earl's childhood, there is no evidence that he was ever the boy's tutor. And if we want to gauge his political allegiance and alliances, the pattern and the tone of his dedications is more significant. As early as 1571, his dedication to the 21-year-old Oxford of Calvin's *Commentaries on the Psalms* shows a problematic relation to the young man: it uses, says Golding's biographer, "very vigorous language ... towards one of the greatest and wealthiest nobles of England."[16] And this— 16 years before the *Trewnesse*—was the last time he would choose Oxford, now

---

Atheists: A Background to Pamela's Refutation of Cecropia," *Bibliothèque d'Humanisme et Renaissance* vol. 17 (1955), 252–77.

[13] Ronald A. Rebholz, *The Life of Fulke Greville, First Lord Brooke* (Oxford: Clarendon Press, 1971), 76–7; Joan Rees, *Fulke Greville, Lord Brooke, 1554–1628: A Critical Biography* (Berkeley: University of California Press, 1971), 46–7, and *Sir Philip Sidney and Arcadia* (Rutherford, NJ: Fairleigh Dickinson University Press, 1991), 121–2.

[14] F.J. Sypher, ed., *A Woorke* etc., facsimile edition (Delmar, NY: Scholars' Facsimiles & Reprints, 1976), ix–xv.

[15] Apart from Sypher, few authors deal with Golding's translations other than the Ovid. For the present purpose, the most useful (apart from Louis Golding's biography) is perhaps James Wortham's "Arthur Golding and the Translation of Prose" *HLQ* XII (1949), 339–67. The biographical facts here mentioned are taken from Louis Golding, *An Elizabethan Puritan: Arthur Golding the Translator of Ovid's Metamorphoses and also of John Calvin's Sermons* (New York: R.R. Smith, 1937).

[16] Golding p. 66. The whole "Epistle Dedicatorie" is written in this urgent admonitory tone: *The Psalmes of David and others, with M. Iohn Calvin's Commentaries* (London: Thomas East and Henry Middleton for Lucas Harison, and George Byshop, 1571), sig. *ii–v^{vo}.

148   *French Connections in the English Renaissance / Kuin*

rapidly going to the bad, as a patron. "It seems clear in fact that as time went on he disapproved of his nephew's wild and spendthrift life, at least he dedicated no more books to him nor is there any record of friendly association" (131). While he continued to dedicate works to his first patron Burghley, most of his dedications now were to what Blair Worden calls the "forward Protestants" or their sympathizers: Hatton, Mildmay, Lord Cobham, the Earls of Huntingdon and Essex, and the Earl of Leicester—his first dedication to whom had been of Ovid's *Metamorphoses* as early as 1565. He seems, indeed, to have distanced himself entirely from Oxford from the mid-1570s on.

A few other points about Golding are worth remembering. Among the translations that must have helped bring him to Sidney's notice were those of the Calvin Psalm Commentaries, of Calvin's *Sermons on Job* (1574), and of Beza's *Tragedie of Adam's Sacrifice* (1577). He had also Englished Caesar's *Commentaries* (1565),[17] a version that, says his biographer, "was warmly received, particularly by students of history and military affairs [which we know Sidney, like Mornay, to have been] and later by the gentlemen volunteers who learned the art of war while fighting in the Netherlands against Spain." This last case presents interesting similarities and contrasts with that of the *Vérité*. The work had been begun by John Brende, the translator of Quintus Curtius, but had been interrupted by Brende's death when only five and a half books had been completed. Cecil suggested Golding finish it; but eventually, after much study and soul searching, the latter yielded to those who had urged him instead to do a whole new translation himself. His dedicatory letter to William Cecil is worth quoting for the insight it gives us into the mind of a sixteenth-century translator in general and of the scrupulous Arthur Golding in particular: it is not without relevance to the Sidney-Mornay *Vérité*.

> This I most humbly desier your honor, that you will take my paines & trauell in that behalfe in good worth. for I haue not done it, because I thought my selfe of more skill and experience than maister Brend (which I confesse my yeeres giue me not) neither because I would in defacing his glory, (which were a point of lewdnesse) goe about (as the Latin prouerb saith) to pricke out the Crowes eyes. But I haue done it, partly mooued by the persuasions aforesayd, and partly because I was desirous to haue the body of the whole story compacted unyforme and one stile throughout. For so I thought it should be both more alowable among such as are of knowledge, and also more acceptable to the Reader, when neither part of the work might be an eye sore to the other. Furthermore forasmuch as it is knowne vnto many, that the sayd Copie was committed vnto mee, I haue forborne to build vpon that foundation, least I might haue ministred occasion to such as loue cauelling, to say I had eyther hatched other byrds Egges, or else presumed to finish the picture of Venus that Appelles left vnperfect. (sig. *iii–iii^v)

---

[17]   *The eyght bookes of Caius Iulius Caesar conteyning his martiall exploytes in the realme of Gallia and the countries bordering vppon the same translated oute of latin into English by Arthur Goldinge G.* (London: Willyam Seres, 1565).

Given the nature and attitude demonstrated here, Golding might easily have done the same thing with Sidney's unfinished translation. But given the same nature and attitude, and the persons involved, and the situation after Sidney's death, it is less than likely that Arthur Golding, that scholarly and honorable forward Protestant gentleman, should have done so and not admitted it: that he should have taken the huge risk of a barefaced lie, both on the title page of the edition and in his dedication to Leicester. Moreover, family lawsuits had left him in the mid-1580s, at the time of the *Trewnesse*, in peculiarly straitened circumstances, and Sidney's request may well have been also a characteristic kindness and a final act of patronage.

We may then, I think, assume that Golding is telling the truth about Sidney's request. The fact that in Thomas Cadman's Stationers' Register entry Sidney is not mentioned, only Golding, is probably explained by the entry's date: November 7, 1586, when Sidney's death was already known. It is certainly not due to any lack of respect on Cadman's part, for it was he also who in the same year printed George Whetstone's accurate and moving memoir of Sidney.[18]

There is a final indication that the *Trewnesse* we have was not a "mercenary book" disapproved of by the Sidney circle. The *Vérité* had a particular place in the *œuvre* of Mornay, in the mind of the author and of his family. It had been written about the time that his, and Sidney's, spiritual father and mentor, Hubert Languet, died in Antwerp; and Languet's last request had been that Mornay should remember him in his next published work. Accordingly, the latter added a moving tribute to the old Huguenot to the Latin (i.e., international) edition of the *Vérité*.[19] And in her Memoir of her husband's life, Charlotte takes pains to mention that their English friend, whom they had gotten to know so well during their singularly happy year in England in 1577–1578, "some time afterward did him [Mornay] the honor of translating into English his work on the truth of the Christian religion."[20]

This is the passage that has suggested to some that there was a full Sidney translation in MS, now lost like his Du Bartas, the *Trewnesse* being the hack Golding's "mercenary book"; but that theory can now be conclusively disproved. When, a few years ago, the Château-Musée at Saumur—where Mornay was governor for over 20 years—bought back a collection of books from his library that had surfaced in Croatia, there was an interesting item among these. Mornay's library contained a core of books, mostly his own works, bound in a sumptuous

---

[18] *Sir Phillip Sidney, his honorable life, his valiant death, and true vertues* (London: [T. Orwin] for Thomas Cadman, 1587).

[19] *De Veritate religionis christianae liber adversus atheos, epicureos, ethnicos, judaeos, mahumedistas et caeteros infideles, a Philippo Mornaeo, Plessiaci domino.. gallice primum conscriptus, latine versus, nunc autem ab eodem accuratissime correctus* (Leiden: F. Raphelengius, 1587).

[20] Lucy Crump (tr. and ed.) *A Huguenot Family in the XVI Century: the Memoirs of Philippe de Mornay, Sieur du Plessis Marly, Written by his Wife* (London: Routledge/New York: Dutton, 1926?), 169.

binding of red morocco, stamped with his arms and initials, and furnished with full-page bookplates of his and Charlotte's arms, hand painted by his resident painter Rudolf Anspach. The recovered collection also contains just such a gorgeously bound copy of the Sidney-Golding *Trewnesse*, printed by Thomas Cadman in 1587, as well as a copy of the second English edition, printed by Robert Robinson in 1592, in a nineteenth-century Mornay family binding. In conjunction with Charlotte's comment on Sidney, this makes it, I think, almost incontrovertible that Mornay himself accepted this translation as the authentic one.

The second question that concerns us about the *Trewnesse* is not "who?" but "how much?" How much did Sidney translate; how much, and which parts, of the published work can be accepted as his? These questions necessarily lead us from the outside to the inside, from external evidence to internal. Briefly to recapitulate, first, the history: Albert Feuillerat, in 1912, compared the *Trewnesse* with Golding's translations of Calvin's *Sermons* of 1574 and Jacques Hurault's *Politicke, Moral and Martial Discourses* of 1595. He found a "literalness," a "tendency to paraphrase, and, more generally, ... [a] toilsome industry"— "a certain honest, heavy mediocrity which smells of the lamp of industrious toil without having any redeeming originality of style."[21] This same style he found in all but six chapters of the *Trewnesse*, while in those six, he says, "the meaning is rendered with astonishing accuracy and yet the writer gives the impression that he is uttering his own thoughts. The terseness of the French is preserved, nay, in many cases, improved" (ibid.)

It is easy to make fun of Feuillerat for what one might see as a projecting of Philipolatry upon the text, and as in any case—dread word!—an "impressionistic" judgment. Yet alternatives are hard to come by. Searching for the accurate, computer-assisted methods for identifying styles, which I assumed must now be available, I learned to my dismay that what is currently called "stylometry" is still a very uncertain business.[22] I did, however, attempt one of its classic methods, now facilitated by electronics: checking for use of certain words that seemed unusual. This method is patchy, as there is no searchable version of any Golding text; although thanks to EEBO there is now one of the *Arcadia*. A preliminary search of the first two books of the *New Arcadia* gave a result that is still very incomplete. One word, *stickler* for the French *arbitre*, turned out to be relatively usual in Sidney. Mornay's splendid phrase "confits en meschanceté," for people who are soaked or preserved in wickedness like comfits, is translated in the *Trewnesse* as

---

[21] Albert Feuillerat, ed., *The Prose Works of Sir Philip Sidney*, vol. III (Cambridge: Cambridge University Press, 1912), ix.

[22] A precursor to much modern work is Samuel Schoenbaum, *Internal Evidence and Elizabethan Dramatic Authorship: An Essay in Literary History and Method* (Evanston, IL: Northwestern University Press, 1966). Also of interest are Anthony Kenny's *The Computation of Style: An Introduction to Statistics for Students of Literature and Humanities* (Oxford: Pergamon Press, 1982) and Jonathan Hope's *The Authorship of Shakespeare's Plays* (Cambridge: Cambridge University Press, 1994). A continuing venue is the journal *Computing and the Humanities*.

"saped in wickedness," which, OED points out, is a Golding word, the first three instances coming from his translations. It is not found in Sidney, or indeed in a dozen other searchable Elizabethan texts. "Othersome" for "Some other(s)" turned out to be fairly rare but not exclusive to anyone, while "to stye up" for *monter* can be found in Book I of Spenser's *Faerie Queene*. So the vocabulary method, like others falsely promising precision, does not free us from impressionism.

Moreover, studying the translation closely with the aid of the original and several early French dictionaries, such as Palsgrave, Holyband, and Cotgrave, at times gives one exactly the same impression as Feuillerat. The first few pages of Chapter I, for example, "That there is a God, and that all men agree in the Godhead," show an ease, a grace and an elegance quite unlike, say, Chapter VIII, "When the world had his beginning." There is, however, a problem. In the first place, impressions are notoriously personal, and one of the reasons I found myself delighted with the beginning of Chapter I was its contrast with what to me seemed the laboriousness of the long Preface—which Feuillerat ascribed to Sidney. Moreover—still impressionistically—I sensed a change of style, back to toilsome industry, about four pages into the chapter, again unlike Feuillerat, who confidently assigned the whole to Philip.

Secondly, before jumping to conclusions in either direction, on the basis of such uncertain notions, it is important to look at the original. One thing that stands out in Mornay's many writings is, precisely, his style. Terse, vigorous, *musclé*, often amusing, it is much the same in his published works as in his enormous correspondence, especially in the large collection of letters to his wife.[23] If the translation, as Duncan-Jones objected, shows few Latinisms, this is in the first instance due to Mornay's refreshingly direct and simple *écriture*. Both translations, though they occasionally show different choices, show essentially the same style, which clearly derives from the original author. Also, in the *Trewnesse* a number of the stylistic changes—from eloquence to humdrum enumeration, for example—are due to the pattern of the original's closely reasoned arguments. Chapter VIII, for instance, is a relatively pedestrian account of the world's beginning and gradual population, interesting for what it relates—Frank Lestringant used it as evidence for a theory about the Huguenots and the New World[24]—but not particularly literary. Chapters XIV and XV, on the other hand, concern the immortality of the soul and are often of considerable eloquence.

Two conclusions can be tentatively drawn. In the first place, Golding in his dedicatory letter to Leicester says that Sidney "had proceeded certeyne Chapters therein" before he went to the wars, but that "beeing thus determined to followe the affayres of Chivalrie, it was his pleasure to commit the performance of this peece

---

[23] In A.-D. de Fontenelle de Vaudoré and P-R. Auguis, eds., *Mémoires et correspondance de Duplessis Mornay*, 12 vols (Paris: Treuttel & Würtz, 1824–1825).

[24] Frank Lestringant, *Le Huguenot et le sauvage: l'Amérique et la controverse coloniale, en France, au temps des Guerres de Religion (1555–1589)* (Paris: Aux amateurs de livres, 1990), 119–26.

of service which he had intended to the Muses or rather to Christes Church and his native Countrie, vnto my charge." I am not sure of those "certeyne Chapters": I suspect it may not have been as neat as all that. There may well have been, in addition to some chapters—and not necessarily the first ones—rough drafts of other passages, which Golding, ever scrupulous about manner as about matter, was left to preserve or to harmonize. As Sypher says, "the preponderance of the evidence indicates that Sidney should be credited with an important share of the printed translation."[25]

The other conclusion that presents itself is that Golding himself was, as a translator at least, a much better writer than he has usually been given credit for. His hack reputation, I suspect, is due to the twentieth-century's perhaps unjust contempt for the fourteener as a metre, in conjunction with the prominence thrust upon his Ovid by its association with Shakespeare. Yet in his prose translations he is a genuinely good writer, and Sidney's choice of him surely reflects a respect for his style as well as for his religion and his professionalism.

Before going from the who to the how, it is time to look at Mornay's other translator and her work. In the case of Mary, Countess of Pembroke, Margaret Hannay's admirable biography[26] has considered the question in detail, and there is little for me to add; I am concerned more with the comparison, and with the function of translation and its relation to both literature and what one may loosely call ideology. It may be appropriate to begin with the original text's author and addressee.

Mornay wrote the *Excellent discours de la vie et de la mort* (as it was titled in its first edition by the Genevan printer Jean Durant in 1576) at Sedan in the Ardennes, the Protestant prince of which, Henri-Robert de la Marck, was dying at the age of 33. After some contacts with the Prince of Condé, Mornay had been working for the Duke of Alençon, youngest brother to King Charles IX, who had sent him on a fruitless mission to Louis of Nassau, William of Orange's younger brother. On Charles's death in 1574, Mornay and his brother, fearing new persecutions of Huguenots, moved to Sedan, where Philippe made the acquaintance of a young widow one year older than himself, Charlotte Arbaleste, whose husband, the "chevalier guerrier" Jean de Paz, had died five years earlier, leaving her with their little daughter, Suzanne.

Charlotte was a remarkable woman. During the St. Bartholomew's Day massacre she escaped on a donkey, disguised as a chambermaid, as far as the Ardennes, where she then led a sober and devout life that belied her inner fire and spirit (her family name means "Crossbow" and their motto was *Scopus mihi sufficit unus*: "I only need one target"). In his biography of his master, Mornay's secretary David de Licques says this about her:

---

[25] Sypher, p. xv.

[26] Margaret P. Hannay, *Philip's Phoenix: Mary Sidney, Countess of Pembroke* (New York and Oxford: Oxford University Press, 1990), 60–63. See also Margaret P. Hannay, Noel H. Kinnamon and Michael G. Brennan, eds, *The Collected Works of Mary Sidney Herbert, Countess of Pembroke* (Oxford: Clarendon Press, 1998), i. 220–54 (introduction and text) and 336–39 (commentary).

> I can say without flattery that there existed not in that time a woman more accomplished in all kinds of virtues. She had a clear intelligence [un esprit net], *judgement* more solid than her sex [usually] bears, a courage that nothing could shake, such a severity against vice that the great feared her: and withal an extreme charity toward the poor: but in the midst of all those virtues there showed a burning zeal for God's glory and the advancement of the church.[27]

She was almost penniless and in exile, supporting her daughter and her mother, but Mornay "preferred her person to several wealthy and profitable matches which from various sides were proposed to him"; and in 1575 they were affianced. "And at that time," Licques writes, "Monsieur du Plessis composed, at the request of his fiancée, the Treatise of Life and Death, soon afterwards printed in Geneva and since then in several places translated into all languages" (31). A few months later he was taken prisoner at the battle of Dormans, and Charlotte at once organized the ransom and sent him "the money and a horse, but not too good a one, so as not to make him appear too valuable" (*pour ne montrer trop de soin de sa personne*) (35).

One's initial surprise at a bright young widow with a seven-year-old being given—indeed, asking for—such a tract as an engagement present should be tempered by two considerations. In the first place Huguenots, while often (like Mornay and Admiral Coligny) personally engaging, were austere in their outlook. Secondly, there was a great deal of death about, and much of Charlotte's life was to be a kind of coda to the *Discours*: she lost two children at the apparently fatal age of three, like Mary Herbert's Katherine, as well as very nearly dying herself while giving birth to twin stillborn boys; and her surviving son, named after his father, was killed in his twenties in the Netherlands.

What Mornay wrote for young Charlotte, and what Mary translated, is commonly seen as a largely neo-Stoic text, originally accompanied by translations of a few of Seneca's letters, and redeemed for Christianity only by its religious ending. This is largely true, and is in part what makes it non-sectarian: a Senecan disparagement of life and a wholly traditional criticism of Courts under the title of Ambition could be agreed upon by moralists of all stripes. Interesting also is the fact that, while congruent with Philippism, it is much less directly Biblically pious than a reading of Melanchthon's *Loci Communes* would lead one to expect. So, a worthy, Senecan, Erasmian, Lipsian piece of *contemptus mundi* culminating in a dignified *ars moriendi*, appropriately written for a grieving widow and aptly translated by a grieving sister (and mother, and daughter). There is, perhaps, more.

In both Philip's and Mary's cases, as in many studies of translation, the *inamoramento* is commonly overlooked. It is easy to see why Philip might have thought worthwhile a text that closely argues the truth value of Christianity from a Protestant, Melanchthonian point of view, against the careless "atheism" certainly

---

[27]   (David de Licques) *Histoire de la vie de Messire Philippes de Mornay, Seigneur du Plessis Marly, &c.* (Leiden: Elsevier, 1647), 31. My translation.

more common at the time than is sometimes supposed.[28] Equally evident is Mary's approval of a discourse meant to reorient the worldly to the values of eternity, particularly after the death of her beloved brother. What, though, provided the affective, the emotional impulse? One of the commonplaces of epistolary writing was the declaration that in reading the author's letter, the addressee seemed to see him in person, and to enjoy his company as if in an actual visit. As regards Philippe de Mornay this is not only true but verifiable over four centuries later. Anyone who knows anything of Mornay will recognize in his writing this tireless, generous, enthusiastic, zealous, and affectionate man, whose style faithfully reflects his extraordinary personality. He delights in wordplay and in painting brisk verbal pictures of things and people under discussion; his French is a pleasure to read aloud, and has the authentic rhythms of amused and passionate speech. A part of him, consequently, resided and remained in the *Vérité* as in the *Excellent discours*; even we can almost hear his voice when we read them. Both Sidney siblings were exceptionally sensitive to style: the *Defence* and the collaborative Psalms amply show it. I contend, then, that for both Philip and Mary the *inamoramento* stemmed from their delighted recognition of their friend's voice in his style.

When we come to examine the how of the two translations, the two are still best studied together. How did Philip and Mary learn their French, how good was it, and what aids did they use for the tricky parts? It seems clear that the Sidney family employed at least one French tutor. Moffett's *Nobilis* says that at the age of seven Philip was given a tutor who furnished him "with a provision of languages"; and there is a 1569 letter from Sir Henry to Cecil sending the latter a tutor to teach French to his daughter Anne, one John (more probably Jean) Tassel who has served Sir Henry long and whom he can recommend.[29] When young Philip went abroad to Paris at the age of 17, wrote his companion Lodowick Bryskett, the French he met were "no less delighted with his ready and witty answers than astonished to hear him speak the French language so well and so aptly, having been so short a while in their country."[30] In his letter files Théophile de Banos from Frankfurt and Jean Lobbet of Strasburg write to him now in Latin, now in French; and with Mornay and his family it is certain that French was spoken. With Languet he corresponded for nine years in Latin, but it seems evident that when they were together they spoke French. As for Mary, Margaret Hannay cautiously limits herself to saying that John Tassel "may have taught Mary and Ambrosia as well" (22); yet when we see her accomplishment in translating both Garnier's *Antonius* and Mornay's *Discours* we may usefully conclude that some sound early tutoring lay at the root of her command of the language.

---

[28] For an excellent discussion of the term and its contemporary implications, see Michael Hunter, "The Problem of 'Atheism' in Early Modern England," *Transactions of the Royal Historical Society*, 5th Ser., vol. 35. (1985), 135–57.

[29] Sir Henry Sidney to Lord Burghley, 26 October 1569. HMC Salisbury I:438.

[30] Lod[owick] Br[yskett], *A Discourse of Civill Life, Containing the Ethike Part of Morall Philosophie* (London: for William Aspley, 1606), 160–61 (sig. X3vo–X4).

As for the aids in translation, it is hard to be sure. Technically available were John Palsgrave's 1530 *L'Esclarcissement de la langue francoise*, Giles DuWes's *Introductory for to learn to read, to pronounce, and to speak French*, possibly from 1532, and several works by the Huguenot immigrant Claude de Sainliens, who delightfully Englished his name as Claudius Holyband. His *French Scholemaster* appeared in 1573 and his *French Littleton* in 1576; his *Treasure of the French tong* and his *Treatise for Declining of Verbes* in 1580, and his *Dictionarie French and English: Published for the benefit of the studious in that language*, in 1593. It is impossible to know exactly what aids the Sidneys used; but Holyband was a Huguenot, and doubtless connected to the French church in London, where Philip stood godfather to Mornay's second daughter in 1578, and one of the ministers of which, Robert le Maçon de la Fontaine, was remembered in Sidney's will. Holyband's *French Scholemaster* was dedicated to the son of Thomas Sackville, Lord Buckhurst, who was a friend of Sir Henry Sidney's. Moreover, while the Sidney library catalogue, now being edited by Germaine Warkentin, is disappointingly sparse for Philip's generation, it does mention a copy of Holyband's *Dictionarie*.[31] In its 1593 printed form this would have been too late for Philip, though it may have served the Countess of Pembroke; more probably they owned, or at least consulted, a manuscript copy or sketch.

Turning now to the translations themselves, the first feature one notices is their skill. Both brother and sister had genuinely excellent, though not perfect, French; and following their versions closely provides a fascinating glimpse into the translator's workshop. Certain phrases stand out as deliberate choices. In the Preface to the *Vérité*, having written of Gentiles and Jews and Turks, Mornay comes closer to home, to "nous, qui preschons le Royaume des Cieux, mais toujours le nez en terre." Here is Philip's briskly splendid Englishing: "What shall I say of the most part of us? Of us I mean which beleeve the Gospell and professe the Christian Religion, and yet live as if we believed it not? Which preach the kingdome of heaven, and have our groynes ever wrooting in the ground?"

Mary, too, is adept at finding equivalents for Mornay's stylistic flourishes. When Mornay says about the body you wear that "il sera plustost usé que toi las d'en user" she elegantly translates, "Thou mayst sooner wear it out, then weary thyself with using, or rather abusing, it" (E1). Some of his sound effects are of course incapable of being put into English: when the air in the mountains takes delight "à fouldroyer et pouldroyer leur superbe hauteur" Mary takes an equally vigorous sidestep and says that it takes pleasure "to thunderbolt and dash into pouder that proude height of theirs" (B4).

The *Trewnesse* cannot, and does not try to, match the French capacity for ellipsis: the sentence structure is "unfolded" into slightly longer models, but this is compensated for by vigorous vocabulary and rhetoric, and a very English pleasure in alliteration. The difficult French "Voire" becomes "Yea,—" and sometimes a French abstraction is Englished with a pleasant metaphor. "Mais si l'impiété meut

---

[31] My thanks to Germaine Warkentin for this information, in a personal communication.

des questions" becomes "But if ungodliness stirre coales,"—Reason will then "open her mouth and shewe, that it was agreable to Gods Justice and necessarie for mans welfare"; "vtile a notre humilité et digne de sa gloire," or, as the *Trewnesse* says, "behoofful for our baseness, and beseeming his glorie."

Mary has other, economical elegances. "Par roides montagnes et par precipices, par deserts et par brigandages" is reduced to a crisp "over ... steepe rockes, and theevish deserts" (A2). Fearing neither life nor the state of death, Everyman says "je crains seulement ce pas qui est entre deux"; Mary's capable hands improve this to "only I fear the midway step" (D4). And of course the delightful French "Povre ignorant que tu es" pithily becomes "Simple soule!" (E1).

Periodically (though not always) she shows herself the poet, and heightens Mornay's choices. God in the French punishes kings when he "les accable de leurs couronnes propres"; Mary finds the heavy crown too cliché'd an image and has God "oftentimes intrapping them in their own crownes" (C1). Even in our evil times some have in them "quelque reste de sinceritê," Mary livens this up and grants them "some sparkes of sinceritie" (C1vo). Mornay talks of the port of death "où nous serons à couvert de tous vents"; Mary gives the more graphic seaman's term: "where we shall ride in safetie from all windes" (D2).

Some problems are perennial: every translator from the French still wrestles with the future perfect tense. Interestingly, Philip (if we may imagine it is he) and Mary choose different solutions: the *Trewnesse* translates it, as do most moderns, with a past tense in English, while the Countess insists on a literal version: "they shall have endured."

A particular test for any translator from the French has always been the notorious impersonal pronoun "on" that every French schoolboy was taught to shun as a "pronom lâche et malhonnête." Mary, with some sophistication, finds four different equivalents for it: in the first place, the passive voice. Courtiers drink in gold and silver ware; but "c'est en celle-là ... qu'on verse, et qu'on boit le poison"—Mary says "but in those ... the poison is prepared and dronke" (B3). Secondly, there is "they." When the avaricious lose their toys, says Mornay, using "on" here not to let the reader escape identification, "Lors vient on à crier, à pleurer, à se tourmenter ..."; Mary either has not seen or does not accept the trap and translates, "Then fall they to cry, to weepe, and to torment themselves" (B1vo). Her third tactic with "on" translates it, interestingly, as "a man"; for the covetous, the drink of possession does not quench thirst: "Or de ceci tant plus on en boit, et tant plus on en seche de soif"—Mary says "Now hereof the more a man drinkes, the more he is a thirst" (B1). And finally, and most interestingly, rather than "they," "on" becomes "we." When Mornay asks, rhetorically, what fear is left for him who hopes for death, and begins "Le pense-on chasser de son pays?" Mary, curiously, puts herself and her reader among the persecutors: "Thinke we to banish him his country?" (E1ᵛ).

She has some interesting vocabulary choices. Some of these are vigorously native, "mere English" as the queen put it; "fascheuses hostelleries" along the way become alliteratively "lothsome lodgings," "abrutis" becomes "blockish," "povres gens" are "seely creatures," and boasting Toby Belches, "ces vaillans à la table," are "these hardie trencher knights." When in the mountains travelers are engulfed in an avalanche, "une vague de neige les enveloppe"; Mary sees it in her mind when it has come to rest and says that "a drift of snowe overwhelmes them." On occasion it is hard to distinguish a writerly choice from a momentary ignorance. When "le paysan s'endort au courant d'un ruisseau," does this peasant sleeping through the brook's peaceful rushing become "the countryman sleepeth at the fall of a great river" from ignorance or for better drama?

This brings us to the places where Homer nods: often trivial but sometimes important. In the *Vérité*'s Preface, for example, the original says "que la verité, quand elle est *relevee*, esclarcit la raison, et la raison s'en esveille pour *appuyer* la verité." Philip (or Golding) seems dyslexically to have misread *relevee* (found or pointed out) as *revelee* (revealed), and reversed the meaning of *appuyer* (prop up or support); rendering the sentence as "... that the truth being *revealed*, enlighteneth reason; and that reason rowseth up herself to *rest upon* truth."

Farther into Chapter I, the truly human insights are enumerated: "namely the perswasion of the Godhead, the conscience of evil, the desire of immortalitie, the longing for felicities, and such other thinges, which in this neather world are incident unto man alone, and in al men, without the which is no more a man"; "*et que l'homme ne sauroit nier qu'en se dementant.*" In the *Trewnesse*'s translation Sidney (or Golding) has clearly taken the verb *se dementir* as *dementer* and instead of writing "and which man cannot deny without *denying himself*" renders the phrase "insomuch that hee cannot deny them except *he be out of his wittes.*"

As for Mary, sometimes her choices lead us to ponder, as it is worth doing with her brother's Mornay translation, on what dictionary she was using and how faithfully she followed it. Mornay's "adolescence" becomes "youth" though in Palsgrave that is the translation of "jeunesse." Suppose the covetous man in pursuit of wealth has "gagné à bon escient"; Mary, opting for what seems to her the specific meaning in this case, says "Suppose he hath gained in good quantitie," even though Holyband's dictionary translates the phrase as "in good earnest." Among the things that make life loathsome are "meurtres, fuites, maladies"; Mary gives this as "murthers, banishments, sicknes" in spite of Holyband's "flights" for "fuites."

The Countess's excellent French is not without flaws. Twice she mistakes the Doctor ("le médecin") for the medicine he brings ("la médecine"); and there are others. Even if the ambitious attain a crown, "ils ont des finages à plaider avec Dieu, et taschent d'empieter sur sa Seigneurie." This is a bit beyond Mary, who does not know or ignores the meaning of "finages": instead of pointing out that they have boundary disputes to settle with God, and try to encroach upon his Lordship (a pun: "Seigneurie" is both the title and the property), she says, more generally and more violently, that "they have cuarels to pleade with God, and indeavour to tread under foot his kingdome" (C1). "Perclusions," which with "gouttes" are the covetous man's punishment in this life, become, in defiance of Holyband's "benumbments," "oppilations," which are obstructions or constipations. And like many a foreigner since, she has trouble with the French word for thirst quenching. "Nous louons sur tous les breuvages qui desalterent," says Mornay; yet while the modern meaning existed since the mid-sixteenth century and Holyband has "to slake thirst," Mary says that "We commend most those drinks that breed an alteration."

All in all, though, it is clear that both brother and sister were remarkably good translators from the French. The fascination of translation is that, when both sides of the equation are extant, we have an unparalleled opportunity to glance into a writer's workshop. The constant choices a translator makes constitute a body of evidence that only the most extensive (and ultra-rare) set of autograph revisions could hope to equal. Any study of translation that looks only at the importing of ideas, emphasizing the matter while neglecting the manner, would bypass a genuine treasure of literary information.

* * *

Finally, though, I should like to return to the why of these two translations, and to that which in this regard unites them. To begin with the *Excellent discours*—the first to be written if the last to be translated—we may usefully examine the situation's ostensible paradox: the presenting by Mornay to his enchanting young widow fiancée of a text filled with the loathsomeness of life. In our rather blasé pointing to the work's neo-Stoic genre and to its difference from the traditional *artes moriendi*, we do not always with sufficient attention read the end. In Mornay's French this reads like a breath of fresh air; and while the Countess's version is tougher and sparer in style—more Wyatt than Marguerite de Navarre, say—there is enough of the original in her *Discourse*'s ending to make it a stirring piece. Moreover, it allows us to see how the Stoic reasoning is completely transformed, *transcoded*, by the Christian hope of Heaven; for what was there a hope for a deliverance out of misery into an unspecified rest, now becomes the entry, not only into some generic harbor, but into the port city of Paradise. And, to return to another ungrammaticality, while Mary certainly in the late 1580s had as much death in her life as Charlotte and may have turned to the *Discours* as an aid in mourning, it seems to me evident that there is much more to her translation of this essay. It is not remotely strange that the poet of the Psalms of David should have taken delight in this vigorous denunciation of the greedy and the toady, in this upright and energetic welcoming of the "midway step" taken in the trust of God; that the sister of Philip should have smiled and thought of foolish kings as she translated "Must wee to fynde true humanitie, flye the society of men, and hide us in forrestes among wilde beastes ... to avoyde these unrulie passions, eschue the assemblye of creatures supposed reasonable? to plucke us out of the evills of the world, sequester our selves from the world?" (C2); and that thinking back to her brother's first prose essay should have brought a special relevance to "the Astrologer lookes up on high, and falles in the next ditch."

Mary, much more than Charlotte Arbaleste de Mornay, was a woman of letters. She had the leisure to be so. And just as her brother had written ruefully to their Uncle, the Earl of Leicester, "your Lordship hath made me a courtier," so brother and sister made each other poets, and the brother made the sister a woman, and a patron, of letters. The intense locus that is the text of the *Discours*, if we study it closely enough and long enough, begins to lift the veil and reveal something of this known and unknown woman: the intensity of being the survivor of a twosome for whom the devotion of their lives was, finally, to the word, as well as to the Word.

As for the *Vérité*, in a number of ways it continues what the *Excellent discours* had so eloquently begun. And Philip certainly chose it for reasons beyond his and Philippe's friendship. The *Vérité*, to invite translation, must correspond, indeed respond, to a situation Sidney discerned in his own *milieu*. The Jews, Paynims, and Mahumetists are clearly a secondary audience; Mornay's primary target are the Atheists (a word he may have coined) and especially the Epicures—those whose groynes are ever wrooting in the ground. In the *Discours* he had already memorably attacked the heedless *mentalité* of the pleasure seekers and the power hungry; here he goes to the implications of their ideology. For a Sidney, an increasingly "Huguenot" member of a court where until recently the Earl of Oxford had been a favorite, this must have had a certain attraction; and for one who was coming to agree with those who had once complained that "my knowledge brings forth toyes," it might be considered an appropriate palinode. But there is more. Sidney's own prose style has elegance and *gravitas*: yet there is something it does perhaps lack. Nowhere in the *Arcadia* do we find the vehemence, the colloquial simplicity, of, for example, sonnet 92 of the *Astrophil and Stella*:

> You say, forsooth, you left her well of late.
> O God, think you that satisfies my care?

In his "songs and sonettes,"[32] Sidney had illustrated the *Defence* by supplying the "*energia* or forcibleness" others lacked, and which he considered indispensable for *moving* the reader. The more one reads the *Trewnesse* in the light of Mornay's *Vérité*, the more one is led to conclude that, indissolubly from the man and the matter, it was also the *manner* of Mornay, his irresistible *energia* that enchanted Sidney and made him want to share with everyone his wonderment.

Let me end, for the pleasure of the translation, with a particularly successful passage. He has been talking about the heavenly bodies, which "direct us incontinently too a Spirit, and this orderlines too a certeine Governer."

> But when wee enter afterward intoo our selves, and finde there an abridgement
> of the whole universall; a bodie fit for all sorts of moving; a soule which (without
> removing) maketh the bodies to moove which way it listeth; a Reazon therein
> which guydeth them everychone in their dooings; and yet notwithstanding, this

---

[32] *Sonetti e canzoni* is the closest approximation the sixteenth century had to a generic name for what we call a sonnet-sequence.

160 *French Connections in the English Renaissance / Kuin*

Soule to bee such as wee can neither see it nor understand it; It ought in all reazon too make us all too understand, that in this great universall masse, there is a soveraine Spirit which maketh, mooveth and governeth all that we see here; by whom wee live, move, and bee; who in our bodies hath framed a Counterfet of the whole world, and in our Soules hath ingraven an image of himself. (sig. A1vo)[33]

No traitors except by necessity, the *inamorati* that are our two translators have framed in their books a Counterfet of the whole text, *and* ingraven in the words— if we could but see clearly—an image of themselves.

---

[33]   Reprinted in Albert Feuillerat, ed., *The Prose Works of Sir Philip Sidney*, 204.

Chapter 8

From "Amours" to *Amores*:
Francis Thorius Makes Ronsard
a Neolatin Lover

Anne Lake Prescott, with Lydia Kirsopp Lake

This is not an essay on the Pléiade's English connections; it is, rather, an essay on Ronsard and a poet-doctor whose career was largely Continental but whose son established a medical career as a Protestant refugee in England. Imagine this study, then, somewhere on the way through the Chunnel between England and France.

Francis Thorius (or de Thoor or Thorie) was a doctor and Neolatin poet of Flemish extraction who spent a good deal of time in France. Writing in the second half of the sixteenth century, he was not English, but he had at least one good English friend with whom he exchanged charmingly affectionate verses: the diplomat and Neolatin poet Daniel Rogers, son of a Marian martyr, admirer of Pierre de Ronsard (he sent a copy of Ronsard's *Œuvres* to the Dutch humanist Dousa), and friend of Philip Sidney.[1] As a Protestant, Thorius became less than comfortable in France

---

[1]   I thank Roger Kuin and my sister, Lydia Kirsopp Lake, who knows even more about classical culture than did Ronsard, for help with transcriptions and Latin and for the latter's notes on classical allusions; the translations from Thorius are largely hers and she must share in the authorship of this essay.

On the Thorius family see Francis Devos, "François Thorius (Thooris) et son fils Raphaël médecins, poètes et mathématiciens de la Renaissance" (<http://home.nordnet. fr/~rgombert/Meteren/FicheN16.htm>), and also Paul Bergmans, "Les Poésies manuscrites de François et Raphaël Thorius," in *Mélanges Paul Thomas: Recueil de mémoires concernant la philologie classique dedié à Paul Thomas* (Bruges: Imprimerie Sainte Catherine, 1930), 29–38. The family, says Bergmans, carried a gold/yellow shield with a chevron in gules (red) and three eagles' heads with necks, in gules, "contournés" sinister (i.e., looking leftward). The title page of Thorius's MS poetry says it is by "Francisco Thorio Bellione Medico." An exchange between Thorius and Rogers found in the MS of the latter's work now at the Huntington Library is worth quoting for its flavor of humanist *amicitia*; I give Roger Kuin's translation in an essay by Professor Kuin and myself, "Versifying Connections: Daniel Rogers and the Sidneys," *Sidney Journal* 18.2 (2000), 1–35:

To Franciscus Thorius, best of men and poets
Here on the road to Orléans from Paris,
Thorius, what great troops of heartfelt wishes
Wanted you at my trudging side, how often,
You can't imagine, friend—by God, you cannot:
For on my way through valleys wide, then anxious,

Staring at cliffs I'd never yet encountered,
Yours was the face I wished I had beside me,
You as our road's companion: I lamented
Loud to the lonely rocks and lonely valleys
I had been snatched away from you, my friend, and
You had been snatched from me, my dear friend, also.
For as I trudged alone through lonely regions,
Only my slow dog following his master,
Sadly I wandered, and I did not miss you,
Thorius, so much for your conversation,
As for your wit, to chase the journey's boredom.
Lord, but that road was long, to Rogers, trudging
Sole through deserted unknown regions, crossing
All by himself the strange and foreign vineyards!
And yet my destination's only twenty
Miles from the city: longer than that voyage
By which not long ago I traveled over
Waves of the tidal sea to kinder England.
But if your Raphael and that Francisca,
Light of your life, your children, now by illness
Swept, had instead not kept you home-bound, grieving,
You would have joined me as my road companion,
You would have also made this trip less boring,
You and your jokes, your sallies and your nonsense.
Curse you, the lot of you: may you go to evil
Regions of fever, evil and malignant.
For it was your decision that alone I
Had to cross lonely lands from Town to Orleans,
Lacking the Thorian wit's volcanic discourse.
And it was all your fault that I should vomit
Horrible verses, by myself and witless. (From the road to Orleans, 17 April 1570)

Ode to Daniel Rogers
By Franciscus Thorius of Bailleul
What, Rogers, honestly, do you want me to
Do for you? With what gift do you want me to
    Adorn your book, already polished
    With gold and pumice and vermilion,
And where I'm asked to look at your other friends'
Grateful inscriptions? And without blushing, as
    I see it marked by hands of poets
    In graceful words and pithy writings?
Those overwhelm me: names such as Sturmius,
Fournier, and Donel, names like Acontio,
    And Beroald, Hugo, Paul, and his, too
    Whose name receives its shining grace from
Flowers and from Christ, and who by the Muses was
Joined to us both (I don't know the others, but
    They all are splendid): all are skilful

From "*Amours*" to Amores

despite his friendships with the great humanist teacher and Neolatin poet Jean Dorat, Ronsard, Rémy Belleau, and Joachim Du Bellay, eventually fleeing for safety to the Low Countries; Rogers wrote an epigram on his friend's problems that was translated into English by Sir Henry Norris, Sidney's lieutenant in the 1586 English expeditionary force in the Netherlands.[2] Thorius's distinguished and much better known son, Dr. Raphael Thorius, who died in 1625, was born in France, spent time at Oxford, but took his degree in Leiden in early 1591 after—or so it is said—a career there of 12 days; his thesis was apparently on dropsy. He settled in London and was a success despite legal troubles for letting one patient vomit herself to death (he pled guilty) and for practicing without a license (offered a choice of prison or a 5-pound fine he went for the latter). He shared his father's taste for Latin, if not for the Pléiade, and sang the pleasures of wine and Indian weed—his once famous seriocomic hymn to tobacco, first composed around 1610 and translated into English in 1626, calls it "Planta beata! decus terrarum, munus Olympi!"[3] At some point he or an agent put together a manuscript (British Library, Sloane MS 1768) of mostly Latin verse by his father and himself; its neatness, with occasional corrections, suggests that someone was preparing it for the press, although there is no evidence it was ever published.[4] I have found, so far, only one extant printed allusion to his verse. This is a fleeting reference in Edward Phillips's *Theatrum poetarum* (London, 1675), an often astute set of comments on a large number of authors and works, which mentions "*Franciscus Thorius Bellio*, his *Varia Carmina*" (sig. Kk3v: as for Raphael, he was "a learned French poet, whose elegant style in Latin Vers. discovers itself in his noted Poem entitled *Hymnus Tabaci*, or *Encomium* of Tobacco," sig. Gg6v). Understandably, Phillips has more to say on Ronsard himself, calling "*Petrus Ronsardus, a French Poet of Vendosme*, the most to be esteem'd in the judgement of *Thuanus*, not only of the French, but of all other Poets that have liv'd since the time of *Augustus*."[5]

> At rhetoric, or they are famous poets.
> Shall, in that crowd of swans in white elegance,
> I be the crow, the black and ridiculous?
> And bray among them, as once the goose did
> Among the tuneful nightingales honking?

[2]   Jan van Dorsten, in his book on northern European humanist networking, quotes Norris's translation of Rogers's poem sympathizing with Thorius's misfortunes (the poem is dated 2 May 1570); see his *Poets, Patrons, And Professors: Sir Philip Sidney, Daniel Rogers, and the Leiden Humanists* (Leiden: Leiden University Press, 1962), 107.

[3]   Raphael Thorius, *Hymnus tabaci* (London: H. Mosley, 1651 edition), sig. B4.

[4]   Sloane 1768; I have worked from Columbia University's microfilm of this MS. Since "John" was a favorite name in the Thorius family (see the DNB on Raphael Thorius), I have been unable to sort out the familial ties between Francis and the John Thorius who figured in the slanging match between Gabriel Harvey and Thomas Nashe. Was Francis his grandfather? Uncle?

[5]   Sig. Gg3v. Belleau, according to Phillips, who is probably taking this from James Howell (see below), comes in third if we agree with those who count "Joachimus Bellaius" [Joachim Du Bellay], author of "many things in Latin, but most in the Mother Tongue," as

It is not clear to what extent Francis knew his son's adopted country; the available sources are either ambiguous or give no evidence. Among the fascinations of Sloane 1768, however, are the filiations it shows between Continental Renaissance poetry and England—and some evidence in its contents that Time or taste had frayed those filiations as far as the son's poetry is concerned, for father and son differ noticeably in their treatment of French verse. Francis's part of Sloane 1768 is classily Franco-Netherlandish and humanist; his son's, for all its elegant Latinity, and despite some lines on Henri IV and a few poems on visiting foreign swells, is more solidly English, if in a Neolatin way, with poems on Bishop George Abbot, a translation from Camden, and some meanly witty anti-Catholic epigrams. There is no trace, so far as I can see, of the Pléiade. Not that the educated English were neglecting Ronsard and the Pléiade in Raphael's day. True, the high tide of that group's popularity in England as a source of verse to be imitated was now ebbing and its cultural glitter was somewhat if not entirely faded, but Ronsard was famous in seventeenth-century England well into the Restoration, often mentioned and occasionally imitated. Robert Codrington, for instance, included a flattering poem on the young Marguerite de Valois—at the time of composition the future wife of Henri de Navarre and by the time of the translation the deceased ex-wife of that same king—in his 1654 translation of Marguerite de Navarre's *Heptaméron*.

Eventually, to be sure, and particularly after the Restoration with a cultural elite more aware than ever of all things French, English taste caught up. The author of a discussion in John Dunton, ed., *The Young-students-library* (London: Dunton, 1692), knows that the famous Ronsard's style was now *passé*: unlike Hebrew, we read, French does not allow lexical transpositions, and "If *Ronsard*, and other Poets of this time made use of such Transpositions, their *French* was but a sorry kind of Latin. Neither could these sorts of Licenses be long suffered, and they are now quite banished from the French Poesie" (p. 295). Dunton is not, perhaps, speaking from personal discovery after pondering Ronsard's works, for what he says clearly echoes the crisp condemnation of the practice by Nicolas Rapin, although the latter does not, in this regard, condemn Ronsard as much as he does elsewhere.[6] Nevertheless, despite the Pléiade's misplaced lexical experiments, the name "Ronsard" was hardly obscure and still often, even near the end of the century, figured in an English understanding of what we would call the "canon" of French poetry. Raphael's indifference to Ronsard and his contemporaries thus seems a puzzle. Perhaps he was informed enough to know, more than did his English friends, that French literary fashion had shifted. Perhaps, more than had his father's faith, his Protestantism shaped his literary preferences. Or perhaps he was trying to distance himself from his father's taste.

---

second, right after Ronsard (sig. Dd6). "Thuanus" is J.-A. de Thou, a French humanist who wrote extensively on French poets.

    [6]   René Rapin, *Reflections on Aristotle's treatise of poesie* ..., trans. Thomas Rymer (London, 1674), section 33.

From "Amours" to Amores   165

Francis, though, had long been dazzled by the Pléiade, as witness a French poem to Pierre de Paschal in Sloane 1768. In what is both a compliment and a self-promoting or self-reassuring claim to know the stars, Thorius writes that "Ronsard, Bellay, Baïf, Grevin, Belleau, Jodelle, I haunted familiarly in Paris, and Turnèbe, and Dorat."[7] And although he did not know Paschal back then and has not met him since, he knows that he is "un bel ornement de la sçavante France" (a handsome ornament of learned France). "Sçavant" indeed: Whatever his taste for Ronsard's love poetry, Dr. Thorius's France is the republic of letters, not the France of the monarchy and its court. It is understandable, therefore, that his translations of Ronsard make that highly erudite French poet even more *sçavant*, in part by moving his stylishly crystalline French into the weightier terms of Renaissance Latin and in part by studding Ronsard's already learned verses with yet more Greco-Roman allusions. In 1558 and 1559, as war clouds began to form, Thorius had translated two poems by Ronsard on peace, but in the poems collected for this manuscript he attends to the amatory sonnets, ignoring, for example, the hymns, the epic, the odes. Whoever prepared the manuscript, in fact, was so impressed by Ronsard's fame that he misattributes at least one poem and perhaps several more to Ronsard that are by others; one, for example, which recounts a dialogue between a lover and Charon ("Hêus ô Charon, charon ô Erebi portitor") is despite its heading a translation of Olivier de Magny's "Holà Charon, Charon, Nautonnier infernal."[8]

Renaissance translations of vernacular literary works into Latin were hardly uncommon, although some instances remain startling. Translating Spenser's *Shepheardes Calender* makes him even more Virgilian, but a tale from the *Decameron* in elegiacs? Chaucer's *Troilus and Criseyde* in Francis Kynaston's Latin rhyme royal? Promoting Du Bartas's French *Sepmaine* into a more epic *Hebdomas* makes some sense, although some might say that to put Milton into Latin, as was done, is *portare carbones ad Novum Castellum*.[9] Nor was Thorius alone in elevating Ronsard's French into Latin; in an important study, I.D. McFarlane appends a catalogue of such translations (including a list of the poems in Sloan 1768 and some valuable if

---

[7]   In this essay I use Ronsard's *Œuvres Complètes*, ed. Jean Céard, Daniel Ménager, and Michel Simonin (Paris: Gallimard, 1993–1994, 2 vols) I, which gives variants. The most available list of Thorius's lyrics, if with some errors in transcription and the omission of a poem headed "Ex Ronsardo" from "Las sans la voir" (Céard I.75; a variant opening of "Par l'œil de l'âme," as is indicated by the Pléiade edition's first-line index but not the notes), is *British Literary Manuscripts from the British Library: Series One: The English Renaissance, c. 1500–1700* (Harvester Press), Appendix I, pp. 67–70; it identifies these lyrics by letter. This is "l."

[8]   Harvester "ss." Nor can I find in Ronsard's poetry the original of a Latin poem ("qq") that begins "Je meurs helas je meurs"; it is not the poem to Paschal in the *Premier livre des amours*, despite the similar opening; it addresses "Lilia."

[9]   I take these examples, except for Du Bartas (which I have seen), from W. Leonard Grant, "European Vernacular Works in Latin Translation," *Studies in the Renaissance* 1 (1954), 120–56; Grant mentions, as well, a twentieth-century translation of Shakespeare's *Sonnets* into Latin. See also J.W. Binns, "Latin Translations from English In Renaissance England, 1550–1640," *Res Publica Litterarum* 1 (1982), 25–40.

brief comments on Thorius's technique).[10] Thorius *was* unusual in translating almost two dozen poems to Cassandre and seven or eight more to Marie (the numbers and hence the proportions are imprecise, for Ronsard sometimes shifted the names of his lady as he revised his works). Other Renaissance admirers—Dorat, Paul Schede (Melissus to his humanist friends), and Edouard Du Monin—turned some sonnets into Latin; none, though, translated as many as did Thorius.

For the remainder of this essay, and with help from Lydia Lake, I will describe some of Thorius's transformations, giving several poems in full, and then raise some questions. One of his efforts raises a small preliminary mystery concerning possible awareness of his work to which I cannot offer an answer: Thorius translates Ronsard's "Je voudroy bien richement jaunissant," a sonnet to Cassandre, but redirects it to a "Phyllis." Phyllis is hardly an uncommon name, particularly in pastoral, yet it seems more than coincidence that Thomas Lodge translated the same sonnet for his 1593 sonnet sequence, *Phillis*.[11] Had Lodge somehow read Thorius? He was a close reader of French Renaissance love poets, as well as of many other French writers, sometimes indulging in what one can plausibly call plagiarism, and he might have been curious to see what Thorius had made of poetry he evidently loved.[12] Or had Thorius read Lodge's sequence? Whether the parallel shifts of name are merely fortuitous or a sign that Thorius's work was circulating, the sonnets provide a chance to see how one sonnet mutated into both English and Latin, so I give the full texts, putting an earlier variant in brackets:

> Je voudroy bien richement jaunissant
> En pluye d'or goute à goute descendre
> Dans le giron de ma belle Cassandre,
> Lors qu'en ses yeux le somne va glissant.
> Puis je voudroy en toreau blanchissant
> Me transformer pour [finement la prendre],
> Quand en Avril par l'herbe la plus tendre
> Elle va, fleur, mille fleurs ravissant.
> Je voudroy bien pour alleger ma peine,
> Estre un Narcisse et elle une fontaine,
> Pour m'y plonger une nuict à sejour:
> Et si voudroy que ceste nuict encore
> Fust eternelle, et que jamais l'Aurore
> Pour m'esveiller ne rallumast le jour. (Céard I.34, with an earlier variant)

---

[10] I.D. McFarlane, "Pierre de Ronsard and the Neo-Latin Poetry of His Time," *Res Publica Litterarum* 1 (1978), 177–205; Malcolm C. Smith, "Latin Translations of Ronsard," in *Acta Conventus Neo-Latini Guelpherbytani*, ed. Stella Revard, Fidel Rädle, and Mario Di Cesare (Binghamton, NY: Renaissance Texts and Studies/MRTS, 1988), 331–7, adds some items.

[11] See the *Premier livre des amours*, no. 20 (Céard I.34–5. Both Thorius and Lodge used an earlier edition: the Latin "Callidus" and English "fineness" translate Ronsard's earlier "finement" to describe the bull's seduction. Lodge's *Phillis* was published in London by James Roberts for John Busbie.

[12] On Lodge's silent and sometimes seemingly surreptitious borrowings from the French see my *French Poets and the English Renaissance: Studies in Fame and Transformation* (New Haven and London: Yale University Press, 1978).

From "Amours" to Amores   167

Lodge gives a fairly close translation but seems more invested than is Ronsard in the persistence of his desire, and after calling Phyllis his "friend," a warm touch not found in Ronsard, he adds the image of himself in the lap of pleasure, or perhaps of Pleasure, as though he were Spenser's Verdant lying in a post-coital slumber while Excess bends over him like a parodic *pieta* (*Faerie Queene* III.xii):

> I would in rich and golden coloured raine,
> With tempting showers in pleasant sort discend,
> Into faire *Phillis* lappe (my lovely friend)
> When sleepe hir sence with slomber doth restraine.
> I would be chaunged to a milk-white Bull,
> When midst the gladsome fieldes she should appeare,
> By pleasant finenes to surprise my deere,
> Whilest from their stalkes, she pleasant flowers did pull:
> I were content to wearie out my paine,
> To bee *Narsissus* so she were a spring
> To drowne in hir those woes my heart do wring:
> And more I wish transformed to remaine:
> That whilest I thus in pleasures lappe did lye,
> I might refresh desire, which else would die. (Sonnet 34, sig. G4)

Thorius is likewise largely faithful and likewise tonally a little different:

> Ex Ronsardo:
> Je vouldroy bien richement jaulnissant &c
> Vellem ego flaventi liquefactus membra metallo
> Auripluas fluere in guttas, mictúmque[13] meæ me
> Phyllidis in gremium pretioso fundere nimbo
> Languidulos illi quum somnus inivit ocellos.
> Vellem ego, pulcra proci mutatus in ora juvenci,
> Tergore candenti per amœna vireta vagari,
> Callidus incautæ ludosque jocosque puellæ
> Ut struerem, violas quum depopulata recentes,
> Semoto comitum procul agmine sola vagatur.
> Vellem ego grata meis quærens solatia poemis,
> Narcissus fieri, mea fons quoque Phyllis ut esset,
> Et totam placide noctem illa mergi in unda:
> Vellem etiam tenebris nox illa perennibus esset
> Obsita, nec roseo unquam Aurora diem ore referret. (Harvester "aa")

> [I would wish (melted to golden metal) my limbs to flow into golden raindrops, and that I, blended with a rich rain cloud, might flow into my Phyllis's lap when sleep has entered her little weary little eyes. I would wish that (changed into the beautiful appearance of a young bull a-wooing), I might wander with gleaming

---

[13]   The manuscript is not entirely clear and "t" could be a "s" (thus giving an older spelling of the verb "to mix") or even a "c," giving "mictum," the urinary suggestion being unfortunate if not irrelevant in terms of flow and color.

168 *French Connections in the English Renaissance / Prescott*

white back through the pleasant greenery, that I might skillfully contrive games and jokes for the unwary maiden when, having cropped the new-blooming violets, she wanders alone, her band of attendants far separated from her. I would wish, seeking welcome comfort in my poems, to become Narcissus, so Phyllis might also be my wellspring, and to bathe peacefully the whole night in that stream. And I would wish that night to be wrapped in eternal shadows, and that Dawn would never bring back the day with her rosy countenance.]

The Latin lingers over the opening fluidity, adding preciousness to a rain cloud ("Pretioso ... nimbo") and preciosity to what had been mere "yeux" and are now "ocellos," or "little eyes"; the bull is more playful—even joke-playing—and Ronsard himself might point out that mentioning Dawn's rosy face is neither Homeric nor necessary. In sum, Thorius's Ronsard, although charming, is more given to mannerism and redundancy.

Aside from Thorius's rendition of Ronsard's decasyllables or alexandrines into various Latin meters, what is particularly striking about his translations is the increased use of Greco-Roman mythological allusion and a desire to convert Ronsard's indirection into explicit reference. Most of us know that "the archer" or "the god" or just "amour" means Cupid. Thorius likes to call a Cupid a Cupid, when he is not calling him something yet more fancy. A good example is a sonnet to Cassandre, the relentlessly erudite "Je ne suis point ma guerriere" (Céard I.26–7; Harvester "t"), a sonnet so studded with classical names and allusions that from a distance it might be mistaken for Neolatin even in its French dress. He is not, says Cassandre's lover, a Myrmidon or a Dolopian soldier, nor yet the archer [Philoctetes] whose homicidal dart killed Cassandra's brother [Paris] and turned the town to ash. No armed camp set to make her a slave leaves the port of Aulis, and she will not see at the foot of her rampart a thousand ships ready to take her away. Alas, the lover is mad Corœbus [a Phrygian prince in love with Cassandra], whose heart lives mortally wounded, not by the hand of the Greek Peneleus [leader of the Bœotians] but by a hundred shots that the little conquering archer thoughtlessly sent into the speaker's heart by way of a path hidden in his eyes. The poem depends for its effect (beyond the effect of making us reach for our Homer, Virgil, a reference book, or Google) on our knowledge of the Trojan Cassandra's genealogy and the fate of her relatives, for this is one of those love poems that gestures toward Ronsard's still unfinished epic, the *Franciade*. By relating his somehow persistently hopeful if painful victimizations by Eros to doomed Troy, the poet positions himself to have his Aphrodite and his Calliope both, his myrtle and his laurel.[14] As Jean-Claude Moisan puts it, "Ces *Amours* seront marquées du sceau de l'epique."[15]

---

[14] See my "The Laurel and the Myrtle: Spenser and Ronsard," in Patrick Cheney and Lauren Silberman, eds, *Worldmaking Spenser: Explorations in the Early Modern Age* (Lexington: University Press of Kentucky), 63–78.

[15] Jean-Claude Moisan, "Le *'Logos'* dans les *Amours de Cassandre* de 1584," in Jean Balsamo, ed., *Mélanges de Poétique et d'histoire littéraire du XVIe siècle offerts à Louis Terreaux*

From "Amours" to Amores 169

Thorius adds yet more weight to the poem's classical learning—further "antiquing" it, as they say in the furniture business, with yet more classical patina. Paris is not simply killed but is sent "sub tartara"; it is not just Cassandre's "ville" Troy that is turned to cinders but her "Pergama"; and Cupid is no longer just a "conquering little Archer," for that "puer insuperabilis" now wounds the lover with a Paphian bow: "paphio … arcu." The result of all this literary strutting, even for the educated, is yet greater distance from the vernacular, not just linguistically but also culturally, as well as a yet firmer settlement within a largely male and transnational networked world of elite *Latinitas*.[16]

In another sonnet, one of Ronsard's most powerful, "Quel dieu malin, quel astre me fyt estre" (Céard I.52), the lover's lament ranges downward from the stars and gods that have betrayed him to the hard rind of the earth where the enviably oblivious dead find surcease and, below that, to the depths with Sisyphus and Tantalus where there is all too much feeling. Under what evil star was he born? Which of the Sisters blackened the thread of his life? What demon suckled him with cares instead of milk? Happy the corpse whose bones the earth keeps and happy those whom the night of Chaos holds in the lap of its "masse brutale." In Thorius's Latin (Harvester "ee"), traditionally a more masculine language, the lover's fate has accumulated more female figures: who was his midwife, what Lucina helped his mother, and what demon with cruel hand rocked his cradle? Again, though, the allusions are spelled out and the lines studded with more classical names: the sisters are the Parcae and the earth no mere French "terre" but the goddess "Tellus" herself. The style is further classicized, and even as the lover wonders about all those feminine names and nouns hovering over his unlucky birth he also substitutes the personification "crudelis Amor" for Ronsard's adjective "amoureux"; it is perhaps an amusing reminder of Thorius's profession that this arrow-pierced lover, unlike Ronsard's, adds that he cannot doctor his wounds: "nec medicari vulnera possum."

(Paris: Champion, 1994), 97–131, 102. What is true in 1584 is, I think, true even in earlier versions. On Ronsard's "obscurité," see the subtle chapter on the matter in Yvonne Bellenger's *Lisez La Cassandre de Ronsard: Etude sur Les Amours (1553)* (Paris: Champion, 1997); she quotes some who think such obscurity unsuitable for love poetry—the same objection, with just as little truth and just as much sexism, that was once made about Donne's love poetry. For a neoclassical French complaint about Ronsard's indecorous Latinity, translated and published in England, see Rapin, *Reflections on Aristotle's treatise of poesie*, section 30: Ronsard was "noble and great," says Rapin, "but this greatness becomes deform'd and odious, by his affectation to appear learned; for he displayes his *Scholarship* even to his *Mistriss*" (L1v).

[16] Women readers could, to be sure, consult Marc-Antoine Muret's learned but clear *Commentaires au premier livre des Amours de Ronsard* (1553), ed. Jacques Chomarat, Marie-Madeleine Fragonard, and Gisèle Mathieu-Castellani (Geneva: Droz, 1985); in a note on "Je ne suis point," sonnet 4, Muret notes that Ronsard addresses Cassandre both as her modern self and as the Trojan princess, much as Petrarch addresses Laura both as herself and as Daphne. For more general theories about Latinity, the vernacular, and gender, see Margaret W. Ferguson, *Dido's Daughters: Literacy, Gender, and Empire in Early Modern England and France* (Chicago Chicago University Press, 2003).

170 *French Connections in the English Renaissance / Prescott*

Another of Thorius's translations, one of his most mannered, keeps the air of the French court but adds a bit more academic density:

> Je vy ma Nymphe entre cent damoiselles,
> Comme un Croissant par les menus flambeaux,
> Et de ses yeux plus que les astres beaux
> Faire obscurcir la beauté des plus belles.
> Dedans son sein les Graces immortelles,
> La Gaillardise, et les freres jumeaux
> Alloient volant, comme petits oiseaux
> Parmy le verd des branches plus nouvelles.
> Le ciel ravy, qui si belle la voit,[17]
> Roses et liz et ghirlandes pleuvoit
> Tout au rond d'elle, au milieu de la place:
> Si qu'en despit de l'hyver froidureux,
> Par la vertu de ses yeux amoureux
> Un beau printemps [s'esclouit] de sa face.
> (Céard, I.81–2, with an earlier variant; later editions have "s'engendra")

Thorius changes the "crescent" Cassandre, promoted to a "nymph," to a moon just as luminous but less curvy, and although keeping, indeed intensifying, the prettiness makes it a trace more classical:

> Ex Ronsardo
> Je vy ma nymphe entre cent demoiselles.
>
> Vidi ego, quum nymphas inter mea numpha trecentas
> Luderet, una suo prælucens lumine cunctis,
> Candida ceu stellas micat inter luna minores.
> Præstabant omnes speciosæ munere formæ,
> Illa sed æthereis oculi fulgoribus omnes
> Vincebat formas, et pulcri sideris instar
> Eximias radiante faces face præstringebat.
> Pectoris in spatio genus immortale sororum
> Ludebat Charitum, quibus intermista Venustas
> Et Gemini fratres Amor, et Lepor, agmine læto
> Ludebant alacres, tepidi ceu tempore veris
> Frondea pervolitant teneræ virgulta volucres.
> Quin pater ipse, meae perculsus imagine nymphæ
> Liliaque, et violas, densis dabat imbribus Æther,
> Sternebatque rosis, et suavibus omnia circum
> Largus opum sola muneribus: nec frigida brumæ
> Tempestas oberat, quin indignantibus auræ
> Flatibus hybernæ, subiti nova veris honestas
> Surgeret, et cœli facies inopina sereni:
> Tantùm sidereis mea nympha valebat ocellis. (Harvester "x")

---

[17] In early versions Heaven is moved by her voice, further suggesting that Thorius used an edition such as that of 1567.

[I saw, when my nymph was frolicking among three hundred nymphs, her alone outshining all with her light, as the brightly fair moon flashes amongst lesser heavenly bodies. They all excelled in the gift of good looks, but she surpassed all beauties in the ethereal gleam of her eye, and like a lovely star eclipsed their exceptional torches with her own radiant flare. In the region of her breast frolicked the immortal race of the sister Graces, mingled with whom Beauty's self and the brethren twins, Love and Charm, eagerly frolicked in a glad company, as delicate birds at the time of warm spring fly about the leafy thickets. Indeed the Father himself, struck by the picture of my nymph, provided frequent showers of lilies and violets, and lavishly strewed the whole ground about with roses and the delightful gifts of plenty: nor was the chill season of winter harmful, but rather (despite the angry breezes of the winter atmosphere) the fresh beauty of the sudden spring sprang up, and the unexpected visage of a fair-weather sky: Such was the power my nymph wielded with her starry little eyes.]

In the Latin the twin brothers are further identified as Amor and Lepor, perhaps to make crystal clear that they are not the stellified Castor and Pollux (traditionally relevant to starry eyes but unapt to flutter like birds), and Ronsard's more abstract "ciel" has become a more personified "Father," although whether Zeus or Jehovah or even the Stoics' Ethereal Father it is hard to say.

Not all of Thorius's changes, though, bring more explicit learning. In one poem, besides adding some "Idalian flames" to Ronsard's ardor, the translator further signals his knowledge of the French literary scene: lying miserably on the hard ground in a lonely wood (Céard I.29; Harvester "dd"), the lover pulls out a picture made by the poet and draftsman Denisot, which seems to help his spirits; Thorius turns the French "Denisot" into "Alcinous," thus signaling his awareness that "Nicolas Denisot liked to go into print anagrammized as the "Conte d'Alcinois." It may have been this desire to show his intimacy with the Pléiade that led Thorius also to rename Ronsard's mere lute strings as "Pindaricis ... nervis." He knows, this implies, that Ronsard was the first in France, as he himself boasted, to write Pindaric odes; perhaps he even knew that Dorat had called "Pierre Ronsard" the "Rose de Pindare."[18] And sometimes Thorius adds a touch of the exotic, an echo, some might say, of early modern European exploration and trade or colonization. When Ronsard explains, for example, that he would not change the hurts Marie has caused for all the gold in the cosmos, all "l'or de l'Univers" (Céard I.201; Harvester "nn"), Thorius specifies the "or" as Attic talents but also as the opulence of the Indies (or "of India"; the adjective is "indianis"). And when Ronsard, wounded by love for Cassandre, asks "quelle plante" might cure him, Thorius wonders about the medical properties of plants in Arabia and, again, the Indies (Céard I.59 Harvester "lll").

Another sonnet that drew his attention glances westward, although briefly and not necessarily all the way to the Americas. Here Cassandre's lover, enjoying an erotic languor that, like Ovid's *Amores*, signals a preference for Cupid over Mars,

---

[18]   "Devant les yeux nuict et jour me revien," Céard I.76; Harvester "cc." On the anagram see Estienne Tabourot, *Les Bigarrures du Seigneur des Accords*, ed. Francis Goyet, 2 vols (Geneva: Droz, 1986, a facsimile of the 1588 edition) I, sig. I12v.

performs the traditional slightly nervous *recusatio* (I am not writing an epic, for I am better suited for love—and, in Ovid's case, he says in *Amores* I.1, cannot do so because Cupid has swooped by, laughing, and stolen the syllable needed for Virgilian dactylic hexameters and thus left the poet only with elegiacs and myrtle). What Ronsard says has a long tradition behind it, for Ovid was not alone:[19]

> Si je trespasse entre tes bras, Madame,
> Je suis content: aussi ne veux-je avoir
> Plus grand honneur au monde, que me voir
> En te baisant, dans ton sein rendre l'ame.
> Celuy dont Mars la poictrine renflame,
> Aille à la guerre, et d'ans et de pouvoir
> Tout furieux, s'esbate à recevoir
> En sa poitrine une Espagnole lame:
> Moy plus couard, je ne requier sinon
> Apres cent ans sans gloire et sans renom
> Mourir oisif en ton giron, Cassandre.
> Car je me trompe, ou c'est plus de bon-heur
> D'ainsi mourir, que d'avoir tout l'honneur,
> Et vivre peu, d'un monarque Alexandre. (Céard I.64)

Thorius's translation is quite close but with a few typical and intriguing shifts:

> Ex Ronsardo
> Si je trespasse entre tes bras madame &c
>
> Si morior, Cassandra, tuis projectus in ulnis,
> Hæc sat erit merces: neque enim mihi major amanti
> Gloria contigerit, quàm, dum tibi basia libo,
> Oppetere, inque tuis animam expirare lacertis.
> Cui Mavors animos ciet, inflammátque juventas,
> Viribus ille suis fidens, et fervidus armis,
> Militiam, pugnásque cruentaque castra sequatur,
> Hesperiúmque furens in pectora provocet ensem.
> Ast ego, degenerem quem mitior aura creavit,
> Nil spero, nihil expecto, nihil amplius opto,
> Quàm bis ut ignavæ post quinque decennia vitæ
> Serà mori tolerer, laudisque et nominis expers,
> Inque tuo, mea vita, sinu deponere vitam.
> Conditio est etenim, (mea me aut sententia fallit)
> Pulcrior, et melior, tali se dedere fato,
> Divite Pellæi, quàm Regis honore potiri,
> Exiguoque frui trabeatæ tempore vitæ. (Harvester "y")

---

[19] The notes in the Céard edition cite Propertius's elegy II.1, and Dr. Lake reminds me of Tibullus I.i, which says the poet is willing to be thought lazy and idle if he could "hold you as I die, with failing hand." Thorius may have been drawn to Ronsard precisely because he heard and enjoyed such frequent echoes.

From *"Amours"* to Amores   173

[If I die, Cassandra, stretched out in your arms, it will be sufficient reward: for no greater glory could befall me as a lover than to die tasting your kisses and breathing out my soul in your embrace. The man whose courage Mars stirs up and whose youth sets him ablaze—that man, trusting his own strength, and ardent in arms, follows war and battles and bloody camps, madly challenging the western sword to try his breast. But I, whom a milder air created base, expect naught, await naught, hope for naught—but that after two times five slow decades of idle life I might bear to die, without praise or fame, and lay down my life—my life—in your lap. For this (or my thoughts deceive me) is a fairer and finer choice, to yield one self to such a fate, than to gain the rich honor of the Pellean king, and enjoy a brief span of a courtly-robed life.]

As one would expect, Thorius edges Ronsard a little closer to the schoolroom. Alexander is now called—accurately but more obscurely—the Pellean king (Pella was the capital of Macedonia) and Ronsard's mere "cent ans" is now twice five decades, which does indeed work out to a century. More interesting is the "Spanish sword," the "Espagnole lame," that will not be killing the lover (note the transposition of adjective and noun, the practice that drew the contempt of critics such as Rapin). The commentary in the Pléiade edition of Ronsard sensibly says that we need not hear in this phrase an allusion to the real Cassandre Salviati's husband fighting in the wars with Spain, but no allusion to a Spanish sword can be quite free from awareness of France's conflicts with that nation or with its earlier Habsburg rulers; whatever the international situation at any given moment it was in Spain that François Ier had been held prisoner. For Thorius himself, the Spanish must have been the persecutors of his fellow Protestants, but he does not specify "Spanish," preferring "Hesperium." The word can mean merely "western"—like Spain or Hispaniola. But even visually it can also provoke associations with the evening star shining over the western horizon and with the Hesperides, the western isle looking toward new worlds. Whatever sword Ronsard himself was imagining, that of Thorius has a more general and perhaps more exotic look to it.

Thorius was entirely capable of sensing words' overtones, and indeed of hearing the possibility of further wordplay. In one sonnet to Cassandre ("Lors que mon oeil," Céard I.128; Harvester "r"), for example, his renaming of Ronsard's "Sœurs" (the sister Muses) suggests an ear for puns. Ronsard has been lamenting that the "vertu" of Cassandre's eye has changed him to stone ("m'em-pierre en un rocher"). Since the lover is already, like Petrarch himself, halfway to being a rock or "Pierre" (de Ronsard), Thorius may have thought, why not underscore the wit of his original by giving the Muses a traditional name that both adds classical bling and advances the French pun: the "Pieriæ"? An even better example comes in Thorius's reworking of Ronsard's "C'est grand cas que d'aimer," from the *Second livre des Amours* (Céard I.139; Harvester "ll"). Love, says Ronsard, is a magician who manipulates time, so that for the poet a day with his girl seems a year. Love also affects the tongue: when Ronsard is alone with Marie his tongue can babble his ardor, but when somebody else is there speech deserts him. Thorius seems to have realized that Ronsard's allusion to being "seul" and talkative with his beloved but silent in company could be reinforced by a more explicit mention of the movement of light through the day that elongates into a year for a lover, suggesting wordplay, missing in Ronsard's sonnet, on "solus" and "sol." So when the lady is "sola" with him and he is "solus," the day seems a year, whereas the presence of others is like Capricorn, which draws in darkness and steals the light. But, Thorius says, circling back to his pun, when he is "solus" and she is "sola," then in effect the sun returns. Thorius was certainly clever. True, he may also be slandering the great Goat, unless he is performing a self-correction as he repeats his wordplay, for as all almanacs agree it is precisely when Sol enters Capricorn at the winter solstice that he begins his northward journey and will now go from strength to strength.

But why choose the love poetry and why Latin at all?

After attempting to trace the variants listed by Ronsard's editors, I have come to think that Thorius worked from a volume or volumes, most likely published before 1572, and perhaps in 1567, that included the *Premier livre des amours* (largely to the elegant and sophisticated Cassandre) and the *Second livre des amours* (less focused but most famous for its poems to the more simple and rustic Angevine flower, Marie, who—like Laura—dies part way through the volume). It is highly probable, I think, that Thorius knew, or knew of, Ronsard's other works. This means in turn that he *chose* the love poetry. Ronsard's amatory verses, moreover, even those to Marie, are already extraordinarily learned, weighty (some have said too weighty) with allusion or with periphrasis that, with pleasant coyness, skirts around the famous old names.

Malcolm Smith has said that one reason for Neolatin translations of Ronsard was a conviction that his content was of the highest importance—although the poems Smith mentions are non-amatory.[20] He also speculates that some translated Ronsard because fascinated by his obvious "excellence," and I agree that Thorius probably hoped to beam Pléiade star-power into his own Flemish (or English) sky. Again, though: why love poetry? McFarlane has noted that many Latin tributes to Ronsard precisely praise his lines to Cassandre. In any case, it may be easier to change Cassandre into Cassandra than it would be to change, say, Spenser's Elizabeth Boyle or Sidney's Stella (already a Roman noun), into Corinna. Significantly, perhaps, Thorius turns one poem to Marie—never named by him as such, and for that matter not often named by Ronsard either—into a poem to "Fausta" (Céard I.293; Harvester "eee"). A "Maria" would do nothing for the tone, whereas Cassandre is one letter away from being the Trojan princess with whom Ronsard so often merges her. No wonder that when Melissus translated a love poem to Marie—"Amour estant marri qu'il avoit ses saigettes"—into Latin

---

[20]   Smith, p. 334. Note 22 also mentions the desire to put Ronsard into a more durable language and, citing McFarlane, a desire to "show off." This last, I might add, and along with playfulness, must underlie such translations as Alexander Lenard's 1960 *Winnie Ille Pu* (New York: Dutton, 1960; the title character, when dragged down the stairs by his owner, goes "Tump, tump").

From *"Amours"* to Amores   175

he addressed his 14 elegiacs to the somewhat more classical sounding (or at least Italian) "Rosina."[21] Thorius does not violate the mood of Ronsard's love poetry so much as return it to one of its spiritual—and *spirituel*—homes and, as I have said, facilitate further its complex and sometimes ironic gestures toward the epic that Ronsard was writing, trying to write, going to finish any day now. Perhaps that is one reason why Thorius avoids the sonnet form, unknown to the ancients, preferring to expand the conceits and to use a variety of Latin meters.[22]

Is there more to say, about the choice of Latin and not Flemish or even English? To give the little archer (Ronsard's "Archerot") more heft by pumping Latin into his biceps or wings would certainly increase his *gravitas*, such as it is. Latin weighs more than French. Latin has words, to borrow the wittily punning title of a book by Judith Anderson, that *matter*. That may be why, as I have suggested elsewhere, Ben Jonson so often glossed the words in his copy of Rabelais's *Gargantua et Pantagruel* with definitions in Latin, as though to make the margins of this comic but learned satire more solid.[23] In 1653 James Howell summed up what seems like a prevalent opinion of the relevant languages in his *German diet, or, The ballance of Europe wherein the power and weaknes ... of all the kingdoms and states of Christendom are impartially poiz'd.* Because this "German diet" is an imaginary council with orations by advocates for the various nations, what Howell writes is not in his own voice; it may, though, represent something like his opinion when he has a speaker report, albeit with some dubious philological history, that St. Jerome left his studies in Gaul for those in Rome so that "he might season the copiousnesse and neatnesse of the *French* speech with the *Roman* gravity" (sig. M2v; as for what has been done in French, Ronsard is first among the "heavenly inspir'd Poets," and "the excellentest that hath bin since *Augustus* his egresse out of this World" [sig. N1]). Such comments need not mean that Latin and Neolatin are "heavy" in the pejorative sense, and indeed for one poet Latin could in fact accelerate a work: Du Bartas writes in a French sonnet to Gabriel de Lerm that the dull lead of his first *Sepmaine* is now gilded by Lerm's Latin translation; dressed in French, he says, the work had lagged behind the *Franciade*, but since it has been put into a "habit estranger" Lerm's glory follows Virgil and Homer close at heels (one understands why in a later edition of the *Franciade* Ronsard himself objected

---

21   I thank Lee Piepho for a photocopy of the poem in the Paris 1586 edition of *Melissi Schediasmata Poetica*, p. 164. Ronsard's sonnet (Céard I.183 and notes), in turn indebted to Latin epigrams, reports that Cupid used his arrows in vain and so threw the bees that had taken up taken up residence in his quiver at Marie's face and "mammelettes," but the bees just made honey from her sweetness; Melissus keeps the face but drops the breastbuds.

22   McFarlane, too, mentions the tendency of most of Ronsard's translators to avoid the sonnet form, noting the formal difficulty of adapting elegiacs to the tercets.

23   Judith H. Anderson, *Words That Matter: Linguistic Perception in Renaissance English* (Stanford: Stanford University Press, 1996); Anne L. Prescott, "Jonson's Rabelais," in James Hirsh ed., *New Perspectives on Ben Jonson* (Madison, NJ; London: Fairleigh Dickinson University Press, 1997), 35–54.

176 *French Connections in the English Renaissance / Prescott*

to the recently intensified fashion for writing in Latin).[24] As for Thorius, even if not edging much closer to Virgil's heels, he approaches being a second Secundus, if not yet a Catullus, Ovid, or Propertius.

If Ronsard's words are now more culturally weighty, are they also gendered male? The lover's sentiments are post-Petrarchan, his erudition is humanist, and his language and style are, if not quite Roman, then something a little closer to Dorat's classroom than to the châteaux of the Loire; they suit an international, masculine, highly educated network of humanist poets, a network that connected Ronsard to Thorius, Thorius to Rogers, Rogers to Sidney, and Sidney to all over the place on both sides of the Manche/Channel.

It is noteworthy, though, if a little discouraging, to observe that those who track the Renaissance desire to put vernacular texts into Latin often explain that such translation meant a wider readership, and it is certainly true that after the first flush of enthusiasm for their own tongues some writers did come to worry about the vernacular's constriction in space and mutability in time. This must have seemed particularly true in England, with a population speaking a still fairly obscure Germanic dialect that had changed confusingly in just a few generations since Chaucer, to say nothing of since King Alfred. But was this true for those writing in French, a language of great *prestige*, known to the *elite* and indeed to all those wanting to show they were *au courant* and could talk with that *je ne sais quoi* demonstrating *savoir-faire*? Apparently so. Claude Faisant quotes some deliciously awful lines to Ronsard by Du Monin fearing "l'âpre dent du porte-fau[x]" (i.e., "the sharp tooth of carry-sickle" Time, the compound noun being another usage that would draw scorn from neoclassical critics) that might undermine the "rempar de ton los."[25] But if to write in nice stable tooth-resistant and rampart-preserving Latin might expand a permanent readership among the highly educated, it also *narrowed* a readership, especially in countries such as France with a tongue that so many (including the Flemish and the English) could understand; and it did so by excluding most women. A valuable modern essay on Latin translations from the vernacular says that one purpose of such enterprises was "to make available to any cultivated reader in Europe works which might otherwise remain unknown or inaccessible to him."[26] Yes, "him." But depending

---

[24] *Guilielmi Salustii Bartassii Hebdomas a Gabriele Lermœo latinitate donata* (London, 1591), dedicated to Queen Elizabeth, sig. A1. On Ronsard's vexation with a lapse in French confidence in the vernacular, see Claude Faisant, "Un des aspects de la réaction humaniste à la fin du XVIᵉ siècle: la paraphrase latine des poètes français," in P. Tuynman, G.C. Kuiper, and E. Kessler, eds., *Acta Conventus Neo-Latini Amstelodamensis* (München: Wilhelm Fink, 1979), 358–70.

[25] Faisant, p. 362.

[26] Grant, p. 120. Grant is not wrong about Englishmen's attitudes. He quotes William Cartwright on Kynaston's Chaucer: "He that hitherto / Was dumbe to strangers and's owne Country too, / Speakes plainly now to all, being more our owne / Ev'n hence, in that thus made to Aliens knowne." Thorius may have thought that he was making Ronsard better known to "Aliens," or at least aware, like so many others, that there was a reputable

on the definition of "cultivated," one can doubt that Latinization made Ronsard more accessible to many an otherwise cultivated "her."

And Thorius? His translations move Ronsard's love poetry into a discourse pleasing to the Belleau/Rogers/Melissus/Sidney network, but less likely to be read by otherwise cultured women with small Latin and less Greek. Perhaps not by Cassandre, or not readily, and certainly not by Marie. In other words, in addition to making Ronsard even more learned, durable, and legible to foreigners, Thorius makes him more what some call homosocial—or, if one prefers phrasing with less ideological freight, more suitable to the universities, the schools of law and medicine, and the world of international diplomacy and correspondence than to, say, Catherine de' Medici's *escadron volant*. Not that there's anything wrong with that. Male humanists are people too. But Thorius's poet is more the Ronsard of international learning, less the courtier of Blois, and that it is *love* poetry that serves this choice makes the learned lines' anguished *eros* all the more poignant.

---

community that knew Latin and did not know French. And yet even outside France many female "Aliens" were apt to read French more comfortably than Latin. (The gendering of Latin and French continued well into the twentieth century. At my childrens' school, boys in the 1950s had been required to learn Latin and girls to learn French.)

Appendix
Ronsard in England, 1635–1699

Anne Lake Prescott

A chapter in my *French Poets and the English Renaissance: Studies in Fame and Transformation* (New Haven and London: Yale University Press, 1978) explores the reception of Ronsard in early modern England as fully as I could then manage. Since then I have found other allusions or imitations, usually later than those in my book, thanks often to a search of Early English Books Online. Because they suggest both the variety of much English comment on Ronsard as well as a trajectory (less clear in England than in France) after the French had turned to a new style of poetry, it seems valuable to describe them briefly, in chronological order but with authors kept together. The list is incomplete, if only because EEBO has yet to make all its texts searchable. The place of publication is London unless otherwise specified; I omit printers, although they can matter in times of political upheaval, and quote only as much as space allows. This is a list, not an essay, so I note only the obvious: first, Ronsard's name remained famous even in the 1690s and, second (particularly in texts translated from French), the growing belief in progress that is observable in political or scientific thinking shows also in the seemingly smug belief that language and literature have improved over time. Unlike Whigs or the Royal Society, though, few critics seem to have asked if there might be further advancement; the focus is rather on Ronsard as facilitating progress but unable himself to reach the Parnassus (or Parisian salon) of true wit.

Gerhard Mercator, *Historia Mundi* … trans. W.S. (1635). The great geographer says of the "Dukedome of Turone" that there lie "the ashes of that great Poet *P. Ronsard*, who they call the French *Homer*, and *Pindar*," and the "Dukedome of Franconia." Some say "Franconia" comes from Francus, whom "*Peter Ronsard*" claims the ancients called "*Astyanacta Francum*, "as it were *Hastigerum*, that is, the speare-bearer" (Gg2v; Hhh1v; Mercator or a research assistant has read the *Franciade*).

Jacques Ferrand, *Erotomania or A Treatise discoursing of … Erotique Melancholy*, trans. Edmund Chilmead (Oxford, 1640). In Chapter 24, on recognizing love through dream interpretation, Ferrand quotes a phrase from Homer and then adds, "that is, as *Ronsard* translates it into French. *Des Dieux, çà bas certaine viennent les Songes. / Et Dieu n'est pas artisan des Mensonges.*" A translation follows: "Those Dreames the Gods us send, have sure event. / For they to cousenage nere give consent" (M2v; *Franciade* ed. Céard IV.181–2, pp. 685–6).

In Chapter 34, on curing marital love melancholy, Ferrand quotes more extensively (III.627–46), but Chilmead omits the lines.[1]

Dudley North, *Forest of Varieties* (1645). A poem in this collection of lyrics and essays by a well-read aristocrat is "Made in imitation of a Sonnet in Ronsard." The lover's sympathy for those who leave an indifferent lady suits a generation of poets less Petrarchan than—in every sense—cavalier; that the lover finally keeps his idealism says something about North. The love poems in *Forest* are dated 1638. I cannot find the original; this may be what one thoughtful poet thought Ronsard would sound like in English:

> Though he that loves with unrequited love,
> And finds his heat ingender no reflection,
> Nor that his plaints can her compassion move,
> That is the object of his true affection,
> May uncondemn'd resume his love again,
> And to a more kind subject it apply
> Himself exempting from unpityed pain:
> Nor doth he wrong whom no desert doth tie,
> Nor doth he faith or constance violate,
> For vertue and folly incompatible be,
> And constant Lovers uncompassionate
> Are foolish guilty of their miserie;
> Nor breaks that Prince his faith who league hath sworn
> Of amity with some great Potentate,
> Who will not after the like oath return
> Of love and faithfull aide unto his State:
> For perfect love in sympathie consists,
> And single Love is but a fatuous fire;
> Yet little merits he, who not persists,
> No victory is gotten by retire.
> I'le love her still, though shee unjust doe prove;
> And happier contentment will I find
> In loving her with unrequited love,
> Then to love one lesse faire, though farre more kind. (F2v)

Robert Baron, *Mirza a Tragedie, Really Acted in Persia, in the Last Age. Illustrated with Historicall Annotations* (EEBO says 1647; the online Oxford Dictionary of National Biography says 1655). A royalist with ties to Gray's Inn and debts to such writers as Jonson, Baron's annotations at one point say that Du Bartas calls lawyers harpies, on which creatures he sends us to "Ronsard in his Hymn of *Calais* and *Zethes*" (R1; Céard II.442–59).[2]

---

[1]   Why would Chilmead drop the passage, no steamier than the chapter itself? For space? See the notes in the translation by Donald A. Beecher and Massimo Ciavolella (Syracuse: Syracuse University Press, 1990).

[2]   My thanks to Adam Katz, graduate student at SUNY Stony Brook, for help with this text.

Appendix   181

William Bosworth, *The Chast and Lost Lovers* (1651). An Introduction by "R.C." to this posthumous edition of the young author's brief verse romances, amatory dixains, and shaped poems argues that if we refer to "the *Divine Mr. Spencer*, the *Divine Ronsard*, the *Divine Ariosto*," much more "Divine" are those "who have made chast Love their Argument" (A2).

James Howell, *A German Diet: or, The Ballance of Europe* (1653; "diet" is of course a congress). The prolific Howell, who often recycled his thoughts (for more allusions to Ronsard see my *French Poets*), says of French literature, "Now for heavenly inspir'd Poets let *Ronsard* appear first, the excellentest that hath been since *Augustus* his egress out of this World." Du Bellay is next, then Belleau, then Dorat. For a fifth, Du Bartas—and we get Ronsard's dubiously ascribed pun that Du Bartas had done more in a *Sepmaine* than had Ronsard in a lifetime (N1; readers could also find this in Simon Goulart's commentary on Du Bartas's "Babylon" in the *Seconde Sepmaine*, trans. Thomas Lodge [1621, Uuu1v]). **Howell**, *Paroimiographia Proverbs, or, Old sayed savves & adages* ... (1659). In a section on cultural history, Howell says that "The *French* began to be polishd in the reign of *Philip de Valois*, *Marot* did something under *Francis* the First, but *Ronsard* under *Henry* the Second did more then both" (sig. **).

Madeleine de Scudéry, *Clelia, an Excellent New Romance* ... trans. George Havers (1655), Book IV (here ascribed, as were many of her other works printed in England, to "the exquisite pen of Monsieur de Scudéry"). Calliope foretells the literary future to Hesiod, judging as she goes. A muse with Neoclassical tastes, she praises earlier poets, chiefly as pioneers. Now "behold the Prince of the *French* Poets," she says, for "he shall be call'd *Ronsard*; his descent shall be noble; he shall be highly esteem'd, and deserve it, in his own dayes; for he shall have a very great genius. He shall also be sufficiently learned; but being he shall be the first in *France* that shall undertake to make handsom Verses, he shall not be able to give his works the perfection necessary to assure him lasting praises. However, it shall alwayes be known by some of his Hymnes, that nature ha's been very liberal to him, and that he merited his reputation. His fortune shall not be bad, and he shall die Superior to poverty." Then Belleau, Du Bellay, Jodelle, Garnier, Desportes, and a few others (X2–X2v).

Charles Sorel, *The Extravagant Shepherd, the Anti-Romance*, trans. **John Davies** (1653).[3] Davies's long introduction is severe. Does the hero Lysis think the "Stars living creatures"? Compare "*Ronsard* in his hymn, who says, they feed in the Plains of Heaven all night, and in the morning the Day-star (who is the Keeper) brings them together, tels them over, and drives them for all day into the shade" (a2v; cf. "Hymne des Astres," Céard II.623ff). Does a swain exaggerate? His "countrymen Ronsard, Marot, and others could have furnished him with much more extravagant and greater contradictions" (a4). Amatory images? Well, Ronsard says that "Love is a *Bird*, that he hath laid *Eggs* in his bosom, and that

---

[3]   The 1660 frontispiece is the famed Petrarchan lady with pearls for teeth, suns for eyes, etc.

when they are *hatch'd*, they'll prey on his *heart*, and when they have done flie away, if he do not lay Bird-lime or nets to catch them, *&c.*" (b2). Where does one character get his nymphs and rural gods? "I might produce whole Odes out of *Des Portes* and *Ronsard*" with such figures (b2v). And if Lysis had read more Ronsard he would know how to make "a Mortal fit for a celestial conversation" (b3). As it is, whatever his extravagance, "his Authors the Poets say as much. *Ronsard* says, *Then shall the Honey from the tall Oakes flow, / And Damask-Roses shall on Ashes grow: / The Ram, that sturdy Emp'rour of th'Down, / Shall march before us in a Scarlet-gown, &c.* What needs this? are not Roses as good, if they grow as they do?" (B4v). "This Poet," concludes Sorel, "would finde a man perpetual Satyre, yet was the most renowned of his time" (d3v).[4]

The anti-romance itself mentions Ronsard from time to time, as when a lackey confuses "sonnets" with the little bells on a morris dancer (F3v). Some satire is of the easy sort that wonders why the gods don't smoke at their banquets, and on occasion Ronsard figures (see L2v on Cassandre's eyes; a passing reference to his eclogues, Y1; or the advice to imitate Ronsard's invitation to Muret to leave a war-torn France for the Fortunate Isles, Gg1). More significant is Book XIII's "Oration of Clarimond against Poetry, Fables, and Romances." Among Clarimond's targets is "the most famous Poet that ever was in *France*: Any one may conceive I mean *Ronsard*: and what reputation soever his works have gotten, I shall venture to encounter them" (Hhh1v).

What follows, too long to quote in full, finds Ronsard's lyrics full of "ancient absurdities," his hymns incoherent, and the *Franciade* "low and poor" (an extensive demonstration follows, including the suggestion that we update mythology and give Cupid a pistol so that a "flaming bullet" could set our hearts afire). The rest of the discussion treats Ronsard no better. This is, however, followed by an oration by Philiris vindicating "Fables and Romances." He will not take the trouble, says Clarimond, to answer these "impertinent reasons" against Ronsard and against those "descriptions which have made *Ronsard* highly famous and esteemed, for the discourses of a *Poet* should not be so *severe* as those of a *Stoick* Philosopher." Not only is Ronsard justly famous for his "sweetness" but he had the "honour of having opened the dore to the advancement of the French Tongue." As for the silly history of the *Franciade*, that is his "Poetical stile"—and besides, the work is unfinished, and beyond that, "being a Poet, he was permitted to feign what he pleased." Pastorals? For a fine example, see Sidney's *Arcadia*, now "crossed the Sea to come and see us" (Kkk1–Kkk2). Aside from Clarimond's other arguments, note again the interest in a literary and linguistic history that shows the sense of *progress* that would change history.

---

[4]   For more, see sig. c1 on Ronsard's breathing in air blowing from Paris "where his Mistress was, which did extreamly enliven him"; c4 on the temple that Ronsard imagines in which lovers will come to worship the statues of his mistress and himself (cf. Donne's "Canonization"); and d3v, an extended denunciation first of "Hercule Chrestien"—"O lewd Poet!" exclaims Davies at Ronsard's comparisons of Christian story to the pagan—and then of the *Franciade*.

Appendix

Robert Codrington (1654). After dedicating this translation of Marguerite de Navarre's *Heptaméron* to Thomas Stanley, Codrington translates a poem on the queen's granddaughter-in-law, Marguerite de Valois, famous in England as the divorced first wife of the widowed queen Henrietta Maria's father, Henri IV, and the author of often-printed memoirs. He calls this epithalamic poem "The true and lively Pourtraicture of the most Illustrious and most Excellent Princess *Margaret* of *Valois*, Daughter to *Henry* the II. Sister to Henry the III. and Wife to *Henry* the IV. of France. Excellently set forth by the inimitable pen of *Peter du Ronsard* ..." and gives bibliographical information. "*La Charite*" begins, "The little God and wild one, a Commander, / Who through the earth, and through the Heavens doth wander, / Viewing the Ladies of the Court one day, / Return'd to Heaven, to whom did *Venus* say, ..." and ends, "Then a more high, and a devouter fire / My re-inforced Courage shall inspire, / To sound your happy Marriage Joyes, as far / As are the fields of flourishing *Navarre*" (B1–B4; Céard I.573–80).

Edward Leigh, *A Systeme or Body of Divinity* ... (1654). In a section on the Creation, a note observes that "*Du Bartas* hath most excellently described the Creation of the world in his Week. *Ronsard* being asked, what he thought of that Book, answered wittily, *Mounsieur* Du Bartas *à [sic] plus fait en une Sepmaine que je n'ay fait en toute ma vie. Bartas* hath done more in one week, then I have done in all my life" (Hh1; the 1662 edition repeats this, Oo3v). Siding with Parliament in the civil war (and an MP until expelled in Pride's Purge), the erudite Leigh also edited the Anglican Lancelot Andrewes and would welcome the Restoration. **Leigh**, *A Treatise of Religion & Learning* (1656; reissued in 1663 as *Foelix Consortium*). In a section on those zealous for true religion or learning, Leigh says of "Joannes Auratus" (Dorat) that he was admired by Charles IX, taught Ronsard, Baïf, and Du Bellay (true) and was "the chiefest Poet of his time" (R2; not so true). In a later such catalogue we find "*Peter Ronsard* Prince of the French Poets. Some call him the French *Homer* and *Pindar*." Leigh quotes Jacques de Thou, citing his *Historia* Vol. 5, Bk 117, part 1 (Rr3–Rr4), and a long note offers yet further praise, in both Latin and French, by Papire Masson, Antoine du Verdier, Etienne Pasquier, and Du Bartas, to the effect that Ronsard, master of many genres, is the French Homer, Theocritus, Pindar, Virgil, Catullus, Horace, and Petrarch. He gives Masson's Latin epitaph ("Hac tegitur *Ronsardus* humo, tot notus in oris / Quot patrius flavas Leda [*sic* for Ledus] percurrit arenas" [Ronsard is covered by earth, known on as many shores as his native stream, le Loir, flows through yellow sands]) and yet more praise from Cardinal Du Perron's funeral oration.[5]

John Collop, *Medici Catholicon* (1656 [1655]), reissued as *Charity Commended, or, A catholick Christian soberly instructed* (1658). A moderately royalist poet, Collop takes Catholics to task for contaminating truth with fable, as witness such "masking foolery" as the Golden Legend, "Monkish Chymæra's, and pious frauds, which for excellence and probability may parallel *Lucian's* true

---

5   The star-studded *Tombeau* is reprinted in Prosper Blanchemain's 1867 edition of the *Œuvres*, p. 270 (available on Google). The Loir (not Loire) was Ronsard's native river. Blanchemain includes the cardinal's oration.

History, render *Pantagruel* Orthodox"; witness, too, "*Ronsard* tenter our Saviours miracles to an analogy with *Hercules* labours" (C5; cf. "Hercule Chrestien," Céard II.525–32, which Ronsard himself thought "vers Chrestiens," l. 286).

William Drummond, *The history of Scotland* (1655). In a section containing some correspondence, Drummond, who knew Ronsard's work well, writes "To his much honoured friend M. A. J. Physitian to the King," that "Neither do I think that a good Piece of *Poesie*, which *Homer*, *Virgil*, *Ovid*, *Petrarch*, *Bartas*, *Ronsard*, *Boscan*, *Garcilasso* (if they were alive) and had that language, could not understand, and reach the sense of the writer" (Kk4v).[6]

Anon. *The Academy of Pleasure* (1656), a miscellany with, says its packed title page, jests, dialogues, songs, "conceits," a "*Dictionary* of all the hard *English words*," and models to help teach all sorts "How to Retort, Quibble, Jest or Joke, and how to return an ingenious Answer upon any occasion whatsoever." An alphabetized list offers useful materials for quick retorts. "C" is for "Cassandra," a "Prophetesse, Daughter to *Priam* King of *Troy*" and beloved of Apollo, who was pained by her rejection, "as is sweetly hinted by the famous French Poet *Ronsard* in one of his most excellent Sonets (translated, and almost fitted for the Presse) to his Mistresse, whom he shadows under the name of *Cassandra, Son. 22.*":

> So sacred *Phœbus* up and down did rove
> On Zincius [sic] banks (by *Ilion* swiftly running)
>   While rivers, woods, and flowry-meads did move,
> Wailing (with him) *Cassandra's* cruell cunning:
>   In vain the pensive God his Harp did plie,
> (Mingling his briny tears with *Zanthus* stream)
>   In vain he taxt his Ladies cruelty,
> Wasting his vitals in an amorous Dream.
>   As thou great God of Science, and of Light,
> Gold-hayr'd *Hyperion* were't once perplexed;
>   So am I stabb'd with dolours day and night,
> With griping care, and sullen sorrow vexed, Etc. (F8v; Céard I.42)[7]

The odd intrusion of Hyperion adds a little more of what might seem learning; but behind the "Etc." is a conclusion in which the poet suffers parallel anguish "on the banks of the Loir near Vendôme." Did the translator think that such French specifics spoiled his lesson in Greek mythology? "Yet at last," he continues, "this love-sick Deity got a grant of his wishes," and he then finishes explaining the rest of the myth. It is good to think of Ronsard the witty lover among the quips, retorts, mannered dialogues, and clever lyrics, published at a time whose moral glumness has been exaggerated. The godly know that "Tis Mirth that fills the veins with blood / More than wine, or sleep, or food" (E5).

---

[6]   I have failed to identify "M.A.J."; Drummond adds that expecting a new form of poetry is like expecting a new form of animal.

[7]   What the anonymous author means by saying the sonnet is almost ready for the press is unclear, as is the number "22" and the spelling of Xanthus in the second line.

Appendix 185

Traiano Boccalini, *I Ragguagli di Parnasso*, trans. Henry Carey, Earl of Monmouth (1656). In one episode of this work that doubles as farce and literary criticism, Dante is seized by ruffians who want to know the true genre of his poem. When he cries for help, his neighbor on Parnassus, Ronsard ("the Prince of French Poets"), arrives with sword in hand and Dante's enemies flee. Told to name the perpetrators he refuses lest he offend them, and after rope and rack do not make him talk he is given that final torture for a Frenchman—put on a slow horse with no whip. He agrees to name names: Carrieri of Padua and Jacapo Mazzoni (Dd2v–Dd3).

Samuel Holland, *Don Zara del Fogo a Mock-Romance* ... by "Baslius Musophilus" (1656), a parody with references to Sidney and Spenser, a masque on Venus and Adonis, and mild indecency ("Let's laugh, and leave this world behind, / And procreate till we are blind" E4). After killing a monstrous bear and, recovered from being "trans-elemented" by thoughts of his lady (the "Metaphysics of her Sex, the very Rule of Algebra"), Zara will go to her balcony "provided with an amorous Canticle, Rivall to best of Petrarchs, Sidney, or Ronsard" (E1).

John Jonston (Johannes Jonstonus), trans **John Rowland**, *A History of the Constancy of Nature* ... (1657). The Polish scholar Jonston defends modern humanity's size, morals, and technological feats against those who see decay; much is an assault on ancient manners, ethics, and "sottish" paganism. The continued power of poetic invention is shown by Ronsard, Buchanan, Du Bartas, Tasso, Spenser, Sidney, Barclay's *Argenis*, Mary Wroth, and some German and Polish writers. Rowland translates Latin lines by "Pasquire" (Etienne Pasquier) showing that Ronsard combines the capacities of Virgil, Catullus, and Petrarch. Jonston (or Rowland) may have found the epigram in Ronsard's 1587 *Œuvres*, but a more likely source is Pasquier's popular *Recherches de la France* (Book VII) or George Hakewill's 1627 *Apologie or declaration of the power and providence of God* (sig. G3v), which likewise argues against decline.[8]

Henry Stubbe, *Clamor, Rixa, Joci, Mendacia, Furta, Cachini, or A Severe Enquiry into the late Oneirocritica published by John Wallis, Grammar-Reader in Oxon* (1657). An anti-Presbyterian minister with republican tendencies until the Restoration, friend of Hobbes, satirist, pamphleteer, Galenist physician, critic of the Royal Society (though a better scientist would not have written in *The Indian Nectar*, K6, that chickens grow from egg whites), and apparently an irritating showoff, Stubbe includes in this diatribe against Wallis some stanzas taken, without credit, from the translated poem on Marguerite de Valois with which Codrington had prefaced his translated *Heptaméron* (see above).[9] The context is an argument over how people or even Spenser's iron Talus can move.

---

[8]   Céard II.1459; on Hakewill, see my *French Poets*, pp. 123–4 and note. I assume that by "Montgomeries Urania" Hakewill means—or should mean—Wroth's *The Countesse of Mountgomeries Urania*.

[9]   H3–H3v; Stubbe changes the typography, but the texts are close, even if Codrington's awkward but accurate "the Wind / Through the wast[e] Regions bouy'd her up as kind" ("les vents gracieux / La soustenoyent par le vague emportée," 23–4) is now "and the winde / Through the vast regions blow'd her up behinde." Ouch.

Stubbe's *The Indian Nectar, or, A Discourse Concerning Chocolate* (1662) explains chocolate's virtues, including its potential as an aphrodisiac (nations that drink it are the "most amorous," K7), relation to the humors, and geographical range. Noting our ability to love "a deformed Person," Stubbe cites "the commendation of *Ronsard* to *Pasithea*, or the Queen of *Navarre*, whom he represents to be *Of complexion rather brown, then faire*," a taste he compares to "the *choice* of *Solomon* in the *Canticles*: *I am black, but lovely*" (L2v).

Richard Flecknoe, *Erminia. Or, The Fair and Vertuous Lady. A Trage-comedy* (1661). The preface to this (understandably) never performed play by a priest, poet, and secondary victim of Dryden's satirical *Macflecknoe*, boasts of his familiarity with the English stage, claims that no one has "seen more of the *Latine, French, Spanish* and *Italian*," and says he is of the "same Profession with *Petre Ronsard* in *France*; *Lopes de Vega* in *Spain*; and the best and famousest Poets in *Italy*" (A3v). **Flecknoe**'s *Epigrams of all Sorts, Made at Divers Times on Several Occasions* (1670) includes one "Out of Ronsard, Of a happy life." Flecknoe gives the French (Céard II.1064) then, in bouncing anapests, "The same in English": "He is not happy, they point at i'th'Streets, / Whom the people does know, and salutes as it meets: / But happy is he who ambition has none, / Nor others to know, nor by others be known."

Philip de Cardonnel, *Complementum Fortunatarum Insularum* ... (1662). The dedication to the Earl of Ossory that prefaces Cardonnel's English version of his epithalamion on the king's wedding to Catherine of Braganza notes hopefully that just as Homer, Ennius, Virgil, and Horace were cherished by the great for giving them respite from their duties, so "on the same account *Ronsard* was esteemed by Charles the ninth of France" (A3). In Cardonell's *Tagus* (1662), his French and Latin versions, the Latin dedication to the Earl of Clarendon notes not that poets can be cherished but rather that the great can serve the muses, citing Michel de l'Hôpital ("Galliae Cancellarium"), the "Angliae literatae decus" More, and Bacon (A3–A3v).

The Works of the famous Mr. Francis Rabelais ... Translated into English by Sr. Thomas Urchard [sic] (1664). This new edition of Urquhart's 1553 translation comes with an unattributed "Life of the Author" that cites praise by a number of French writers, statesmen, and scholars, among them "*Peter Ronsard* Prince of Poets" (A5v).

Théophraste, Eusèbe, and Isaac Renaudot, *A General Collection of Discourses of the Virtuosi of France*, trans. George Havers (1664). Commenting on social hierarchy, one speaker cites Ronsard's suggestion that when Deucalion and Pyrrha, divinely instructed, threw stones behind them to repopulate the world after the flood, the precious stones turned into "the Nobility" and the ordinary ones into "the vulgar" (Dd3v–D4).

Obadiah Walker, *Of Education, Especially of Young Gentlemen* ... (Oxford, 1673). For this Oxford classicist, scientist, Stuart loyalist, and future Catholic convert, Christian consolation transcends secular erudition: "The gentle spirit of *Petrarch* also long before his death quitted his *Helicon* and *Muses* for mount

Olivet and *Divinity. Card. du Perron* kept not so much as any book of humanity (tho formerly a great Poet and Orator) either Poetry, Oratory, or History in his Library. *Jo Picus Miranduia*, extreamly repented his love verses; so did *Bembus, Ronsard, Marc-Ant. Muretus, Laur. Gacubaro, and Cavalier Marini.*" More examples follow (E9v).

René Rapin, *Reflections on Aristotle's Treatise of Poesie*, trans. Thomas Rymer (London, 1674). As Rapin pronounces on genres and those who have attempted them, Ronsard does not come out well. The epic? "*Ronsard* who had a Talent for Lyrick Verse in *Scaliger*'s opinion, and who got Reputation by his Odes, fell short extremely in his *Franciad*, which is dry and barren throughout, and has nothing of an *Heroick ayre* in it" (C2v). The best speech is clear and modest, but "Dubartas and Ronsard, who would heighten their Conceits with *great* words after their fashion, *compounded* according to the manner of the *Greek*, and of which the *French* Tongue is not capable" and so "made themselves *barbarous*."[10] Ronsard's violates literary "decorum" by making his shepherds too "gross" (F1). As for the epic, "For the *French* Poets who have writ in *Heroick* Verse, *Dubartas* and *Ronsard*, had all the *Genius* their Age was capable of; but the *French* Poets being ignorant, they both affected to appear learned, to distinguish them from the common; and corrupted their *wit* by an imitation of the *Greek* Poets ill understood: they were not skillful enough to place the *sublime* manner of the *Heroick* Verse in *things*, rather than in *words*; nor were so happy to apprehend that the *French* Tongue is not capable of those compounded words, which they made after the example of the *Greek*, and with which they stufft their Poems; and it was by this indiscreet affectation to imitate the *Ancients*, that both became barbarous; but besides, that the contrivance of the Fable of *Ronsard* in his *Franciad* is not natural, the sort of Verse he took is not enough Majestick, for an *Heroick* Poem" (G3v). Eclogues? "*Ronsard*, amongst the *French*, hath nothing tender or delicate" (K4v). Odes? "*Ronsard* is noble and great; but this greatness becomes deform'd and odious, by his affectation to appear learned; for he displays his *scholarship* even to his *Mistriss*" (L1v). There is a linguistic issue: "*Ronsard* in the Preface of his Poem of the *Franciad*" cannot accept that French has "a Character proper to bear in its expression" (L4). Languages have their own nature, and French cannot allow transposed words, for example; good writers accommodate themselves to a tongue's capacities. What readers of Rapin would *not* have found was the now common narrative of a barbarous language and literature improved by the likes of Ronsard but needing further refinement and truer wit.

Edward Phillips, *Theatrum Poetarum* (1675). In his catalogue of "The Modern Poets" Phillips includes "*Petrus Ronsardus*, a French Poet of *Vendosme*, the most to be esteem'd in the judgement of *Thuanus*, not only of the French but of all other Poets that have liv'd since the time of *Augustus* (Gg3v); it is Marot, however, whom "*Antoin Verd* in his Bibliothec stiles the Poet of Princes, and the Prince of the Poets of this time" (Bb1v).

---

[10] E1. Rapin means such "mots composés" as "le flot mine-rive" ("Eden," 484), in England associated with Du Bartas and his chief translator, Joshua Sylvester.

François Hédelin, Abbot d'Aubignac, *The Whole Art of the Stage ...* (1684; no translator named). The tone toward the vernacular past is predictably condescending. True, "In the Reign of *Henry* the Second in *France*, divers *French* poets made *Eclogues* in their own Language, of which we have some Examples in *Ronsard*" (S3v). As for drama, there were then no rules: "I have seen some of eight and forty Acts or Scenes, without any other distinction. In the time of Ronsard," though, "Comedy [does this mean drama?] was a little more regular," being cultivated by such writers as "*Jodelle, Garnier, Belleau*, and some others. Now Cardinal Richelieu's generosity and our poets' labor is improving the dramatic genre"—a compliment to his patron (T1v–Y2).

César Oudin, *The Extravagant Poet. A Comical Novel*, trans. G.R., Gent. (1681). Oudin (d. 1625), best known for translating *Don Quixote* into French, imagines a penniless poet, his confusing novel, and his wretched lyrics ("*Phillis*, like Tobacco I esteem you ... [but] in the Flambeau of my pipe, / I will extinguish all your charms" (D1v).[11] Author of "An Heroick *Poem* for Monsieur *Rondeau*" (B2v; a genre joke), the poet claims superiority to a long list of French writers; most are seventeenth century, but he includes Desportes and Ronsard (C1v). None, he adds, merits more than five or six hundred readers.

Michel de Montaigne, *Essays*, trans. Charles Cotton (1685–1686). Montaigne comments on some poets in terms that in Cotton's time were sometimes applied to Ronsard himself: "Since *Ronsard* and *du Bellay* have given Reputation to our *French* Poesie, every little Dabler, for ought I see, swells his Words as high, and makes his Cadences very near as they. *Plus sonat quam valet* [more noisy than effective]" ("Of the Education of Children," V2; Montaigne is quoting Seneca Ep. 40.5). The fault is not Ronsard's: "As to the French poets, I believe they have raisd it to the highest pitch to which it can ever arrive; and in those Parts of it wherein *Ronsard* and *du Bellay* excell, I find them little inferiour to the Ancient perfection" ("Of Presumption," Mm1v–Mm2; titles cited are not Cotton's).

Nathaniel Lee, *The Princess of Cleve* (London, 1689). This dramatization of La Fayette's novel changes the author's cool moral insight for late Restoration swagger. Vexed by Lady Tournon's wrinkle-inducing virtue, Nemours tells her that "now thou put'st me in Poetick Rapture, / And I must quote *Ronsard* to punish thee" (B3v). He does not do so.

Sir William Temple, *Miscellanea. In Four Essays* (London, 1690). The disquisition on poetry in this "second part" of the famous and prolific Temple's essays mentions, somewhat at arm's length, those "first Refiners" of an art fallen into *Gothick* Fashion," including "Petra[r]ch, Ronsard, Spencer," who "met with much Applause upon the Subjects of Love, Praise, Grief, Reproach." Ariosto and Tasso attempted the epic but lacking wings of their own merely imitated Virgil, and there follow some (vexing) thoughts on Spenser's supposedly transparent didacticism.

---

[11] Or, as admirers of Rudyard Kipling's "The Betrothed" in *Departmental Ditties*, used to say, "A woman is just a woman, but a good cigar is a smoke."

Appendix 189

Anon., *A Catalogue of Ancient and Modern Musick Books*, … (1691), a list of books "which will be sold at Dowing's Coffee House" that December; item 156 is "*French* songs for 4 voices, D.P.D. Ronsard" (A4).

Gerard Langbaine, *An Account of the English Dramatick Poets* (1691). The author, who spent much of his career tracking down sources and analogues, praises Thomas Stanley's translations from an impressive list of authors; French sources are "St. Amant, Tristan, Ronsard, Theophile, and De Voiture" (H5–H5v).[12]

William Walsh, *A Dialogue Concerning Women, being a Defence of the Sex Written to Eugenia* (1691, with a preface by Walsh's coffee-house friend John Dryden). The land on Parnassus is as poor as that in Ireland, says Walsh, and poets are a discontented lot, always complaining of women's misbehavior, including their supposed greed. Take "Ronsard, *among* the French," and a note quotes "*Celuy devroit mourir de l'Eclat du Tonnerre / Qui premier descouvrit les Mines de la Terre. Ronsard.* El. 8. 'Tis all against the love of money" (C4; in Céard II.330 these lines begin Elegie IV).

John Dunton, *The Young-Students-Library* … (1692). Dunton argues that Hebrew does not permit quantitative verse (which he calls "metrick"), for that requires a freedom to transpose words that Hebrew lacks. So does French—and "If Ronsard, and other Poets of his time made use of such Transpositions, their *French* was often but a sorry kind of *Latin*. Neither could these sorts of Licenses be long suffered, and they are now quite banished from the French Poesie" (4P2).

Edmund Bohun, *The Character of Queen Elizabeth* … (1693), taken largely, Bohun says, from **R. Johnstone's** 1655 *Historia rerum britannicarum*. Noting Elizabeth's linguistic prowess, Bohun repeats the story that "She gave *de Ronsard*, a *French* Poet, a Diamond of great Value, as a Testimony of Her approving his elegant and splendid Poems in that Tongue" (B5v).

Samuel Wesley, *The Life of our Blessed Lord & Saviour Jesus Christ. An Heroic Poem* (1693). In a long preface on the epic arguing that it does not require fiction or an always-virtuous hero, Wesley (father of the founder of Methodism) mentions Sannazaro, Vida, Tasso, Ariosto, Spenser, and Milton. Irritated by French critics' indifference to English poets, however, he says of the critic René Rapin that "since he has been so partial, as not to take any notice of our Writers, who sure as much deserve it as their *Dubartas* and *Ronsard*" (A4v), he will now turn to his own countrymen; he begins with Spenser and has much on his favorite, Cowley.

The Works of F. Rabelais, *M.D. … Done out of French by Sir Tho. Urchard, Kt., and Others* (1694). "Others" means primarily **Peter Motteux**, who finished Urquhart's translation of Book III and then translated Books IV and V.

---

[12] A shift in views of authorship and originality may explain the accusatory tone of his *Momus triumphans: or, The plagiaries of the English Stage Expos'd* (London, 1687), an in fact useful catalogue of English dramatists and, when detectable, their sources. I assume that Stanley does not "plagiarize" but translates; on his 1647 version of "Jeune beauté, mais trop outrecuidée" see my *French Poets*, 116–18. He credits Ronsard, setting off his version with italics.

190 *French Connections in the English Renaissance / Prescott*

The anonymous prefatory "Life of Dr. Francis Rabelais" (not the same as that in the 1664 edition but clearly indebted to it) and Motteux's long Preface name Ronsard, but with a difference—listed in the "Life" among those who praised Rabelais, he is now "*Peter Ronsard*, once Prince of the French Poets" (b3). The author says he will omit Ronsard's epitaph for Rabelais because it is too long but gives a number of brief ones by others and then again includes Ronsard among Rabelais's admirers (b3–b4). Far more significant is Motteux's signed "Preface," which judges by standards much affected by French Neoclassical criticism. Commenting on *Pantagruel*'s scholar who talks pseudo-erudite Latinate French until Panurge shakes him back into his native Limousine dialect, Motteux thinks of Ronsard. Citing a real scholar given to "*Pedantic Jargon*," he quotes Boileau: "*Ronsard en Francois parlant, Grec et Latin* (speaking Greek and Latin in *French*) thought to have refin'd his Mother Tongue." Rabelais's aim in his satire is to "prevent the spreading of that Contagion" (d11). Some pages later Motteux comments on the difficulty, a difficulty Rabelais overcomes, of exercising "the nicest Judgment" so as to "manage" a farce that "extends beyond Nature," for "Extravagant and monstruous Fancies are but sick Dreams." Thus the judicious Pasquier wrote of Ronsard that Rabelais won praise by "folastrant sagement" ("wise Drolling," f6v–f7).

Nicolas Boileau and **Peter Motteux**, *Ode de M. sur la Prise de Namur avec une Parodie de la Mesme Ode* (1695). Motteux has accosted an arrogant Boileau, asking for "two words" (I translate the French). "Write against me! ... Do you know who I am?" "I'm going to publish." "Leave my ode alone!" Eventually Boileau says Namur is taken, so wind it up and "take my ode." The parody that follows, in French and juxtaposed against the original, mentions Ronsard: Boileau asks, "Est-ce Apollon, Neptune / Qui sur ces Rocs sourcilleux ... ?" And Motteux: "Est-ce Ronsard le Gothique ...?" (Ronsard the Gothic). Elsewhere, for Motteux, Ronsard is too Humanist and word-drunk for his own good; here he is Medieval (A2v–A3).

Claude Fleury, *The History, Choice, and Method of Studies* (1695; no translator named). Sketching a rapid history of learning and its literary impact (a narrative still largely with us, if with inevitable biases), Fleury notes that some loved the ancients not wisely but too well: "They thought themselves happy, if they could attain to the making good Verses in *Latin*; they have also composed some in *Greek*, at the peril of not being understood by any Body: And they, who, as *Ronsard* and his *Followers*, began to make *French Verses*, after their Reading of the *Ancients*, have fill'd them with their *Words*, their *Poetical Phrases*, their *Fables*, their *Religion*, without concerning themselves, whether such *Poems* might please those who had not Studied as they had done: It was sufficient, that they made them Admired for their Profound Learning" (E1).[13]

René Le Bossu, *Monsieur Bossu's Treatise of the Epick Poem* ... trans. W.J. (1695). Together with some flattering comments on the Arthurian epics of his dedicatee, Richard Blackmore, the preface by "W.J." summarizes earlier criticism

---

[13] Hence, he might add, the annotated editions by Muret and Belleau of Ronsard's early love poetry. Fleury comments astutely on the "War amongst the Learned" over the value/threat of humanist scholarship.

on the heroic genre, noting that far from admiring Du Bartas and Ronsard, Rapin "taxes them with such imperfections that one may reasonably dispute with them the name of *Epick* Poets" (a2). Published with this is a disquisition on pastoral by Bernard le Bovier de Fontenelle, translated by Peter Motteux, that objects to giving shepherds aptitudes above their station. Theocritus gives his speakers long descriptions, and "*Ronsard* and *Belleau* his Contemporary, have made some that are yet longer" (u2v).

The Works of Virgil, trans. **John Dryden** (1697). The dedicatory epistle outlines a debate over the action's duration, siding against the "Ronsardians" (d2v–d3). Dryden later writes that, once preferring decasyllables, the French "since *Ronsard's* time, as I suppose," found "their Tongue too weak to support their Epick Poetry without the addition of another Foot" ([e]2). As a crack at the effete French, the anatomical pun is witty, but Ronsard himself blamed his troubles completing the *Franciade* on being told by the king, against his own instinct, to forego alexandrines for—decasyllables.

John Evelyn, *Numismata, A Discourse of Medals*, … (1697). In a section on the famous, Evelyn lists "Poets, Wits and Romancers"; the French include [Du] Bartas, [Du] Bellay, Corneille (but no Racine), Desportes, Dorat, D'Urfé, Marot, Molière, Muret, Passerat, Pibrac, Rabelais, Rapin, Ronsard, and Voiture (Oo2v). No Montaigne.

Jean de La Bruyère, *The Characters* … "Made English by Several Hands" (1699). The author's magisterial-sounding, fashionably opinionated comments on social types, books, news-mongering, and so forth include literary verdicts. "*Ronsard* and *Balzac* have each in their kind good and bad things, enough to form after 'em very great Men in Verse or Prose." Yet "*Ronsard* and his Contemporaries were more prejudicial than serviceable to Stile. They kept it back in the way to perfection, and expos'd it to the danger of being always defective. 'Tis surprizing that *Marot's* Works, which are so easy and natural, had not taught *Ronsard*, otherwise full of Rapture and Enthusiasm, to make a greater Poet than *Marot* or himself …." It is remarkable that after such corruption the French language "should be so quickly recover'd" (C2).[14]

---

[14] The same passage asserts that "*Marot* and *Rabelais* are inexcusable for scattering so much Ribaldry in their writings." Despite his talent, "*Rabelais* is incomprehensible: his Book is an inexplicable *Enigma*, a meer Chimera; it has a Woman's face, with the feet and tail of a Serpent, or some Beast more deform'd: 'Tis a monstrous collection of Political and ingenious Morality, with a mixture of Beastliness: Where 'tis bad 'tis abominable, and fit for the diversion of the Rabble; and where 'tis good 'tis exquisite, and may entertain the most delicate" (C2–C2v).

Bibliography:
Scholarship on the Anglo-French Renaissance

Adams, Marjorie. "Ronsard and Spenser: The Commentary." In *Renaissance Papers: A Selection of Papers Presented at the Renaissance Meeting in the Southeastern States*. Durham, NC: Duke University, 1954. 24–9.

Alatorre, Sophie. "The Translation of French Literature at the Renaissance: England in Search of an Identity." In *Translating Identity and the Identity of Translation*, edited by Madelena Gonzalez and Francine Tolron. Newcastle Upon Tyne: Cambridge Scholars Press, 2006. 175–91.

Anzai, Tetsuo. *Shakespeare and Montaigne Reconsidered*. Tokyo: Renaissance Institute, Sophia University, 1986.

———. "Shakespeare to Montaigne." *English Literature and Language* 5 (1968): 80–98.

Balestrieri, Elizabeth. "Prison/Anti-Prison: The Writings of Elizabeth I and Marguerite de Navarre." In *Continental, Latin-American and Francophone Women Writers, Vol. II*, edited by Ginette Adamson and Eunice Myers. Lanham, MD: University Press of America, 1987. 115–22.

Barkan, Leonard. "Ruins and Visions: Spenser, Pictures, Rome." In *Edmund Spenser: Essays on Culture and Allegory*, edited by Jennifer Klein Morrison and Matthew Greenfield. Aldershot, UK; Burlington, VT: Ashgate, 2000. 9–36.

Beauchamp, Virginia Walcott. "Sidney's Sister as Translator of Garnier." *Renaissance News* 10.1 (1957): 8–13.

Bedouelle, Guy. "L'image de Marguerite de Navarre dans l'Angleterre du XVIᵉ siècle." In *La Femme lettrée à la Renaissance/De geleerde vrouw in de Renaissance/Lettered Women in the Renaissance*, edited by Michel Bastiaensen. Louvain: Peeters, 1997. 95–106.

———. "Une adaptation anglaise des *Epistres et Evangiles* de Lefèvre d'Etaples et ses disciples." *Bibliotheque d'Humanisme et Renaissance* 48.3 (1986): 723–34.

Bellussi, Germano. "L'absolutisme politique et la tolérance religieuse dans l'oeuvre de Jean Bodin et de Thomas Hobbes." In *Jean Bodin*, edited by Georges Cesbron. Angers: Presses Universitaires d'Angers, 1985. 43–7.

Belsey, Catherine. "Iago the Essayist: Florio between Montaigne and Shakespeare." In *Renaissance Go-Betweens: Cultural Exchange in Early Modern Europe*, edited by Andreas Höfele and Werner von Koppenfels. Berlin: de Gruyter, 2005. 262–78.

Bésineau, Jacques. "Montaigne to Shakespeare." In *Shakespeare to Sono Jidai*, edited by Peter Milward and Shonosuke Ishii. Tokyo: Aratakie, 1981. 105–17.

Biot, Brigitte. "Barthèlemy Aneau, lecteur de l'*Utopie*." *Moreana: Bulletin Thomas More* 32.121 (1995): 11–28.

Bornstein, Diane. *The Countess of Pembroke's Translation of Philippe De Mornay's* Discourse of Life and Death. Detroit: Michigan Consortium for Medieval and Early Modern Studies, 1983.

———. *The Feminist Controversy of the Renaissance: Guillaume Alexis, an Argument Betwyxt Man and Woman (1525); Sir Thomas Elyot, the Defence of Good Women (1545); Henricus Cornelius Agrippa, Female Pre-Eminence (1670)*. Delmar, NY: Scholars' Facsimiles and Reprints, 1980.

———. "The Style of the Countess of Pembroke's Translation of Philippe de Mornay's *Discours de la Vie et de la Mort*." In *Silent but for the Word: Tudor Women as Patrons, Translators, and Writers of Religious Works*, edited by Margaret Patterson Hannay. Kent, OH: Kent State University Press, 1985.

Bradshaw, Graham, Tom Bishop, and Peter Holbrook, editors. *The Shakespearean International Yearbook 6: Special Section, Shakespeare and Montaigne Revisited*. Aldershot, UK; Burlington, VT: Ashgate, 2006.

Brady, Andrea, and Emily Butterworth, editors. *The Uses of the Future in Early Modern Europe*. New York: Routledge, 2010.

Brown, Georgia E. "Translation and the Definition of Sovereignty: The Case of Elizabeth Tudor." In *Travels and Translations in the Sixteenth Century*, edited by Mike Pincombe and Arthur F. Kinney. Aldershot, UK; Burlington, VT: Ashgate, 2004. 88–103.

Brown, Huntington. "Ben Jonson and Rabelais." *Modern Language Notes* 44.1 (1929): 6–13.

———. *Rabelais in English Literature*. Cambridge, MA: Harvard University Press, 1933.

Brown, Richard Danson. "Forming the 'First Garland of Free Poësie': Spenser's Dialogue with Du Bellay in Ruines of Rome." *Translation and Literature* 7.1 (1998): 3–22.

———. *The "New Poet": Novelty and Tradition in Spenser's* Complaints. Liverpool: Liverpool University Press, 1999.

Clarke, Danielle. "The Politics of Translation and Gender in the Countess of Pembroke's *Antonie*." *Translation and Literature* 6.2 (1997): 149–66.

Coldiron, A.E.B. *English Printing, Verse Translation, and the Battle of the Sexes, 1476–1557*. Farnham, UK; Burlington, VT: Ashgate, 2009.

———. "How Spenser Excavates Du Bellay's Antiquitez: Or, the Role of the Poet, Lyric Historiography, and the English Sonnet." *Journal of English and Germanic Philology* 101.1 (2002): 41–67.

———. "Journey and Ambassadorship in the Marriage Literature for Mary Tudor (1496–1533)." In *Renaissance Tropologies: The Cultural Imagination of Early Modern England*, edited by Jeanne Shami. Pittsburgh: Duquesne University Press, 2008. 143–65.

———. "Translation's Challenge to Critical Categories: Verses from French in the Early English Renaissance." *Yale Journal of Criticism* 16.2 (2003): 315–44.

Collette, Carolyn. *Performing Polity: Women and Agency in the Anglo-French Tradition, 1385–1620.* Turnhout, Belgium: Brepols, 2006.

Comorovski, Cornelia. "Contributions à une étude sur Joachim du Bellay et le sonnet de la Renaissance." In *La Poésie angevine du XVIe siècle au début du XVIIe siècle,* edited by G. Cesbron, Robert Aulotte, and Gabriel Spillebout. Angers: Centre de Recherche de Littérature et de Linguistique de l'Anjou et des Bocages, Université d'Angers, 1982. 37–49.

Conley, Tom. "Institutionalizing Translation: On Florio's Montaigne." In *Demarcating the Disciplines: Philosophy, Literature, Art,* edited by Samuel Weber. Minneapolis: University of Minnesota Press, 1986. 45–58.

Cox, John D. "Shakespeare and the French Epistemologists." *Cithara: Essays in the Judaeo-Christian Tradition* 45.2 (2006): 23–45.

Daly, Peter M. "The Case for the 1593 Edition of Thomas Combe's Theater of Fine Devices." *Journal of the Warburg and Courtauld Institutes* 49 (1986): 255–7.

De Gooyer, Alan. "'Their Senses I'll Restore': Montaigne and *The Tempest* Reconsidered." In *The Tempest: Critical Essays,* edited by Patrick M. Murphy. New York: Routledge, 2001. 509–31.

Divay, Gaby. "Montaigne's Influence on Bacon: No More Than a Speck of Evidence." In *Proceedings of the 11th Annual Northern Plains Conference on Early British Literature,* edited by Michelle M. Sauer. Minot, ND: Minot State University, 2003. 149–62.

Dozo, Björn-Olav. "Jean Le Blond, premier traducteur Français de l'*Utopie.*" *Lettres romanes* 59.3–4 (2005): 187–210.

El-Gabalawy, Saad. "The Trend of Naturalism in Libertine Poetry of the Later English Renaissance." *Renaissance and Reformation/Renaissance et Reforme* 12.1 (1988): 35–44.

Ellrodt, Robert. "Self-Consciousness in Montaigne and Shakespeare." *Shakespeare Survey* 28 (1975): 37–50.

———. "Self-Consistency in Montaigne and Shakespeare." In *Shakespeare and the Mediterranean,* edited by Tom Clayton, Susan Brock, Vincente Forès, and Jill Levenson. Newark, DE: University of Delaware Press, 2004. 37–50.

Engar, Ann W. "Hamlet in a Western Civilization Course: Connections to Montaigne's *Essays* and Cervantes's *Don Quixote.*" In *Approaches to Teaching Shakespeare's Hamlet,* edited by Bernice W. Kliman. New York: Modern Language Association of America, 2001. 134–7.

Engel, William E. "Aphorism, Anecdote, and Anamnesis in Montaigne and Bacon." *Montaigne Studies* 1 (1989): 158–76.

Evans, G. Blakemore. "Belleforest and the Gonzago Story: *Hamlet,* III. ii." *Shakespeare Association Bulletin* 24 (1949): 280–82.

Farmer, Norman. "Spenser's Homage to Ronsard: Cosmic Design in *The Shepheardes Calender.*" *Studi di letteratura francese* 12 (1986): 249–63.

Ferguson, Margaret W. "'The Afflatus of Ruin': Meditations on Rome by Du Bellay, Spenser, and Stevens." In *Roman Images,* edited by Annabel Patterson. Baltimore: Johns Hopkins University Press, 1984. 23–50.

———. *Dido's Daughters: Literacy, Gender, and Empire in Early Modern England and France*. Chicago and London: University of Chicago Press, 2003.

———. *Trials of Desire: Renaissance Defenses of Poetry*. New Haven: Yale University Press, 1983.

Fitzgerald, James. "Know Ye Not This Parable? The Oxford-Du Bartas Connection." *Oxfordian* 2 (1999): 76–116.

Françon, Marcel. "Sur la tragédie du mouchoir dans les *Essais* de Montaigne (II, 23) et dans l'*Othello* de Shakespeare." *Bulletin de la Société des Amis de Montaigne* 16 (1968): 55–6.

Gibson, Jonathan. "French and Italian Sources for Ralegh's 'Farewell False Love.'" *Review of English Studies* 50 (1999): 155–65.

Grady, Hugh. "Shakespeare's Links to Machiavelli and Montaigne: Constructing Intellectual Modernity in Early Modern Europe." *Comparative Literature* 52.2 (2000): 119–42.

———. *Shakespeare, Machiavelli, and Montaigne: Power and Subjectivity from Richard II to Hamlet*. Oxford: Oxford University Press, 2002.

Gray, Floyd. "The Essay as Criticism." In *The Cambridge History of Literary Criticism, III: The Renaissance*, edited by Glyn P. Norton. Cambridge: Cambridge University Press, 1999. 271–7.

Greenblatt, Stephen. "Fiction and Friction." In *Reconstructing Individualism: Autonomy, Individuality, and the Self in Western Thought*, edited by Thomas C. Heller, Morton Sosna, David E. Wellbery, Arnold I. Davidson, Ann Swidler, and Ian Watt. Stanford: Stanford University Press, 1986. 30–52.

Greene, Thomas M. *The Light in Troy: Imitation and Discovery in Renaissance Poetry*. New Haven: Yale University Press, 1982.

Gregory, E.R., Jr. "Du Bartas, Sidney, and Spenser." *Comparative Literature Studies* 7 (1970): 437–49.

Grève, Marcel de. "Limites de l'influence linguistique de Rabelais en Angleterre au XVIᵉ siècle." *Comparative Literature Studies* 1 (1964): 15–30.

———. "La légende de Gargantua en Angleterre au XVIᵉ siècle." *Revue belge de philologie et d'histoire/Belgisch Tijdschrift voor Philologie en Geschiedenis* 38 (1960): 765–94.

Hall, Joan Lord. "'To Play the Man Well and Duely': Role-Playing in Montaigne and Jacobean Drama." *Comparative Literature Studies* 22.2 (1985): 173–86.

Hamlin, William M. "Florio's Montaigne and the Tyranny of 'Custome': Appropriation, Ideology, and Early English Readership of the *Essayes*." *Renaissance Quarterly* 63 (2010): 491–544.

———. *The Image of America in Montaigne, Spenser, and Shakespeare*. New York: St. Martin's, 1995.

Hampton, Timothy. *Fictions of Embassy*. Ithaca: Cornell University Press, 2009.

———. *Writing from History: The Rhetoric of Exemplarity in Renaissance Literature*. Ithaca: Cornell University Press, 1990.

Harmon, Alice. "How Great Was Shakespeare's Debt to Montaigne?" *PMLA* 57.4 (1942): 988–1008.

Harrison, T.P., Jr. "Spenser, Ronsard, and Bion." *Modern Language Notes* 49.3 (1934): 139–45.

Helgerson, Richard. "Introduction." In *Joachim Du Bellay: "The Regrets," with "The Antiquities of Rome," Three Latin Elegies, and "The Defense and Enrichment of the French Language,"* edited and translated by Richard Helgerson. Philadelphia: University of Pennsylvania Press, 2006. 1–36.

Henderson, W.B.D. "Montaigne's *Apologie* and *King Lear*." *Shakespeare Association Bulletin* 25 (1940): 40–54.

Hieatt, A. Kent. "The Genesis of Shakespeare's *Sonnets*: Spenser's Ruines of Rome: By Bellay." *PMLA* 98.5 (1983): 800–814.

Hillman, Richard. "La création du monde et The Taming of the Shrew: Du Bartas comme intertexte." *Renaissance and Reformation/Renaissance et Reforme* 15.3 (1991): 249–58.

———. *French Origins of English Tragedy*. Manchester: Manchester University Press, 2010.

———. *Shakespeare, Marlowe, and the Politics of France*. Basingstoke, Hampshire: Palgrave, 2002.

Hodgen, Margaret T. "Montaigne and Shakespeare Again." *Huntington Library Quarterly* 16 (1952): 23–42.

Hooker, Elizabeth Robbins. "The Relation of Shakespeare to Montaigne." *PMLA* 17.2 (1902): 312–66.

Hosington, Brenda M. "England's First Female-Authored Encomium: The Seymour Sisters' *Hecatodistichon* (1550) to Marguerite de Navarre. Text, Translation, Notes, and Commentary." *Studies in Philology* 93.2 (1996): 117–33.

Hovey, Kenneth Alan. "'Mountaigny Saith Prettily': Bacon's French and the Essay." *PMLA* 106.1 (1991): 71–82.

Johnson, Christopher. "Florio's 'Conversion' of Montaigne, Sidney and Six Patronesses." *Cahiers Elisabéthains* 64 (2003): 9–18.

Johnson, William C. "Philip Sidney and Du Bellay's *Jugement de l'oreille*." *Revue de Littérature Comparée* 60.1 (1986): 21–33.

Jones-Davies, Margaret. "Paroles intertextuelles: lecture intertextuelle de *Parolles*." In *All's Well That Ends Well: Nouvelles Perspectives Critiques*, edited by Jean Fuzier and François Laroque. Montpellier: Publications de l'Université de Paul Valéry, 1985. 65–80.

Jones-Davies, Marie-Thérèse. *La Satire au temps de la Renaissance*. Paris: Touzot, 1986.

Jourdan, Serena. *The Sparrow and the Flea: The Sense of Providence in Shakespeare and Montaigne*. Salzburg: Institut für Anglistik und Amerikanistik, Universität Salzburg, 1983.

Jusserand, Jean-Jules. *Shakespeare in France under the Ancien Régime*. London: T. Fisher Unwin, 1899.

Kaiser, Walter. *Praisers of Folly: Erasmus, Rabelais, Shakespeare*. Cambridge, MA and London: Harvard University Press; Gollancz, 1963.

Kennedy, William J. "Audiences and Rhetorical Strategies in Jodelle, Shakespeare, and Lohenstein." *Assays* 1 (1981): 99–116.

———. *Authorizing Petrarch*. Ithaca and London: Cornell University Press, 1994.

———. "'Les langues des hommes sont pleines de tromperies': Shakespeare, French Poetry, and Alien Tongues." In *Textual Conversations in the Renaissance: Ethics, Authors, Technologies*, edited by Zachary Lesser and Benedict S. Robinson. Aldershot, UK; Burlington, VT: Ashgate, 2006. 99–116.

———. *The Site of Petrarchism*. Baltimore and London: Johns Hopkins University Press, 2003.

Kirsch, Arthur. "Virtue, Vice, and Compassion in Montaigne and *The Tempest*." *SEL: Studies in English Literature, 1500–1900* 37.2 (1997): 337–52.

Klause, John. "The Montaigneity of Donne's *Metempsychosis*." In *Renaissance Genres: Essays on Theory, History, and Interpretation*, edited by Barbara Kiefer Lewalski. Cambridge, MA: Harvard University Press, 1986. 418–43.

Kocher, Paul H. "François Hotman and Marlowe's *The Massacre at Paris*." *PMLA* 56.2 (1941): 349–68.

Kuin, Roger. "A Civil Conversation: Letters and the Edge of Form." In *Textual Conversations in the Renaissance: Ethics, Authors, Technologies*, edited by Zachary Lesser and Benedict S. Robinson. Aldershot, UK; Burlington, VT: Ashgate, 2006. 147–72.

———. "More I Still Undoe: Louise Labé, Mary Wroth, and the Petrarchan Discourse." *Comparative Literature Studies* 36.2 (1999): 146–61.

La Garanderie, Marie-Madeleine de. "Guillaume Budé lecteur de l'*Utopie*." In *Miscellanea Moreana: Essays for Germain Marc'hadour*, edited by Clare M. Murphy, Henri Gibaud, and Mario Di Cesare. Binghamton: Medieval and Renaissance Texts and Studies, 1989. 327–38.

Law, Robert A. "Belleforest, Shakespeare, and Kyd." In *Joseph Quincy Adams Memorial Studies*. Washington, DC: Folger Shakespeare Library, 1948.

Lee, John. "Unreasonable Men? Categories and Metaphor in Shakespeare and Montaigne." In *Where Are We Now in Shakespearean Studies? III*, edited by Graham Bradshaw, John M. Mucciolo, Tom Bishop, Angus Fletcher, and Frank Kermode. Aldershot, UK; Burlington, VT: Ashgate, 2003. 268–81.

Lee, Sidney. *The French Renaissance in England: An Account of the Literary Relations of England and France in the Sixteenth Century*. New York: Oxford University Press, 1910.

Lepage, John Louis. "Sylvester's Du Bartas and the Metaphysical Androgyny of Opposites." *ELH* 51.4 (1984): 621–44.

Logan, Marie-Rose and Peter L. Rudnytsky, eds. *Contending Kingdoms: Historical, Psychological and Feminist Approaches to the Literature of Sixteenth-Century England and France*. Detroit: Wayne State University Press, 1991.

Mack, Peter. "Rhetoric, Ethics and Reading in the Renaissance." *Renaissance Studies* 19.1 (2005): 1–21.

Manley, Lawrence. "Spenser and the City: The Minor Poems." *Modern Language Quarterly* 43.3 (1982): 203–27.

Marquis, Lou-Ann. "L'abbaye de Thélème de Rabelais et le discours utopique." In *Critique des savoirs sous l'Ancien Régime: érosion des certitudes et émergence de la libre pensée*, edited by Yves Bourassa, Alexandre Landry, Marie Lise Laquerre, and Stéphanie Massé. Quebec: Presses de l'Université Laval, 2008. 173–83.

Martin, Catherine Gimelli. "'Boundless Deep': Milton, Pascal, and the Theology of Relative Space." *English Literary History* 63.1 (1996): 45–78.

Martin, Robert M. "Early Modern Interiority." *Dalhousie Review* 85.2 (2005): 161–320.

Mayer, Jean-Christophe, ed. *Representing France and the French in Early Modern English Drama*. Newark, DE: University of Delaware Press, 2008.

McClelland, John. "From Shakespeare to Rabelais: What Would Life Be without Arithmetic?" In *Proceedings of the 11th Annual Northern Plains Conference on Early British Literature*, edited by Michelle M. Sauer. Minot, ND: Minot State University, 2003. 18–42.

McDiarmid, Matthew P. "The Influence of Robert Garnier on Some Elizabethan Tragedies." *Etudes Anglaises* 11 (1958): 289–302.

McLoughlin, Cathleen T. *Shakespeare, Rabelais, and the Comical-Historical*. New York: Peter Lang, 2000.

Melehy, Hassan. "Antiquities of Britain: Spenser's 'Ruines of Time.'" *Studies in Philology* 102.2 (2005): 159–83.

———. *The Poetics of Literary Transfer in Early Modern France and England*. Farnham, UK; Burlington, VT: Ashgate, 2010.

———. "Spenser and Du Bellay: Translation, Imitation, Ruin." *Comparative Literature Studies* 40.4 (2003): 415–38.

———. "Du Bellay and the Space of Early Modern Culture." *Neophilologus* 84.4 (October 2000): 508–10.

Menninghaus, Winfried. "Zwischen Bandello und Shakespeare: Pierre Boaistuaus *Romeo und Julia*-Version." *Poetica* 19.1–2 (1987): 3–31.

Minta, Stephen. *Petrarch and Petrarchism: The English and French Traditions*. Manchester: Manchester University Press, 1980.

"Montaigne in England." *Montaigne Studies* 24.1–2 (2012).

Mulryan, John. "The Function of Ritual in the Marriage Songs of Catullus, Spenser and Ronsard." *Illinois Quarterly* 35.2 (1972): 50–64.

Murray, Timothy. "Translating Montaigne's Crypts: Melancholic Relations and the Sites of Altarbiography." *Bucknell Review* 35.2 (1992): 121–49.

Nakagawa, Tokio. "Montaigne to Shakespeare." In *Eibungaku to No Deai*, edited by Naomi Matsuura. Kyoto: Showado, 1983. 259–61.

Olivier, T. "Shakespeare and Montaigne: A Tendency of Thought." *Theoria* 54 (1980): 43–9.

Paris, Jean. *Hamlet et Panurge*. Paris: Seuil, 1971.

Parker, Fred. "Shakespeare's Argument with Montaigne." *Cambridge Quarterly* 28.1 (1999): 1–18.

Paster, Gail Kern. "Montaigne, Dido, and *The Tempest*: 'How Came That Widow In?'" *Shakespeare Quarterly* 35.1 (1984): 91–4.

Patterson, Annabel. "Re-Opening the Green Cabinet: Clément Marot and Edmund Spenser." *English Literary Renaissance* 16.1 (1986): 44–70. Rpt. in *The Classical Heritage: Vergil*, edited by Craig Kallendorf. New York: Garland, 1993. 115–44.

Paulson, Michael G. "A Possible Source of William Shakespeare's *Othello*: Alexandre Hardy's *Mariamne*." *Papers on French Seventeenth Century Literature* 14.2 (1987): 151–82.

Picard, Louis. "L'art de la manière et la pratique de la pointe dans les *Sonnets* de Shakespeare et le premier livre des *Amours* de Ronsard." *Etudes épistémè* 9 (2006): 161–83.

Prescott, Anne Lake. "The Countess of Pembroke's Ruins of Rome." In *Mary Sidney, Countess of Pembroke*, edited by Margaret P. Hannay. Farnham, UK; Burlington, VT: Ashgate, 2009. 223–39.

———. "Divine Poetry as a Career Move: The Complexities and Consolations of Following David." In *European Literary Careers: The Author from Antiquity to the Renaissance*, edited by Patrick Cheney and Frederick A. De Armas. Toronto: University of Toronto Press, 2002. 206–30.

———. "Donne's Rabelais." *John Donne Journal: Studies in the Age of Donne* 16 (1997): 37–57.

———. "Du Bartas and Renaissance Britain: An Update." *Œuvres et Critiques* 29.2 (2004): 27–38.

———. "Du Bellay in Renaissance England: Recent Work on Translation and Response." *Œuvres et Critiques* 20.1 (1995): 121–8.

———. "English Writers and Beza's Latin Epigrams: The Uses and Abuses of Poetry." *Studies in the Renaissance* 21 (1974): 83–117.

———. *French Poets and the English Renaissance: Studies in Fame and Transformation*. New Haven: Yale University Press, 1978.

———. "Hills of Contemplation and Signifying Circles: Spenser and Guy Le Fèvre De La Boderie." *Spenser Studies* 24 (2009): 155–83.

———. "Housing Chessmen and Bagging Bishops: Space and Desire in Colonna, 'Rabelais,' and Middleton's Game at Chess." In *Soundings of Things Done: Essays in Early Modern Literature in Honor of S.K. Heninger Jr.*, edited by Peter E. Medine, Joseph Wittreich, and Stuart Curran. Newark, DE; London: University of Delaware Press; Associated University Press, 1997. 215–33.

———. *Imagining Rabelais in Renaissance England*. New Haven: Yale University Press, 1998.

———. "Intertextual Topology: English Writers and Pantagruel's Hell." *English Literary Renaissance* 23.2 (1993): 244–66.

———. "Is There a Reader in This Response? The Case of Robert Burton." In *Rabelais in Context*, edited by Barbara C. Bowen. Birmingham, AL: Summa, 1993. 181–95.

Bibliography 201

————. "Jonson's Rabelais." In *New Perspectives on Ben Jonson*, edited by James Hirsh. Madison, NJ; London: Fairleigh Dickinson University Press; Associated University Press, 1997. 35–54.

————. "The Laurel and the Myrtle: Spenser and Ronsard." In *Worldmaking Spenser: Explorations in the Early Modern Age*, edited by Patrick Cheney and Lauren Silberman. Lexington: University Press of Kentucky, 2000. 63–78.

————. "Making the *Heptaméron* English." In *Renaissance Historicisms: Essays in Honor of Arthur F. Kinney*, edited by James M. Dutcher and Anne Lake Prescott. Newark, DE: University of Delaware Press, 2008. 69–84.

————. "Male Lesbian Voices: Ronsard, Tyard and Donne Play Sappho." In *Reading the Renaissance: Ideas and Idioms from Shakespeare to Milton*, edited by Marc Berley and Edward W. Tayler. Pittsburgh: Duquesne University Press, 2003. 109–29.

————. "Mary Sidney's Antonius and the Ambiguities of French History." *Yearbook of English Studies* 38.1–2 (2008): 216–33.

————. "Mary Wroth, Louise Labé, and Cupid." *Sidney Journal* 15.2 (1997): 37–41.

————. "The Pearl of the Valois and Elizabeth I: Marguerite de Navarre's *Miroir* and Tudor England." In *Silent but for the Word: Tudor Women as Patrons, Translators, and Writers of Religious Works*, edited by Margaret Patterson Hannay. Kent, OH: Kent State University Press, 1985. 61–76.

————. "Rabelaisian (Non)Wonders and Renaissance Polemics." In *Wonders, Marvels, and Monsters in Early Modern Culture*, edited by Peter G. Platt. Newark, DE; London: University of Delaware Press; Associated University Press, 1999. 133–44.

————. "The Reception of Du Bartas in England." *Studies in the Renaissance* 15 (1968): 144–73.

————. "The Reputation of Clement Marot in Renaissance England." *Studies in the Renaissance* 18 (1971): 173–202.

————. "Reshaping *Gargantua*." In *L'Europe de la Renaissance: cultures et civilisations*, edited by J.M. Martinet. Paris: Touzot, 1989. 477–91.

————. "Spenser (Re)Reading Du Bellay: Chronology and Literary Response." In *Spenser's Life and the Subject of Biography*, edited by Judith H. Anderson, Donald Cheney, and David A. Richardson. Amherst: University of Massachusetts Press, 1996. 131–45.

————. "The Stuart Masque and Pantagruel's Dreams." *ELH* 51.3 (1984): 407–30.

————. "The Thirsty Deer and the Lord of Life: Some Contexts for *Amoretti* 67–70." *Spenser Studies: A Renaissance Poetry Annual* 6 (1985): 33–76.

————. "Through the Cultural Chunnel: The (Robert) Greeneing of Louise Labé." In *Opening the Borders: Inclusivity in Early Modern Studies*, edited by Peter C. Herman and Edward W. Tayler. Newark, DE; London: University of Delaware Press; Associated University Press, 1999. 133–46.

————. "*Translatio Lupae*: Du Bellay's Roman Whore Goes North." *Renaissance Quarterly* 42.3 (1989): 397–419.

————. "Two Annes, Two Davids: The Sonnets of Anne Locke and Anne de Marquets." In *Tradition, Heterodoxy and Religious Culture: Judaism and Christianity in the Early Modern Period*, edited by Chanita Goodblatt and Howard Kreisel. Beersheba: Ben-Gurion University of the Negev Press, 2006. 311–29.

————. "An Unknown Translation of Du Bartas." *Renaissance News* 19.1 (1966): 12–13.

Prosser, Eleanor. "Shakespeare, Montaigne, and 'the Rarer Action.'" *Shakespeare Studies* 1 (1965): 261–64.

Quitslund, Jon A. *Spenser's Supreme Fiction: Platonic Natural Philosophy and "The Faerie Queene."* Toronto: University of Toronto Press, 2001, 120–21, 240.

Reiss, Timothy J. *Mirages of the Selfe: Patterns of Personhood in Ancient and Early Modern Europe*. Stanford: Stanford University Press, 2003.

————. "Utopie versus état de pouvoir, ou Prétexte du discours politique de la modernité: Hobbes, lecteur de la Boétie?" In *Utopia 1: 16th and 17th Centuries*, edited by David Lee Rubin and Alice Stroup. Charlottesville, VA: Rookwood, 1998. 31–83.

Richmond, Hugh M. *Puritans and Libertines: Anglo-French Literary Relations in the Reformation*. Berkeley: University of California Press, 1981.

————. "Ronsard and the English Renaissance." *Comparative Literature Studies* 7 (1970): 141–60.

Salingar, Leo. "King Lear, Montaigne and Harsnett." *The Aligarh Journal of English Studies* 8.2 (1983): 124–66.

Sanderson, John. *"But the People's Creatures": The Philosophical Basis of the English Civil War*. Manchester: Manchester University Press, 1989.

Satterthwaite, Alfred W. "Moral Vision in Spenser, Du Bellay, and Ronsard." *Comparative Literature* 9.2 (1957): 136–49.

————. *Spenser, Ronsard, and Du Bellay: A Renaissance Comparison*. Princeton: Princeton University Press, 1960.

Schwartz, Jerome. "Aspects of Androgyny in the Renaissance." In *Human Sexuality in the Middle Ages and Renaissance*, edited by Douglas Radcliffe-Umstead. Pittsburgh: Center for Medieval and Renaissance Studies, University of Pittsburgh, 1978. 121–31.

Sedley, David L. *Sublimity and Skepticism in Montaigne and Milton*. Ann Arbor: University of Michigan Press, 2005.

Sellevold, Kirsti. "Paraphrasing *Utopia* for French Readers." In *Urban Preoccupations: Mental and Material Landscapes*, edited by Per Sivefors. Pisa: Fabrizio Serra, 2007. 203–15.

Silcox, Mary V. "The Translation of La Perrière's *Le Théâtre des bons engins* into Combe's *The Theater of Fine Devices*." *Emblematica* 2.1 (1987): 61–94.

Sinfield, Alan. "Sidney and Du Bartas." *Comparative Literature* 27.1 (1975): 8–20.

————. "Sidney, Du Plessis-Mornay and the Pagans." *Philological Quarterly* 58 (1979): 26–39.

Bibliography

Skretkowicz, Victor. "Sidney's Defence of Poetry, Henri Estienne, and Huguenot Nationalist Satire." *Sidney Journal* 16.1 (1998): 3–24.

Snyder, Susan. "Guilty Sisters: Marguerite de Navarre, Elizabeth of England, and the *Miroir De l'âme pécheresse*." *Renaissance Quarterly* 50.2 (1997): 443–58.

Sokol, B.J. "Holofernes in Rabelais and Shakespeare and Some Manuscript Verses of Thomas Harriot." *Etudes rabelaisiennes* 25 (1991): 131–5.

Sproxton, Judith. "D'aubigné, Milton and the Scourge of Sin." *Journal of European Studies* 11.4 (1981): 262–78.

Stabler, Arthur P. "King Hamlet's Ghost in Belleforest?" *PMLA* 77.1 (1962): 18–20.

———. "Melancholy, Ambition, and Revenge in Belleforest's *Hamlet*." *PMLA* 81.3 (1966): 207–13.

Stapleton, M.L. "Spenser, the *Antiquitez de Rome*, and the Development of the English Sonnet Form." *Comparative Literature Studies* 27.4 (1990): 259–74.

Stein, Harold. *Studies in Spenser's Complaints*. New York: Oxford University Press, 1934.

Stevens, Scott Manning. "'Unaccommodated Man': Essaying the New World in Early Modern England [Europe]." In *Multicultural Europe and Cultural Exchange in the Middle Ages and Renaissance*, edited by James P. Helfers. Turnhout, Belgium: Brepols, 2005. 123–38.

Sutch, Susie Speakman. "Translation as Transformation: Olivier de La Marche's *Le Chevalier délibéré* and its Hapsburg and Elizabethan Permutations." *Comparative Literature Studies* 25.4 (1988): 281–317.

Taylor, Andrew W. "Between Surrey and Marot: Nicolas Bourbon and the Artful Translation of the Epigram." *Translation and Literature* 15.1 (2006): 1–20.

Taylor, George C. "Montaigne-Shakespeare and the Deadly Parallel." *Philological Quarterly* 22 (1943): 330–37.

Thomas, David H. "Rabelais in England: John Eliot's Ortho-Epia Gallica (1593)." *Etudes Rabelaisiennes* 9 (1971): 97–126.

Upham, Alfred Horatio. *The French Influence in English Literature: From the Accession of Elizabeth to the Restoration*. New York: Columbia University Press, 1908.

Walter, Melissa. "Constructing Readers and Reading Communities: Marguerite de Navarre's *Heptaméron* 32 in England." *Renaissance and Reformation/ Renaissance et Reforme* 27.1 (2003): 35–59.

Ward, H.G. "Joachim Du Bellay and Sir Thomas Browne." *Review of English Studies* 5.17 (1929): 59–60.

Westling, Louise. "Montaigne in English Dress from Florio to Cotton." *Pacific Coast Philology* 13 (1978): 117–24.

Williams, Deanne. *The French Fetish from Chaucer to Shakespeare*. Cambridge: Cambridge University Press, 2004.

Woodhead, M.R. "Montaigne and *The Tempest*: An Addendum." *Notes and Queries* 29.2 (1982): 125.

Yachnin, Paul. "Eating Montaigne." In *Reading Renaissance Ethics*, edited by Marshall Grossman and Theodore B. Leinwand. New York: Routledge, 2007. 157–72.

Yates, Frances. *The French Academies of the Sixteenth Century*. London: Warburg Institute, 1947.

Zarucchi, Jeanne Morgan. "Du Bellay, Spenser, and Quevedo Search for Rome: A Teacher's Peregrination." *French Review* 71.2 (1997): 192–203.

Zuber, Roger. "Eloge du Dialogue des Morts: John Donne et le pamphlet gallican." In *La Satire au Temps de la Renaissance*, edited by Marie Thérèse Jones-Davies. Paris: Touzot, 1986. 127–38.

Index

Abbot, George, 164
Adam of Usk, 35
Adorno, Theodor, 76
Alciato, Andrea, 106
Alexis, Guillaume
    Debat de l'homme et de la femme
      [*Interlocucyon, with an an*
      argument, betwyxt man and
      woman], 8, 15–25 passim
Alfred, King, 176
Almain, Jacques, 107
Anderson, Benedict, 140
Anderson, Judith, 175
Anne of Bohemia, 27, 28, 31, 42
Anspach, Rudolf, 150
Ariès, Philippe, 29
Ariosto, Ludovico, 181, 188, 189
Aristotle, 82n30
    on friendship, 74, 102, 104, 105–6,
      110, 115–16, 129–32
Arundel, Archbiship, 35
Ascham, Roger, 136
Auerbach, Erich, 133n53
Augustine, Saint, 103–4, 105–6
Auvergne, Gaspard d', 70–71

Bacon, Francis, 68, 84, 89, 113
Baïf, Jean-Antoine de, 165, 183
    Amours, 69
Bandello, Matteo, 8–9, 119–41 passim
Banos, Théophile de, 154
Barclay, William, 96–7, 185
Baron, Robert, 180
Belleau, Rémy, 71, 163, 165, 177, 181,
    188, 190n
Belleforest, François de, 119, 127–34, 141
Berger Jr., Harry, 52, 57n
Beza, Thédore, *see* Bèze, Théodore de
Bèze, Théodore de, 67, 91, 97–8, 148
Blackmore, Richard, 190–91
Boaistuau, Pierre, 119, 127, 129–31

Boccaccio, Giovanni, 16n3, 125, 133,
    139, 165
Boccalini, Traiano, 185
Bohun, Edmund, 189
Boileau, Nicolas, 190
Bolingbroke, Henry, 35
Bolton, Robert, 108
Bonciani, Francesco, 120
Bonnefon, Paul, 69, 71n18
Bornstein, Diane, 16n3, 18, 25
Borris, Kenneth, 11
Bosán, Juan, 184
Bossy, Michel-André, 17n4, 24
Bosworth, William, 181
Brende, John, 148
Broughton, G.H., 28
Brown, Huntington, 10
Brown, Michael, 27
Buchanan, George, 96, 102, 105, 108, 109,
    110, 115, 185
Burghley, Baron (William Cecil), 146n10,
    148, 154

Cadman, Thomas, 149, 150
Caesar, Julius, 148
Calvin, Jean, 97–8, 110, 111, 147, 148, 150
Calvinism; *see also* Huguenots;
    Protestantism
    political thought in, 95–8, 105–10,
    115–16
Camden, William, 164
Camus, Jean-Pierre, 128
Cappel, Guillaume, 70–71
Cardonnel, Philip de, 186
Carteret, Anna, 27
Catherine de' Medici, 71, 177
Catherine de Valois, 31
Catherine of Aragon, 32n22, 46n63
Catherine of Braganza, 186
Catholic League, 67, 112
Catullus, 4, 176, 183, 185

206   *French Connections in the English Renaissance*

Caxton, William, 15
Cent nouvelles nouvelles, Les, 131
Cervantes, Miguel de, 139, 188
chanson d'aventure
     and English literature, 20–21
Charlemagne, 114
Charles I (of England), 91, 95, 96
Charles II (of England), 3
Charles IX (of France), 112–13, 152,
     183, 186
Charles d'Orléans, 31, 44
Charles Martel, 114
Charles V, Emperor, 92
Charles VI (of France), 28, 36
Chaucer, Geoffrey, 5, 6, 35, 44, 135,
     165, 176
Christine de Pizan, 16n3, 25
Chronicque de la traïson et mort de
     Richart Deux roy Dengleterre,
     La [*Chronicle of the Betrayal*
     and Death of Richard King of
     England], 45–6
Cicero, 72, 74n23, 82n30, 86, 102, 103–4,
     106, 114
Clarendon, Earl of (Edward Hyde), 186
Clarke, Mary Cowden, 36
Clifford, Lady Anne, 38
Cobham, Baron (William Brooke), 148
Codrington, Robert, 164, 183, 185
Coldiron, A.E.B., 8, 12
Coleridge, Samuel Taylor, 6
Coligny, Gaspard de, 153
Collette, Carolyn, 11–12
Collop, John, 183–4
Company of Stationers, the, 15
Constantine, Emperor, 113
Corneille, Pierre, 191
Cotgrave, Randle, 151
Cotton, Charles, 188
Cowley, Abraham, 189
Curtius, Quintus, 148

Daniel, Samuel, 37, 38–9
Dante Alighieri, 185
Davies, John, 181
de Thou, Jacques-Auguste, 69–70, 112,
     114, 164n5, 183
de Worde, Wynkyn, 15–25
Della Casa, Giovanni, 139

Denisot, Nicolas, 171
Dennis, John, 3
der Noot, Jan van, 55, 59
Descartes, René, 89
Deschamps, Eustache, 16n3
Desportes, Philippe, 181, 188, 191
Diodati, Charles, 100–101
Dodge, Guy, 108
Dolet, Etienne, 132
Dorat, Jean, 71, 163, 165, 166, 176, 181, 191
Dorislaus, Isaac, 100
Dorsten, Jan van, 146
Dousa, Janus, 161
Drake, Sir Francis, 139
Drayton, Michael, 4
Drummond, William, 184
Dryden, John, 3, 4, 5, 186, 189, 191
Du Bartas, Guillaume, 138, 144n4, 146,
     149, 165, 175, 180, 181, 183, 184,
     185, 187, 191
Du Bellay, Joachim, 5, 6, 10, 51–64
     passim, 132, 163, 165, 181,
     183, 191
     Antiquitez de Rome, Les [*The*
         Antiquities of Rome], 59, 60
     Deffence et Illustration de la Langue
         Françoyse, La [*The Defense*
         and Illustration of the French
         Language], 1–2, 52–3
     Olive, 69
     Songe, 59
du Haillan, Bernard, 87–8, 111
Du Monin, Edouard, 166, 176
du Vair, Guillaume, 72
du Verdier, Antoine, 183
Duncan-Jones, Katherine, 146, 147, 151
Dunton, John, 164, 189
Duplessis-Mornay, Charlotte (Charlotte
     Arbaleste), 149, 152–3, 159
Duplessis-Mornay, Philippe, 7, 9, 67, 98–9,
     105, 111, 113, 116n54, 137
     De la vérité de la religion chrestienne
         [*The Trewnesse of the Christian*
         Religion], 143–60 passim
     Excellent discours de la vie et de la
         mort [*Excellent Discourse on Life*
         and Death], 152, 154, 158
     Vindiciae contra Tyrannos [*Vindications*
         against Tyrants], 97, 98, 112–13

Durant, Jean, 152
DuWes, Giles, 155

Ecclesiastes, Book of, 35
Edward III, 34
Edward VI, 3
Edward de Vere, Earl of Oxford, 145, 146,
    147–8, 159
Edward the Black Prince, 34
Eleanor d'Aquitaine, 31
Eleanor de Provence, 31
Elias, Norbert, 140
Elizabeth I, 2, 3, 30, 31, 109, 116, 145,
    176n24
Ellrodt, Robert, 11
Elyot, Thomas, 16n3
England
    and nationhood, 1, 4–5, 30, 52–3
Ennius, Quintus, 186
Erasmus, Desiderius, 3, 84, 116
Essex, Earl of (Robert Devereux), 148
Estienne, Charles, 70
Estienne, Robert, 132
Evelyn, John, 191

Faisant, Claude, 176
Fenton, Geoffrey, 119, 134–9, 141
Ferguson, Margaret W., 10, 11, 169n16
Ferrand, Jacques, 179–80
Feuillerat, Albert, 150, 151
Ficino, Marsilio, 11
Fiorato, A.C., 127
Flecknoe, Richard, 186
Fletcher, Angus, 51n1, 55–6
Fletcher, Richard, 35
Fleury, Claude, 190
Florio, John, 10, 119n2, 138, 141, 143
Fontenelle, Bernard Bovier de, 191
Fortescue, John, 106
Foucault, Michel, 65n2
France
    François d'Anjou et d'Alençon, 145, 152
    and nationhood 4–5, 30
François Ier, 173, 181
    cultural program of, 1
Franklin, Julian H., 97n8, 99n15, 100n19,
    106, 109, 113n47
freedom
    in social bond, 75–81

and state, 74–5
French Revolution, the, 6, 66
friendship: as social bond, 74, 81–4, 93
Froissart, Jean, 28–9, 30n15, 31–2, 33, 34,
    37, 38–9
Fulke Greville (Lord Brooke), 146

Galilei, Galileo, 101
Garcilaso de la Vega, 184
Garnier, Robert, 154, 181, 188
gender
    and cultural transfer, 8, 13–47
Gerson, Jean, 107
Ghisi, Carlo, 120–21
girlhood
    as social category, 27–47
Golding, Arthur, 146–9, 150, 151–2, 157
Golding, Thomas, 147
Gooch, G.P. 68
Goodman, Christopher, 105, 110
Gosynhill, Edward, 16
Gotti, Vincenzo, 145
Gough, J.W., 102
Goulart, Simon, 181
    Mémoires de l'Estat de France, sous
        Charles Neufiesme, 67
Gower, John, 35
Greenblatt, Stephen, 140
Greene, Thomas M., 10
Grévin, Jacques, 165
Grotius, Hugo, 95, 145
Guez de Balzac, Jean-Louis, 88, 191
Gurr, Andrew, 27

Habermas, Jürgen, 15n
Hakewill, George, 185
Hamilton, A.C., 143–4
Hamlin, William M., 11
Hampton, Timothy, 10–11
Hannay, Margaret, 152, 154
Harvey, Gabriel, 163n4
Hatton, Christopher, 148
Hédelin, François, 188
Hegel, G.W.F.: on freedom, 78
Heitsch, Dorothea, 8–9
Helgerson, Richard, 52n7
    on nationhood, 2, 4
Henri II, 69, 181, 183, 188
Henri III, 112–13

208   *French Connections in the English Renaissance*

Henri IV (Henri de Navarre), 88, 144,
     164, 183
Henrietta Maria, 95, 96, 183
Henry IV (of England), 35, 41, 43–4, 47
Henry V, 31, 43, 44
Henry VII, 46n63
Henry VIII, 3
Heraud, John A., 36
Herbert, Mary, 153
Herodotus, 81
Hill, Christopher, 97n6, 111
Hobbes, Thomas, 65–93 passim, 185
     Behemoth, 73–4, 77, 82, 89–90, 92–3
     De Cive, 74, 89, 93
     Elements of Law, Natural and Politic,
        The, 73–4, 93
     Leviathan, 68, 74, 77, 84, 93
Holbein, Hans, 41
Holland, Samuel, 185
Holyband, Claudius (Claude de Sainliens),
     151, 155, 157–8
Homer, 4, 157, 168, 175, 183, 184, 186
Hooker, Elizabeth Robbins, 10
Hooker, Richard, 102
Horace, 4, 183, 186
Horkheimer, Max, 76
Hotman, François, 67, 97, 98, 99–100, 103,
     105, 111, 112–13, 114
Howard Jean, 27, 37
Howell, James, 175, 181
Hughes, Merritt Y., 95n, 96n2, 102, 105,
     110, 112–13, 115
Huguenots; *see also* Calvinism; Henri IV
     (Henri de Navarre); Reformation
     and political discourse, 2, 8, 68,
     95–116 passim
Hugues Capet, 114
Humanism; *see also* Protestantism
     and nationhood, 3
     political thought in, 65–93 passim,
     105–10
Hundred Years War, the, 33
Huntingdon, Earl of (George Hastings), 148
Hurault, Jacques, 150
Hus, John, 112

imitation
     poetics of, 1–2, 51–64 passim
Isabeau de Bavière, 28, 31

Isabelle d'Angoulême, 31
Isabelle de France, 8, 27–47 passim
Isabella d'Este, 121

James I, 2, 109
James II, 3
Jameson, Anna, 36
Jeanne d'Arc, 7
Jerome, Saint, 16n3, 20, 175
Joan the Fair Maid of Kent, 34
Jodelle, Etienne, 71, 165, 181, 188
Johnstone, R., 189
Jonson, Ben, 175, 180
Jonston, John, 185
Jusserand, Jean-Jules, 9
Justinian, Emperor, 106
Juvenal, 4

Kaske, Carol, 11
Kennedy, Jacqueline, 27
Kennedy, John F., 27
Kennedy, William J., 11
Keohane, Nannerl O., 68n6, 77n28, 83n
Kipling, Rudyard, 188
Knox, John, 96, 105, 108, 109, 110,
     111, 115
Kojève, Alexandre, 86
Kuin, Roger, 9, 137n80, 161n

La Boétie, Etienne de, 2, 8, 65–91
La Bruyère, Jean de, 191
La Marck, Henri-Robert de, 152
la Torre, Sigismondo Fanzino de, 121
Labé, Louise, 2, 12
Lafayette, Madame de
     Princess of Cleve, The [*La Princesse*
     de Clèves], 188
Lake, Lydia Kirsopp, 9, 161n, 172
Lake, Peter, 109n41, 111–12
Langbaine, Gerard, 189
Langland, William, 35
Languet Hubert, 97, 145, 146, 149
Le Bossu, René, 190–91
Le Maçon de la Fontaine, Robert, 155
Le Roy, Louis, 11, 72, 106
Lee, Nathaniel, 188
Lee, Sidney, 10
Leicester, Earl of (Robert Sidney), 148,
     149, 151–2, 159

Leigh, Edward, 183
Lerm, Gabriel de, 175
Lestringant, Frank, 151
L'Hôpital, Michel Hurault de, 72, 88–9,
    116, 186
Licques, David de, 144n5, 152–3
literary canon
    formation of, 8
    and nationalism, 9
    political function of, 1, 52–4, 55, 57
Lobbert, Jean, 154
Locke, John, 73n21, 77, 102n25, 116
Lodge, Thomas, 166, 181
Lope de Vega, Artur Félix, 186
Louis XII, 107
Louis of Nassau, 152
Louis, Prince of Condé, 152
Lucan, 4
Lur-Longa, Guillaume, 69
Luther, Martin, 110
Lyly, John, 136, 137n77

Machiavelli, Niccolò, 68–72, 76, 77, 81,
    84, 93, 110, 114, 115
Magna Carta, the, 114, 115
Magny, Olivier de, 165
Mair, John, 107
Malory, Thomas, 6
Malraux, André, 27
Map, Gauthier, 16n3
Margaret d'Anjou, 31
Marguerite de Navarre, 12, 133, 158, 164,
    183, 185
Marguerite de Valois, 164, 183, 185
Mariana, Juan de, 67
Marlowe, Christopher, 30n17
Marot, Clément, 9, 59, 181, 191
    and Petrarch, 1–2, 5
Marsilius of Padua, 106
Martin, Catherine Gimelli, 8
Marvell, Andrew, 4
Masson, Papire, 183
Mathéolus, 16n3, 20
McFarlane, I.D., 165, 174
Melanchthon, Philipp, 153
Melehy, Hassan, 8, 12, 27n1, 65n1, 132
Mercator, Gerhard, 179
Mildmay, Anthony, 148
Miller, Leo, 100

Millis, Juan de, 119, 141
Milton, John, 3, 4, 5, 6, 8, 95–116 passim,
    165, 189
    Areopagitica, 98, 101, 111–12
    Commonplace Book, 95, 101n22, 110,
        113, 115
    Defensio pro Populo Anglicano, 101,
        102, 111, 115
    Defensio Secunda, 102
    Eikonaklastes, 98, 105
    History of Britain, 115
    *Likeliest Means to Remove Hirelings
        from the Church, The*, 98
    Lycidas, 102
    Of True Religion, 98
    Paradise Lost, 3, 105
    Readie and Easy Way, The, 103, 105,
        113, 114
    Samson Agonistes, 98
    Tenure of Kings and Magistrates, The,
        98, 102–4, 105
Moffett, Thomas, 154
Moisan, Jean-Claude, 168
Molière, 191
Monarchomachs, *see* Bèze, Thédore de;
        Hotman, François; regicide
Montaigne, Michel de, 2, 5, 10, 12, 68–70,
        90, 138, 188, 191
    on friendship, 74
Montmorency, Anne de, 69
More, Sir Thomas, 3
Motteux, Peter, 189–90
Muret, Marc-Antoine, 71, 169n16, 182,
        190n, 191

Nashe, Thomas, 163n4
nationhood
    and cultural transfer, 5
    and poetry, 4
    and Rome, 6
Norman Conquest, the, 33, 95
Norris, Henry, 163
North, Dudley, 180

Orgel, Stephen, 27n1, 30n16, 34, 35
Ossory, Earl of (Thomas Butler), 186
Ostovich, Helen, 28
Oudin, César, 188
Ovid, 4, 58, 148, 152, 176, 184

Palsgrave, John, 151, 155, 157
Parker, Henry, 99–100
Paschal, Pierre de, 165
Pasquier, Etienne, 90, 183, 185, 90
Pasquier, Nicolas, 90
Passerat, Jean, 191
Patterson, Annabel, 105
Paz, Jean de, 152
Peletier du Mans, Jacques, 119n1, 141
Petrarch (Francesco Petracco)
    and Clément Marot, 1–2, 5
    and the sonnet tradition, 1, 74n23, 173,
        183, 184, 185, 188
Philippe de Valois, 181
Phillips, Edward, 5, 116, 163, 187
Phillips, John, 111
Piaget, Arthur, 22
Pibrac, Seigneur de (Guy du Faur), 191
Picot, Emile, 22
Pindar, 183
Plantin, Christophe, 145
Plato, 74n23, 82n30, 86
Pléiade, the, 9, 11, 161, 164
    and national poetry, 1
Plutarch, 70
poetics
    and allegory, 54–5
    and transformation, 56–64
Pogson, Kathryn, 27
Pole, Reginald, 68
Poncet, John, 105, 112
Ponsonby, William, 147
power, *see* state
Pratt, Mary Louise, 15n
Prescott, Anne Lake, 9, 10, 11, 12, 144
Propertius, 176
Protestantism; *see also* Calvinism;
        Huguenots; humanism
    as poetic subject, 143–60
Prynne, William, 96–7
Psalms, the, 146, 147, 154, 158
Puritan Revolution, the, 95, 102
Pynson, Richard, 15

Quitslund, Jon, 11

Rabelais, François, 5, 9, 10, 82n30, 83,
        175, 186, 189–90, 191
Racine, Jean, 191

Rackin, Phyllis, 27, 37
Raleigh, Sir Walter, 4
Raphelingius, Franciscus, 145
Rapin, Nicolas, 164, 173, 187, 189, 191
Rebholz, Ronald, 147
Rees, Joan, 147
Reformation, *see* Calvinism; Huguenots;
        humanism; Protestantism
regicide: legitimacy of, 67, 91, 95–100,
        103–4, 109–10, 111–15
Reiss, Timothy J., 8, 11
Renaudot, Eusèbe, 186
Renaudot, Isaac, 186
Renaudot, Theeophraste, 186
Reveille matin des François, 67
Richard II (historical figure), 27–47
Ringler, William, 15
Rogers, Daniel, 145, 161–3, 176, 177
Rome
    and nationhood, 6
    as poetic subject, 59–63
Ronsard, Pierre de, 1, 10, 179–91 passim
    Amours, 167–77 passim
    Franciade, La (Ronsard), 168, 175,
        179, 182n, 191
    Odes, 69
Rousseau, Jean-Jacques, 6, 77
Rowland, John, 185
Rudolph II, Emperor, 144
Ruth, Book of, 43–4
Rutherford, Samuel, 96, 102, 105, 110

Sackville, Thomas, 155
Said, Edward W., 127
St. Bartholomew's Day massacre, the, 99,
        109, 152
Salamonio, Mario, 106
Salviati, Cassandre, 173
Sannazaro, Jacopo, 189
Satterthwaite, Alfred W., 10
Saul, Nigel, 31, 33
Saumaise, Claude de, 3, 6, 101, 103, 110,
        111, 112, 114
Schede, Paul (Melissus), 166, 177
Scudéry, Madeleine de, 181
Sébillet, Thomas, 132
Secundus, 176
Sedley, David L., 11
Seneca, 74n23, 82n30

Index

Severus, Sepulcius, 113
Seyssel, Claude de, 111
Shakespeare, William, 2, 4, 5, 8, 9, 10, 11,
    12, 63n25, 152
   Henry V, 7
   King John, 31
   Measure for Measure, 30n14
   and nationhood, 6
   Richard II, 8, 27–47 passim
   Romeo and Juliet, 46–7
Sidney, Anne, 154
Sidney, Henry, 154, 155
Sidney, Mary, 9, 37, 137, 138, 143–60
   passim
Sidney, Philip, 2, 3, 4–5, 7, 9, 10, 143–60,
   161, 174, 176, 177, 185
   Arcadia, 3, 145, 146, 150
   Astrophil and Stella, 145
   Defence of Poesie, 4, 144, 154, 159
   Lady of May, The, 145
   New Arcadia, 150
Sir Gawain and the Green Knight, 35
Skinner, Quentin, 99, 100, 106, 107, 108,
   109, 113, 114, 115
Skottowe, Augustine, 36
Smith, Malcolm, 69–70, 74n24, 166n10, 174
Smith, Sir Thomas, 68
Socrates
   on friendship, 74n23
Somerset, Duke of (Edward Seymour), 147
Sorel, Charles, 181–2
Spenser, Edmund, 2, 5, 9, 165, 174, 181,
   185, 188, 189
   Cantos of Mutabilitie, 8, 51–64
   Complaints, 10, 59–64
   Faerie Queene, The, 4, 6, 8, 10, 11,
    59–64 passim, 151, 167
   Ruines of Rome, 59, 61–4
   Ruines of Time, The, 61
   Shepheardes Calendar, The, 165
   Visions of Bellay, 59
Stanley, Thomas, 183, 189
state
   and freedom, 74–5
   and law, 77
   and political thought, 66
   and power, 90–91
Statius, 4

Stein, Harold, 10
Sterne, Laurence, 10
Stevens, Wallace, 40
Strauss, Leo, 71n19, 73, 86n
Strickland, Agnes, 28, 29, 33, 36
Stubbe, Henry, 185–6
Suttie, Paul, 51n1, 55
Sylvester, Joshua, 138
Sypher, F.J., 147, 152

Tassel, John, 154
Tasso, Torquato, 10, 185, 188, 189
Tate, Nahum, 37
Temple, Sir William, 188
Theocritus, 183
Theophrastus, 16n3
Thomas, Sian, 27
Thorius, Francis, 9, 161–77
Thorius, Raphael, 163
translation
   as act of love, 142, 154–5
   and cultural transfer, 1, 5, 7, 8–9, 10,
    15–25, 119–41 passim, 143–60
    passim, 161–77 passim, 179–91
    passim
   fidelity of, 143
   and ideology, 152
   in Spenser's practice, 55
   theory of, 128–9
Tree, Ellen (Mrs. Charles Kean), 27
Trivulzio, Giangiacomo, 121
Trotti, Giovanna, 120–21
Tuck, Richard, 99n14, 105, 108, 113
Turnèbe, Adrien, 165
tyranny; *see also* regicide
   and sovereignty, 71–2, 79–81, 92

Upham, Alfred H., 10
Ure, Peter, 27n2, 42
Urfé, Honoré d', 191
Urquhart, Thomas, 186, 189–90

Vida, Marco Girolamo, 189
Villon, François, 23
Virgil, 4, 168, 175–6, 183, 184, 185, 186
Virgin Mary, the, 33, 40
Voiture, Vincent, 191
Voltaire, 4, 6

Walker, Obadiah, 186–7
Walpole, Horace, 27
Walsh, William, 189
Walsingham, Francis, 146
Walzer, Michael, 109
Warkentin, Germaine, 155
Warner, Beverly E., 36
Wesley, Samuel, 189
Whetstone, George, 149
William of Ockham, 107
William of Orange, 152
William the Conqueror, 103, 114, 115
Williams, Deanne, 8, 9n4, 11

Withals, John, 39
Worden, Blair, 148
Wordsworth, William, 6
Wroth, Mary, 2, 185
Wyatt, Thomas, 158
Wycliffe, John, 112

Xenophon, 74n23

Yates, Frances, 11

Zacharias, Pope, 114
Zimmer, Patriz, 145

CPSIA information can be obtained
at www.ICGtesting.com
Printed in the USA
BVHW01*0537310118
506749BV00007B/33/P